D1561011

The
American Revolution

DOCUMENTS DECODED

The ABC-CLIO series *Documents Decoded* guides readers on a hunt for new secrets through an expertly curated selection of primary sources. Each book pairs key documents with in-depth analysis, all in an original and visually engaging side-by-side format. But *Documents Decoded* authors do more than just explain each source's context and significance—they give readers a front-row seat to their own investigation and interpretation of each essential document, line by line.

TITLES IN ABC-CLIO'S DOCUMENTS DECODED SERIES

The Democratic Party: Documents Decoded
Douglas B. Harris and Lonce H. Bailey

The Republican Party: Documents Decoded
Douglas B. Harris and Lonce H. Bailey

1960s Counterculture: Documents Decoded
Jim Willis

Founding Documents of America: Documents Decoded
John R. Vile

Presidential Power: Documents Decoded
Brian M. Harward

The Early Republic: Documents Decoded
John R. Vile

The Jacksonian and Antebellum Eras: Documents Decoded
John R. Vile

Freedom of Speech: Documents Decoded
David L. Hudson Jr.

The Civil War and Reconstruction Eras: Documents Decoded
John R. Vile

Church and State: Documents Decoded
David K. Ryden and Jeffrey J. Polet

Alexander Hamilton: Documents Decoded
Christina Villegas

Equal Protection: Documents Decoded
David L. Hudson Jr.

The
American
Revolution

DOCUMENTS DECODED

Neil Gould

An Imprint of ABC-CLIO, LLC
Santa Barbara, California • Denver, Colorado

Library of Congress Cataloging-in-Publication Data

Names: Gould, Neil, 1943– author.
Title: The American Revolution : documents decoded / Neil Gould.
Description: Santa Barbara, California : ABC-CLIO, 2018. | Includes bibliographical references and index.
Identifiers: LCCN 2018014201 (print) | LCCN 2018016527 (ebook) | ISBN 9781440839474 (ebook) |
ISBN 9781440839467 (alk. paper)
Subjects: LCSH: United States—History—Revolution, 1775–1783—Sources.
Classification: LCC E203 (ebook) | LCC E203 .G64 2018 (print) | DDC 973.3—dc23
LC record available at https://lccn.loc.gov/2018014201

ISBN: 978-1-4408-3946-7 (print)
978-1-4408-3947-4 (eBook)

22 21 20 19 18   1 2 3 4 5

This book is also available as an eBook.

ABC-CLIO
An Imprint of ABC-CLIO, LLC

ABC-CLIO, LLC
130 Cremona Drive, P.O. Box 1911
Santa Barbara, California 93116-1911
www.abc-clio.com

This book is printed on acid-free paper ∞

Manufactured in the United States of America

For Alan and Nathan: This is your heritage.

Contents

Introduction, xi

SECTION I
THE ROAD TO REVOLUTION

Contemporary Reports of the Boston Massacre (March 5, 1770)	5
Samuel Adams: Report on the Meeting of the Boston Committee of Correspondence (1772)	10
The Tea Act (1773)	13
The New York Sons of Liberty Tea Resolutions (1773)	19
Three Accounts of the Boston Tea Party (1773)	21
Maryland's Reaction to the Intolerable Acts (1773–1774)	25
The Committee of Correspondence (May 31, 1774)	27
The Suffolk Resolves (1774)	30
Thomas Jefferson's Summary View of the Rights of British America (August 1774)	36
Patrick Henry's Speech to the Virginia House of Burgesses (March 23, 1775)	46
Letter from Thomas Jefferson to Dr. Small (May 7, 1775)	48
Congress Grants Washington Command of the Continental Army (July 3, 1775)	50
Declaration of the Causes and Necessity of Taking Up Arms (July 6, 1775)	52
Letter from Thomas Jefferson Hoping for Reconciliation with Britain (August 25, 1775)	59
Thomas Paine: *Common Sense* (1776)	61
John Adams: "Thoughts on Government" (April 1776)	76
The Virginia Declaration of Rights (June 12, 1776)	80
The Unanimous Declaration of the Thirteen United States of America (July 4, 1776)	83
The American Crisis Papers #1 (December 19, 1776)	85
Paul Revere's Account of His Ride (1783)	86

SECTION II
BATTLES OF LIBERTY

Letters on Lexington and Concord (1775)   91

Bunker's Hill (1775)   106

The Invasion of Montreal and Quebec (1775)   123

The Siege of Boston (1775)   129

The Battle for Long Island, Northern Manhattan, and White Plains (1776)   137

The Battle of Trenton (1776)   141

The Skirmish of Sag Harbor (1777)   147

The Battles of Brandywine, Valley Forge, and the Paoli Massacre (1777–1778)   150

The Battle of Monmouth (1778)   157

The Battle of Saratoga (1777)   162

The Battle of Yorktown (1781)   180

SECTION III
A NATION OF AMAZONS

Patriotic Sentiments of an American Woman in Advocacy of the Revolution (June 1780)   203

The Voice of Aristocracy: Mary Morris (June 10, 1780)   205

Eyewitness to Independence: The Adams's Correspondence (July 1776)   206

"Dirty Kate": The Hero of the Battle of Fort Washington (1779)   209

Mercy Otis Warren: Poet and Propagandist (1774)   212

Phillis Wheatley: Young Black Phenomenon (1773)   214

Anna Winslow: A Boston Schoolgirl Writes Home (1771)   216

A Soldier's Daughter's Pride (1876)   218

Nancy Hart: Terror of the Georgia Tories   220

Deborah Sampson Gannett: A Wolf in Wolf's Clothing   222

Prudence Wright and the Women's Guard   225

Patience Lovell Wright: Sculptress and Spy   226

SECTION IV
THE SONGS OF LIBERTY

Peter St. John's "American Taxation" (1765)   231

"The World Turned Upside Down" (1767)   237

"The Liberty Song" and Its Parodies (1768)   239

"To Our Ladies" (1769)   241

"A New Song" (1774)   243

Meshech Weare's "India Tea" (1774)   245

"Pennsylvania Song" (1775)   246

"Alphabet for Little Masters and Misses" (1775)   248

"Adam's Fall, or the Trip to Cambridge" (1775)   250

Verses from "Yankee Doodle" (1775)   252

John Mason's "Liberty's Call" (1776)   254

Benjamin Dearborn's "A War Song" (1776)   256

"Off from Boston," or Military Song (1776)   258

Jonathan Sewall's "On Independence" (1776)   260

"To the Commons" (1776)   262

The British Lamentation or "The Dying Redcoat" (1776)   263

The Battle of Trenton: A Drinking Song (1777)   265

"A Fable" (1778)   267

"Our Women" (1780)   270

"Address to the Vile Traitor" (1780)   271

"Cornwallis Burgoyned" (1781)   273

"Thanksgiving Hymn" (1783)   275

Timeline of Events   277

Further Reading   281

Index   283

About the Author   291

Introduction

The American Revolution, like all great moments in human history, was a series of events that involved both hearts and minds: the hearts and minds of the Englishmen settled in the New World, and those of the Englishmen who were determined to rule them from the fastness of their tight little island beyond the sea.

The documents that follow reflect events and feelings, without which it is doubtful that the unlikely colonial triumph over Great Britain would have occurred. We hear the voices not only of the founding fathers who speak to us with unforced eloquence, but also the barely literate recollections of simple soldiers whose blood supplied the lubricant that drove the engine of revolt, from the hopeful springtime of Lexington and Concord to the glorious autumnal victory at Yorktown. We hear also the childish innocence of a young girl witness to the depredations of the redcoats encamped on Boston Common, and the songs and ballads of a people inured to pain and loss whose response was a mocking rebuke to tyranny.

"I hear America singing, what varied carols she sings," Walt Whitman wrote. How often the American response to hard times is expressed in song and verse. Those first songs were songs of revolution.

"By the rude bridge that arched the flood
Their flag to April's breeze unfurled
Here once the embattled farmers stood
And fired the shot heard round the world."

Emerson's eulogy to the minutemen in his "Concord Hymn" gave us that famous phrase. And indeed, the American Revolution was the first shot of an international movement of men and women determined to break free of political and economic restraint. It was a tidal wave in a revolutionary flood that engulfed France, Austria, Italy, Prussia, and Russia; by the first decades of the 20th century, that flood had washed away forever the seemingly rock solid basis of Western civilization that had persisted for a millennium.

The American Revolution was not just a war for independence; it was also a civil war. Americans were divided. There were Tories loyal to the Crown, and patriots who would hear nothing of cooperation. There was a sectional split between northern and southern interests that anticipated the cataclysm of the 1860s. Tragically, this split was reflected on a smaller scale within families, brother against brother, father against son. But for all that, this was not a conflict of classes, for among the elite of society, as well as among journeyman and farmers, there were patriots and loyalists. There was also a philosophical basis for revolution penned most famously in the Declaration of Independence. Americans proclaimed their rights both as Englishman and as human beings, "natural rights" guaranteed by God.

That the intellectual fathers of the revolution (Adams, Jefferson, Paine, and Hamilton) were essentially conservatives is reflected in the fortunate fact that despite the miseries that attend all armed conflict, the American Revolution never deteriorated into government-sponsored horrors like the reign of terror. Of course, there were massacres and carnage, but by and large the great battles of the war were fought according to the battle ordinances practiced by civilized nations. If it is possible to speak of "decent" warriors, such were those who fought the revolution.

To tell the story of the American Revolution in an objective way, it was necessary to divide the task in order to conquer it. It was necessary to collect and choose between a vast corpus of memoirs, letters, diaries, and writings, then to arrange these into topic areas, some of which have been extensively explored, others less so. The first section of this volume is devoted to the run-up to revolution and gives historical and philosophical context to the events that led to the outbreak of armed conflict. The second section naturally follows, presenting accounts of both major battles and minor skirmishes. For both of these sections I have chosen multiple accounts of actions, seen from both the American and British perspectives. These first sections present materials that have been widely discussed for over 250 years.

For many years, historians agreed that the cause of the American Revolution was the passage by Parliament of a series of acts designed to force the colonies to raise money to help pay for the protection Britain had provided during the French and Indian War. The war resulted in the defeat of French colonial ambitions in the North American territory. It removed a threat to the inhabitants of British America. Wars are expensive. Parliament felt justified in forcing the colonials to pay for their own defense. But Parliament's actions restricted the activities of the colonists who, because of their physical separation from the mother country, had for more than a century grown accustomed to exercising their economic and political freedoms. The colonists saw Parliament's actions as an attempt to increase control over them.

These actions did provoke revolt, but the seeds of revolution had been germinating for many years. The colonies were fertile ground for revolt; they were filled with men and women who were self-reliant and long accustomed to directing their own affairs. Americans interpreted the actions of Britain as an unwarranted attempt to dominate them. By the time armed revolt broke out, the economic, political, and social interests of Britain and America had moved in separate and competing directions. Two peoples who shared a common heritage now felt that the fraternal bonds that held them together were stretched to the breaking point. When Britain decided to establish a military occupation, the colonies objected and the physical presence of the redcoats in New England became a ready target for the festering resentments of the colonials. When a series of increasingly controlling acts (Tea, Sugar, Townsend, Boston Port) were added to the mix, the explosion of war was inevitable.

For many years, this theory about the causes of the revolution went unchallenged. But in recent decades, two competing schools of thought have gained support. The idea has been expressed that the revolution was not only political but also ideological, based on new ideals of freedom unleashed by a century of enlightenment thought in France and England. The other viewpoint emphasizes economic and social tensions as the motive force behind the revolution. This doctrine challenged the accepted wisdom that prevailed through the 19th century. It was a point of view that reflected the forces set in motion in American society between 1898 and 1920, the so-called Progressive Era. That brief period in American history saw the rise to prominence of a new professional class. For the first time, America had grown wealthy enough to pay for the services of new professionals. The progressives were determined to remake America and lead it to a new understanding of itself and its origins. These professionals were doctors and lawyers, of course, but also professors. And professional historians saw economic and social forces at work as not only the appropriate focus for progressive activity in the new 20th century but also as the motive force in society as early as colonial and revolutionary days.

Later, other interpreters once again started to emphasize political philosophy and the influence of enlightenment thought as the trigger of the revolution. More recently, historians again recognize economic and social forces at work.

It is impossible to separate these factors in seeking to understand the cause of the revolution. The social, economic, and philosophical elements in society are inextricable. They feed on each other, and they reinforce one another. Indeed, it is questionable whether each could maintain an independent vitality. The truth lies not in any single element. All of these factors occurring and maturing at a single time and place gave birth to "a new nation, conceived in liberty and dedicated to the proposition that all men are created equal."

Sections III and IV of this book deal with aspects of the conflict less often stressed. The role of women in the revolution is frequently portrayed as supportive, if not secondary: daughters of liberty who supported the cause by knitting homespun cloth and refusing to drink "curséd tea." However, there was an active role for women as battle-tested soldiers, as patriots who dressed in men's uniforms and bound their breasts with cotton bands so they could join the troops, fight side by side with them, and escape detection. Women who, when their husbands fell in battle, took over their places and fired grape shot at the enemy. Women who served as spies in London gathered important military information, and sent messages back to headquarters in Philadelphia. Southern women who tricked redcoats into their homes held them at bay at the point of rifles, and handed them over to patriots who then lynched them. And the unique story of a black slave, abducted from her home in West Africa, who became an internationally famous poet of the conflict. These women constituted a "nation of Amazons" as Abigail Adams said. Section IV reviews the mocking ballads of the revolution, many composed by women. These songs and verses throw a new light on the people who created America and created the American type. Their stories are here.

The materials in this volume (letters, memoirs, printed broadsides, excerpts from newspapers, and archival treasures) are all contemporaneous. They let us see the revolution as those who fought it, saw it. As much as possible, the original language of the documents has been preserved.

John Adams asked: "What do we mean by revolution? The war? That was no part of the revolution; it was only an effect and consequence of it. The revolution was in the minds of the people."

This volume is an attempt to provide the reader insight and appreciation of that revolution of the mind that created the American spirit: independent, creative, and free.

The American Revolution

SECTION I

The Road to Revolution

Introduction

The men and women who fought the revolution in many ways resembled the Pilgrim Fathers. They were white, Protestant, courageous, and independent-minded. But over the years that stretched from the earliest settlements to the unsettled decade of 1765–1775, the colonials had changed in a distinctive way. They no longer saw themselves as Englishmen. They saw themselves as Americans of British descent, with all the traditional rights and privileges that went with that designation. Among these were "life, liberty" and although Jefferson would write "the pursuit of happiness," the original phrase was "life, liberty and property." By "property," the Americans understood the right to govern their own economic affairs.

For most of the colonial period, they had prospered unmolested by what they eventually perceived as economic tyranny from London. They had grown wealthy from fishing, ship building, and agriculture and so long as their activities had proven mutually beneficial to Crown and colony, all was well. But during the 10 years immediately preceding the outbreak of armed insurrection at Lexington and Concord, increased tensions rose as a long-established tradition of colonial self-government came into conflict with ever-increasing attempts by king and Parliament to control colonial commercial activities. The British government was suffering from the economic depression that followed the successful prosecution of the French and Indian War. Since Britain had incurred huge debt in part from the defense of the American colonies, it seemed fair that the Americans should pay for the benefits they enjoyed because of the defeat of the French. After all, the argument ran, weren't they Britons who enjoyed the protection of the Crown? This was the defining question that divided mother and daughter countries. In 1700, the answer might have been very different from the one given in April 1775, but after so many years of independent development, the inevitable answer was arrived at not through dialogue but through war.

By 1775, colonial society had developed a fixed demographic. It was 90 percent agricultural. There was a small upper class made up of merchants (in the North) and planters (in the South); a large middle class of small businessmen (yeomen) and farmers who owned their land; and a lower class of workers and renters of land. As Britain insisted on maintaining its mercantilist economic philosophy with respect to its colonies under which economic activity was controlled to serve the interests of the mother country, Parliament passed a series of laws which segments of colonial society perceived as unreasonably oppressive.

The Navigation Acts from 1651 to 1660 limited colonial mercantile activities by restricting shipments exclusively to British-owned vessels. These acts are often cited as the beginning of the conflict.

But they were for the most part mutually beneficial, since they produced a monopoly for both British and colonial business interests. For example, the New England shipping industry progressed largely because of the protection provided by the Navigation Acts. It was only after 1700, when an attempt was made to use fines for violation of the acts as a form of taxation, that resistance grew.

The Sugar or Molasses Act of 1733 was an attempt to protect the supply of sugar that was needed for the production of rum to British commercial interests. Several acts were amended over time to discourage smuggling of sugar from competing (largely Spanish) suppliers. When bonding regulations were enacted that forced ship's captains to post bonds on all goods in their cargoes before the articles were boarded, colonial masters were outraged. The long-established custom had been to load first and then pay the bond. Under the new regulations, unbonded cargo was subject to confiscation by British inspectors.

John Hancock was one of the most zealous of the revolutionary leaders. When his ship, the *Liberty*, was seized by the customs commissioners, all hell broke loose. The British had chosen to offend the wrong man.

The amount of revenue raised by the Sugar Acts was insufficient to support the maintenance of the British Army in America. Parliament then made the near-fatal decision to place a stamp tax (1765) on all legal documents, newspapers, almanacs, playing cards, and dice. When the colonials protested, Parliament refused to acknowledge their petition, for it had been long-established practice to not receive protests against revenue acts. But the colonists saw the direct imposition of a tax on the colonies as an attack on self-government. Englishmen, they felt, could only be taxed by their own elected representatives. The Stamp Act was an attack on self-rule. For Britain the issue was economic; for the colonists it was political.

Delegates from nine colonies met in New York and formed a Stamp Act Congress. They declared they could only be taxed by their own local assemblies. This Congress was the first formal expression of a need for national unity. It produced such a storm of opposition that Parliament nullified the Stamp Act. But the political damage had already been done.

Charles Townsend was the British chancellor of the exchequer (equivalent to our secretary of the Treasury) in 1767 when the four acts associated with his name were passed. The first was directed at the New York Assembly. It temporarily halted all its legislative activities until it agreed to support the Quartering Act, which forced colonies to provide housing and provisions to British soldiers stationed in the colonies. The colonists saw in this act the potential for Britain to control all local legislative authority. The second and third acts were revenue acts that set up a mechanism in Boston for collecting duties on various goods, including tea. The money raised was to be used to pay the salaries of judges and governors appointed by the king. Previously, officials had been supported by appropriations from local assemblies. This new arrangement was a direct attack on colonial home rule and self-government and was seen as a first step toward tyranny. Resistance was fierce and included evasion of the taxes and physical abuse of the tax collectors. By September 1768, the Boston commissioners felt it necessary to ask for troops to put down the colonial resistance. It was a segment of these troops that was involved in the Boston Massacre.

Tea imported to the colonies had been taxed by Britain as early as 1723. In 1770, the Tea Act canceled the duties so that tea left England duty-free. But another Revenue Act imposed a tax to be collected at colonial ports. In spite of opposition, tea continued to be imported to the colonies. In 1772, a new regulation permitted the East India Company, which was suffering from competition, to export tea directly to the colonies, thus giving it a needed commercial advantage. The tea ships carrying taxed cargoes became another symbol of British tyranny. The residents of Boston, New York, Philadelphia, and Charleston organized to prevent the landing of the tea. The most famous of these efforts was the "tea party" at Boston, but it was only one of many that united the colonies in opposition to Parliament and Crown.

As king and Parliament by stages became increasingly oppressive, colonial leaders of resistance pushed back until finally in 1775 Massachusetts was declared in rebellion. By then, several colonies had formed two Continental Congresses. And though the colonists were by no means united in the desire for independence (Tories, those loyal to the king, made up a sizable proportion of the population), it was but a short step to Jefferson's Declaration of July 1776.

Contemporary Reports of the Boston Massacre

(March 5, 1770)

INTRODUCTION

As tensions rose between the citizens of Boston and the occupying British troops, it became clear that one incident might ignite the whole town. The date was March 5, 1770. The actual facts of the confrontation are harder to verify.

Two contemporary reports on the events of March 5 follow. They differ in emphasis depending on the perspective and political agenda of the author.

Relating to the Massacre of Citizens of Boston by British Troops[1]

. . . one of the causes which led to the massacre of the 5th of March, was the affray[2] between the inhabitants and the British soldiers, an account of which was related to me shortly after the event, by one who was an eye witness.

At that time there was only one house on the east side of what is now called Pearl street, in which then resided Charles Paxton, esq. On the west side of the street stood four or five rope-walks,[3] extending from the upper to the lower end of the street, which were all burnt in 1794. On Saturday afternoon, on the 3rd March, 1770, a British soldier of the 29th regiment, accosted a negro who was employed in one of the rope-walks, by inquiring "whether his master wanted to hire a man." (The soldiers who were mechanics were sometimes hired as journeymen[4]). The negro answered that his "master wished to have his vault[5] emptied and that was a proper work for a Lobster."[6] This produced a conflict between the soldier and the negro, and, before relief came to his assistance, the negro was very severely beaten . . . Mr. Gray, the foreman of the walk, came up and parted them. Mr. Gray . . . told the soldier that "as he had obtained satisfaction for the insult, he had better go back to his barracks." The soldier "damned him" and said that "for six-pence he would drub him as he had done the negro." A contest then took place between

[1] The American view of the events leading up to the Boston Massacre places responsibility on the shoulders of the British.

[2] Public noisy quarrel.

[3] Long alleys where workers laid strands of hemp and bound them to form rope.

[4] Experienced workers.

[5] Outhouse.

[6] "Lobster" was an insult used by Bostonians to refer to the British soldiers, who often wore red uniforms.

them in which the soldier received a much worse beating than the negro, and went off to his barracks . . . swearing revenge. In about half an hour the soldier returned with about seventy of his comrades, who came over the hill huzzahing, armed with pipe staves split into bludgeons . . . and made the attack with great fury.

Each party was brave and intrepid, but the science in this kind of warfare, which the rope-walk men had obtained in their "Pope Day" battles[7] gave them a decided superiority and in their pursuit of the soldiers they halted on Fort-hill and gave three cheers in token of victory. The noise of the shouting. . . resounded far around, and excited the curiosity of those at a great distance . . .

There was a mast yard a little south and several wood wharfs, on all which were also employed hardy laborers, who, together with the blacksmiths, clockmakers, and other athletic mechanics in the neighborhood, (whose brawny arms could wield a club with as much dexterity as a Highlander could manage his broadsword), all ran towards the scene of combat. The bravery of the soldiers was not doubted, and accordingly, preparations were made to repel another attack which was expected and in which they were not disappointed. The shouting of the soldiers, issuing from the barrack-yard, to the number of more than three hundred . . . soon gave the alarm. The soldiers pulled down the fence in High street . . . The rope-walk men pulled down the fence on the opposite side in Pearl street, when both parties rushed on each other with equal intrepidity. But the Herculean strength of virtuous labor, united with the activity and science of the Yankees, soon obtained a triumph over an idle, inactive, enervated, and intemperate, though brave soldiery.[8]

The effect of this recanter[9] was seen in the countenances and conduct of the soldiers the next and following day, who looked vengeance on the inhabitants . . . those of them, who were friendly to the citizens, advised them to remain at home on Monday evening, as revenge would then be taken.

The soldiers asserted on Sunday morning that one of their men had died of his wounds, but as the body was never shewn it was supposed to be only a pretence to justify the horrid scene, which ensued on the Monday evening following. So much has been written on the subject of the massacre of the 5th of March, 1770, that it is unpleasant to repeat "ugly recollections" respecting that horrid scene . . . The

[7] In this period of colonial history, there was widespread discrimination against Roman Catholics, commonly referred to as "papists." Pope Day was what is known today as St. Patrick's Day. It was characterized by heavy drinking and brawling.

[8] The writer describes the "intrepidity" (bravery) of both sides but characterizes the British soldiers as "idle," "inactive," and "enervated" ("weak"). The Yankees, by contrast, are described as attacking with "strength," "virtue," and "science" on their side.

[9] Hostile meeting.

threats of the soldiers . . . were put in execution on Monday evening the 5th of March, 1770, by insulting and abusing many inhabitants in various parts of the town, which resulted in what was called the "horrid massacre," by which four persons were instantly killed, one died of his wounds a few days succeeding, and about seventeen in the total killed and wounded.

Language cannot describe the horror and indignation which was excited through the town by this dreadful event. The bells rang a terrific peal, which roused the whole population. More than five thousand citizens were collected in State street . . . Lieut. Governor Hutchinson, and the king's council, were assembled in the council chamber, even at the solemn hour of midnight! Many of the venerable citizens repaired to them and demanded the surrender of the criminals to justice. The high-sheriff appeared in the balcony of the state house and ordered silence! An awful stillness ensued; when, with a loud voice, he declared, that he was authorized by his honor the Lieutenant Governor and his majesty's council, with the consent of col. Dalrymple, to say that Capt. Preston and the men who had committed the outrage, should be immediately delivered to the civil power, and requested the citizens to retire peaceably to their dwellings; which, after the soldiers had marched off, was complied with . . .[10]

The result of this melancholy affair was, that all the troops were ordered out of town, and the culprits[11] brought to a trial, and acquitted, excepting two who were found guilty of manslaughter. The trial was one of the most important that had ever come before an American tribunal, especially as the public mind was wrought up to the highest tone of indignation. It established the character of the judiciary for purity and independence, which had been questioned by the Tories. The law was triumphant,[12] but the needless barbarity of the act never doubted. The funeral of the unfortunate victims was attended with great pomp and parade. Thousands came from the country; and the whole number that followed them to the grave, was supposed to exceed ten thousand! It was supposed by many, that the above recited horrid event, did more to effect an alienation of the affection of the people of New England from the British government, than any other whatever . . .

[10]In this period, Massachusetts was governed by a royal charter that created a "great and general court" consisting of a governor and assistants (magistrates) who met four times a year to adopt rules for governing, imposing taxes, and conduct other business, including the expulsion of "undesirables" from the colony. Gov. Thomas Hutchinson's stubborn insistence that tea be landed free of duty led to the Boston Tea Party. Col. Dalrymple was commander of the British troops in Boston. Captain Thomas Preston was in charge of the troops involved in the Boston Massacre. He tried to reason with the mob, but when they refused he was later accused of ordering his men to fire on the citizens.

[11]The soldiers who had fired on the crowd.

[12]One of the consistent themes of the intellectual fathers of the revolution was the desire to establish a polity characterized by a "government of laws, not of men." The purpose of creating such a state was to prevent the establishment of a tyranny over individual activity such as the colonial leaders saw in the actions of King George III and his parliament.

Source: H. Niles, *Principles and Acts of the Revolution in America.* (Baltimore, 1822), 480–482.

[14]The social tensions in Boston were of several kinds. There was animosity between British troops and colonials; between those loyal to the Crown and those who supported rebellion; there were class conflicts among the colonists themselves. All these were exacerbated by the actions of the colonial governors who were in the habit of promising to deal fairly with the citizens of Boston and then reneging on those promises. In short, the city was a hotbed of dissent and conflict.

[15]"Boughes" was an archaic term for gallows.

The Events of the Boston Massacre as Reported in London[13]

On the evening of Monday, being the current, several soldiers of the 29th regiment, were seen parading the streets with their drawn cutlasses and bayonets, "abusing and wounding numbers of the inhabitants."[14] A few minutes after nine o'clock, four youths, named Edward Archbald, Wm. Merchant, Francis Archbald, and John Leech, jun. came down Cornhill together, and separating at Dr. Loring's Corner, the two former, in passing a narrow alley, where a soldier was brandishing a broad sword, of an uncommon size, against the walls, out of which he struck fire plentifully, and a person of a mean countenance, armed with a large cudgel, by him, Edward Archbald bade Mr. Merchant take care of the sword, on which the soldier turned round, struck Archbald on the arm, and then pushed at Merchant.

Merchant then struck the soldier with a short flick, and the other person ran to the barrack, and brought with him two soldiers one armed with a pair of tongs, the other with a shovel; he with the tongs pursued Archbald back through the alley, collared, and laid him over the head with the tongs. The noise brought people together, and John Hicks, a young lad, coming up, knocked the soldier down, but let him get up again; and more lads gathering drove them back to the barrack, where the boys stood some time as it were to keep them in. In less than a minute ten or twelve soldiers came out, with drawn cutlasses, clubs, and bayonets, and set upon the unarmed boys, who, finding the inequality of their equipment, dispersed.

On hearing the noise, one Samuel Atwood came up to see what was the matter, and met the soldiers aforesaid rushing down the alley, and asked them if they intended to murder people? They answered, yes, by G—d, root and branch! With that one of them struck Mr. Atwood with a club, which was repeated by another, and, being unarmed, he turned to go off, and received a wound on the left shoulder, which reached the bone. Retreating a few steps, Mr. Atwood met two officers, and said, gentlemen, what is the matter? They answered, you'll see bye and bye. Immediately after, these heroes appeared in the square, asking where were the Boughes?[15] Where were the cowards? Thirty or forty persons, mostly lads, being by this means gathered in King-Street, Capt. Preston, with a party of men, with charged bayonets, came from the main guard, and taking their stations by the Custom-House, began to push and drive the people off, pricking some, and threatening others; on which the people grew clamorous, and, it is said, threw snow-balls. On this the captain commanded his men to fire, and more snow-balls coming, he again said, D—n you, fire be the consequence what it will! One soldier then fired, and a townsman, with a cudgel, struck him over the hands with such force that he dropped his firelock, and, rushing forward, aimed a blow at the captain's head, which grazed his hat, and fell pretty heavy upon his arm: However, the soldiers continued the fire successively, till seven or eight, or, as some say, eleven, guns were discharged.

By this fatal manoeuvre, several were laid dead on the spot, and some lay struggling for life; but what shewed a degree of cruelty unknown to British troops, was an attempt to fire upon, or stab with their bayonets, the persons who undertook to remove the slain and wounded! At length, Mr. Benjamin Leigh, of the Delpht manufactory,[16] came up, and, after some conversation with Capt. Preston, relative to his conduct, advised him to draw off his men; with which he complied.

[16]The Delpht manufactory was where ceramic cups with ornamental decorations were produced. These were used at society tea parties.

Source: *The London Magazine*, xxxix. (London: Printed by C. Ackers, 1770), 222.

Samuel Adams: Report on the Meeting of the Boston Committee of Correspondence

(1772)

INTRODUCTION

Samuel Adams was one of the most zealous supporters of colonial liberties. In 1772, he organized the Boston Committee of Correspondence and published "The Natural Rights of the Colonists as Men." Soon New England established similar committees throughout its territory, and Adams became the recognized leader and spokesman for the revolutionary movement. Natural rights are those which an individual possesses by virtue of his or her existence—they are not bestowed by government. The concept is based on John Locke's *Second Treatise of Government* and was supported by clergy in New England. Adams believed that natural rights were guaranteed by the British Constitution, not created by it.

The doctrine of natural rights runs through much of the literature of the revolutionary period. Although most famously expressed by Jefferson in the Declaration of Independence as "life, liberty, and the pursuit of happiness," it derives from John Locke's *Second Treatise* where it is expressed as "life, liberty, and property." By "natural" is understood an inborn characteristic inseparable from created man and, by extension, the intent of the Creator or "natural God."

Among the natural rights of the Colonists are these: First, a right to life; Secondly, to liberty; Thirdly, to property, together with the right to support and defend them in the best manner they can . . . All men have a right . . . in case of intolerable oppression, civil or religious, to leave the society they belong to, and enter into another . . . Every man . . . has a right peaceably and quietly to worship God according to dictates of his conscience . . . In regard to religion, mutual toleration in the different professions thereof is what all good and candid minds in all ages have ever practised . . . The natural liberty of man is to be free from any superior power on earth, and not to be under the will or legislative authority of man, but only to have the law of nature for his rule . . .[1]

The Rights of the Colonists as Subjects

A commonwealth or state is a body politic, or civil society of men, united together to promote their mutual safety and prosperity by means of their union. The absolute rights of Englishmen and all freemen, in or out of civil society, are principally personal security, personal liberty, and private property. All persons born in the British American Colonies are, by the laws of God and nature and by the common law of England . . . well entitled . . . to all the natural, essential, inherent, and inseparable rights, liberties, and privileges of subjects born in Great Britain . . . Among those rights are the following, which no man or body of men, consistently with their own rights as men and citizens, or members of society, can for themselves give up or take away from others.

First, The first fundamental, positive law of all common wealths or states is the establishing of the legislative power . . . Secondly, The Legislative has no right to absolute, arbitrary power over the lives and fortunes of the people . . . The Legislative cannot justly assume to itself a power to rule by extempore arbitrary decrees;[2] but it is bound to see that justice is dispensed, and that the rights of the subjects be decided by promulgated, standing, and known laws . . .[3]

[2]Despotic decrees made without previous preparation.

[3]Again, an expression of the desire to form a government of laws, not men.

Thirdly, the supreme power cannot justly take from any man any part of his property, without his consent in person or by his representative . . .

It is utterly irreconcilable to these principles and to many other fundamental maxims of the common law, common sense, and reason that a British House of Commons should have a right at pleasure to give and grant the property of the Colonists . . . The words of the Massachusetts charter are these . . . "our will and pleasure is, and we do hereby grant and establish for us . . . that all and every of the subjects of us . . . shall have and enjoy all liberties and immunities of free and natural subjects" . . . Now what liberty can there be where property is taken away without consent? Can it be said with any color of truth and justice, that this continent of three thousand miles in length . . . in which . . . there are five millions of people, has the least voice, vote, or influence in the British Parliament? Have they all together any more weight or power to return a single member to that House of Commons who have not inadvertently, but deliberately, assumed a power to dispose of their lives, liberties, and properties, than to choose an Emperor of China? Had the Colonists a right to return members to the British Parliament, it would only be hurtful, as, from their local situation and circumstances, it is impossible they should ever be truly and properly represented there. The inhabitants of this country, in all probability, in a few years, will be more numerous than those of Great Britain and Ireland together; yet it is absurdly expected by the promoters of the present measure that these, with their posterity to all generations, should be easy, while their property shall be disposed of by a House of Commons at three thousand mile's distance from them, and who cannot be supposed to have the least care or concern for their real interest . . .

The Colonists have been branded with the odious names of traitors and rebels only for complaining of their grievances. How long such treatment will or ought to be borne, is submitted.

Source: Harry Alonzo Cushing, ed., *The Writings of Samuel Adams*, Volume 2, 1770–1817. (New York: G.P. Putnam's Sons, 1906).

The Tea Act

(1773)

INTRODUCTION

Tea shipped to the American colonies was taxed by several acts of Parliament. This had been the practice since as early as 1723 when tea was taxed in England before shipment. In 1767, a Revenue Act provided for an American tax to replace the domestic levy to be collected at New York, Boston, Philadelphia, and Charleston. This tax produced political pushback in the colonies and first expressed itself as agitation against the drinking of tea.

An act to allow a drawback of the duties of customs[1] on the exportation of tea to any of his Majesty's colonies or plantations in America; to increase the deposit on bohea tea[2] to be sold at the India Company's sales; and to empower the commissioners of the treasury to grant licenses to the East India Company to export tea duty-free.

[1] A cancellation of the tax in England.

[2] The best quality Chinese black tea, named after the hilly region where it was grown.

I

WHEREAS by an act, made in the twelfth year of his present Majesty's reign, (entitled, An act for granting a drawback of part of the customs upon the exportation of tea to Ireland, and the British dominions in America; for altering the drawback upon foreign sugars exported from Great Britain to Ireland; for continuing the bounty on the exportation of British-made cordage; for allowing the importation of rice from the British plantations into the ports of Bristol, Liverpool, Lancaster, and Whitehaven, for immediate exportation to foreign parts; and to empower the chief magistrate of any corporation to administer the oath, and grant the certificate required by law, upon the removal of certain goods to London, which have been sent into the country for sale;) it is amongst other things, enacted, That for and during the space of five years, to be computed from and after the fifth day of July, one thousand seven hundred and seventy-two, there shall be drawn back and allowed for all teas which shall be sold after the said fifth day of July, one thousand seven hundred and seventy-two, at the public sale of the united company of merchants of England trading to the East Indies,[3] or which after that time shall be imported, by license, in pursuance of the said therein and hereinafter mentioned act, made in the eighteenth year of the reign of his late majesty King George the Second, and which shall be exported from this kingdom, as merchandise, to Ireland, or any of the British colonies or plantations in America, three-fifth parts of the several duties of customs which were paid upon the importation of such teas; which drawback or allowance, with respect to such teas as shall be exported to Ireland, shall be made to the exporter, in such manner, and under such rules, regulations, securities, penalties, and forfeitures, as any drawback or allowance was then payable, out of the duty of customs upon the exportation of foreign goods to Ireland; and with respect to such teas as shall be exported to the British colonies and plantations in America, the said drawback or allowance shall be made in such manner, and under such rules, regulations, penalties, and forfeitures, as any drawback or allowance payable out of the duty of customs upon foreign goods exported to foreign parts, was could, or might be made, before the passing of the said act of the twelfth year of his present Majesty's reign, (except in such cases as are otherwise therein provided for:) and whereas it may tend to the benefit and advantage of the trade of the said united company of merchants of England trading to the East Indies, if the allowance of the drawback of the duties of customs upon all teas sold at the public sales of the said united company, after the tenth day of May, one thousand seven hundred and seventy-three, and which shall be exported from this kingdom, as merchandise, to any of the British colonies or plantations in America, were to extend to the whole of the said duties of customs payable upon the importation of such teas; may it therefore please your Majesty that it may be enacted; and be it enacted by the King's most excellent majesty, by and with the advice and consent of the lords spiritual and temporal, and commons,[4] in this present parliament assembled, and by the authority of the same, That there shall be drawn back and allowed for all teas, which, from and after the tenth day of May, one thousand seven hundred and seventy-three, shall be sold at the public sales of the said united company, or which shall be imported by license, in pursuance of the said act made in the eighteenth year of the reign of his late majesty King George the Second, and which shall, at any time hereafter, be exported from this kingdom, as merchandise, to any of the British colonies or plantations in America, the whole of the duties of customs payable upon the importation of such teas; which drawback or allowance shall be made to the exporter in such manner, and under such rules, regulations, and securities, and subject to the like penalties and forfeitures, as the former drawback or allowance granted by the said recited act of the twelfth year of his present Majesty's reign, upon tea exported to the said British colonies and plantations in America was, might, or could be made, and was subject to by the said recited act, or any other act of parliament now in force, in as full and ample manner, to all intents and purposes, as if the several clauses relative thereto were again repeated and re-enacted in this present act.[5]

II

And whereas by one other act made in the eighteenth year of the reign of his late majesty King George the Second, (entitled, An act for repealing the present inland duty of four shillings per pound weight upon all tea sold in Great Britain; and for granting to his Majesty certain other inland duties in lieu thereof; and for better securing the duty upon tea, and other duties of excise;[6] and for pursuing offenders out of one county into another,) it is, amongst other things, enacted, That every person who shall, at any public sale of tea made by the united company of merchants of England trading to the East Indies, be declared to be the best bidder for any lot or lots of tea, shall, within three days after being so declared the best bidder or bidders for the same, deposit with the said united company, or such clerk or officer as the said company shall appoint to receive the same, forty shillings for every tub and for every chest of tea; and in case any such person or persons shall refuse or neglect to make such deposit within the time before limited, he, she, or they, shall forfeit and lose six times the value of such deposit directed to be made as aforesaid, to be recovered by action of debt, bill, plaint, or information, in any of His Majesty's courts of record at Westminster,[7] in which no essoin,[8] protection, or wager of law, or more than one imparlance,[9] shall be allowed; one moiety[10] of which forfeiture shall go to his Majesty, his heirs and successors, and the other moiety to such person as shall sue or prosecute for the same; and the sale of all teas, for which such deposit shall be neglected to be made as aforesaid, is thereby declared to be null and void, and such teas shall be again put up by the said united company to public sale, within fourteen days after the end of the sale of teas at which such teas were sold; and all and every buyer or buyers, who shall have neglected

[5]The Townsend Revenue Acts (1767). There were four Townsend Acts associated with Charles Townsend, chancellor of the exchequer. The one referenced here put a tax payable at colonial ports on lead, paper, glass, and tea. The money raised was to be used to pay the salaries of colonial judges and governors, which had previously been paid by colonial assemblies. By removing officials from their dependence on colonials, the act aimed at weakening colonial self-government and political liberty by placing officials beyond colonial control.
[6]A tax placed on exports.

[7]Seen by the colonists as another abuse: cases are now to be tried in British courts rather than colonial.
[8]An excuse for not appearing in court.
[9]Imparlance is the time granted to a party for making a settlement; delay of a suit or a request for such a delay.
[10]Portion.

to make such deposit as aforesaid, shall be, and is and are thereby rendered incapable of bidding for or buying any teas at any future public sale of the said united company: and whereas it is found to be expedient and necessary to increase the deposit to be made by any bidder or bidders for any lot or lots of bohea teas, at the public sales of teas to be made by the said united company; be it enacted by the authority aforesaid, That every person who shall, after the tenth day of May, one thousand seven hundred and seventy-three, at any public sale of tea to be made by the said united company of merchants of England trading to the East Indies, be declared to be the best bidder or bidders for any lot or lots of bohea tea, shall, within three days after being so declared the best bidder or bidders for the same, deposit with the said united company, or such clerk or officer as the said united company shall appoint to receive the same, four pounds of lawful money of Great Britain for every tub and for every chest of bohea tea, under the same terms and conditions, and subject to the same forfeitures, penalties, and regulations, as are mentioned and contained in the said recited act of the eighteenth year of the reign of his said late Majesty.

III

And be it further enacted by the authority aforesaid, That it shall and may be lawful for the commissioners of his Majesty's treasury, or any three or more of them, or for the high treasurer for the time being, upon application made to them by the said united company of merchants of England trading to the East Indies for that purpose, to grant a license or licenses to the said united company, to take out of their warehouses, without the same having been put up to sale, and to export to any of the British plantations in America, or to any parts beyond the seas, such quantity or quantities of tea as the said commissioners of his Majesty's treasury, or any three or more of them, or the high treasurer for the time being, shall think proper and expedient, without incurring any penalty or forfeiture for so doing; any thing in the said in part recited act, or any other law, to the contrary notwithstanding.

IV

And whereas by an act made in the ninth and tenth years of the reign of King William the Third, (entitled, An act for raising a sum not exceeding two millions, upon a fund, for payment of annuities, after the rate of eight pounds per centum per annum;[11] and for settling the trade to the East Indies,) and by several other acts of parliament which are now in force, the said united company of merchants of England trading to the East Indies are obliged to give security, under their common seal, for payment of the duties of customs upon all unrated[12] goods imported by them, so soon as the same shall be sold; and for exposing such goods to sale, openly and fairly, by way of auction, or by inch of candle,[13] within the space of three years from the importation thereof: and whereas it is expedient that some provision should be made to permit the said company, in certain cases, to export tea, on their own account, to the British plantations in America, or to foreign parts, without exposing such tea, to sale here, or being charged with the payment of any duty for the same;[14] be it therefore enacted by the authority aforesaid, That from and after the passing of this act, it shall and may be lawful for the commissioners of his Majesty's treasury, or any three or more of them, or the high treasurer for the time being, to grant a license or quantity of licenses to the said united company, to take out of their warehouses such quantity or quantities of tea as the said commissioners of the treasury, or any three or more of them, or the high treasurer for the time being, shall think proper, without the same having been exposed to sale in this kingdom; and to export such tea to any of the British colonies or plantations in America, or to foreign parts, discharged from the payment of any customs or duties whatsoever;[15] anything in the said recited act, or any other act to the contrary notwithstanding.

V

Provided always, and it is hereby further enacted by the authority aforesaid, That a due entry shall be made at the custom-house, of all such tea so exported by license, as aforesaid, expressing the quantities thereof, at what time imported, and by what ship; and such tea shall be shipped for exportation by the proper officer for that purpose, and shall, in all other respects, not altered by this act, be liable to the same rules, regulations, restrictions, securities, penalties, and forfeitures, as tea penalties, &c. exported to the like places was liable to before the passing this act: and upon the proper officer's duty, certifying the shipping of such tea to the collector and comptroller of his Majesty's customs for the port of London, upon the back of the license,

[11]A fixed income of 8 percent per year.

[12]Untaxed.

[13]An auction on which bidding is open only for a short time—as long as it takes for a candle to burn down one inch.

[14]The purpose of this was to create a monopoly for the East India Company by creating a commercial advantage. Having to pay no duty permitted them to undersell competition.

[15]Again, the purpose of this was to create a monopoly for the East India Company by creating for it a commercial advantage.

and the exportation thereof, verified by the oath of the husband[16] or agent for the said united company, to be wrote at the bottom of such certificate, and sworn before the said collector and comptroller of the customs, (which oath they are hereby empowered to administer,) it shall and may be lawful for such collector and comptroller to write off and discharge the quantity of tea so exported from the warrant of the respective ship in which such tea was imported.

VI

Provided nevertheless, That no such license shall be granted, unless it shall first be made to appear to the satisfaction of the commissioners of his Majesty's treasury, or any three or more of them, or the high treasurer for the time being, that at the time of taking out such teas, for the exportation of which license or licenses shall be granted, there will be left remaining in the warehouses of the said united company, a quantity of tea not less than ten millions of pounds weight; anything herein, or in any other act of parliament, contained to the contrary thereof notwithstanding.

Source: Danby Pickering, *The Statutes at Large . . . [from 1225 to 1867]*. (London: Cambridge, 1762–1869).

The New York Sons of Liberty Tea Resolutions

(1773)

INTRODUCTION

The colonists saw the Tea Act as an attempt by King George to assert his authority. Samuel Adams and the Sons of Liberty used the issue to foment rebellion, boycotts, and smuggling. A program of intimidation was focused on the five tea ports and erupted into the violent action we know as the Boston Tea Party in December 1773. The Boston Tea Party was the first of many such organized activities. New York, Annapolis, Portsmouth (New Hampshire), and Edmonton (North Carolina) all had "parties" involving the turning-away or burning of the tea ships. At Charleston, tea was seized, sold on the open market, and the profits used to pay for revolutionary activity. The Tea Resolutions of New York are typical of the organized resistance to what was seen as British economic tyranny.

To prevent a calamity which, of all others, is the most to be dreaded-slavery and its terrible concomitants—we, the subscribers, being influenced from a regard to liberty, and disposed to use all lawful endeavors in our power, to defeat the pernicious project, and to transmit to our posterity those blessings of freedom which our ancestors have handed down to us; and to contribute to the support of the common liberties of America,[1] which are in danger to be subverted, do, for those important purposes, agree to associate together, under the name and style of the sons of New York,[2] and engage our honour to, and with each other faithfully to observe and perform the following resolutions, viz.

1st. Resolved, that whoever shall aid or abet, or in any manner assist, in the introduction of tea from any place whatsoever, into this colony, while it is subject, by a British Act of Parliament, to the payment of a duty, for the purpose of raising a revenue in America, he shall be deemed an enemy to the liberties of America.

2d. Resolved, that whoever shall be aiding, or assisting, in the landing, or carting of such tea, from any ship, or vessel, or shall hire any house, storehouse, or cellar or any place whatsoever, to deposit the

[1] This statement anticipates the preamble to the Constitution "and secure the Blessings of Liberty to ourselves and to our posterity."

[2] Sons of Liberty were organizations that existed throughout the colonies in reaction to the Stamp Act but more generally as a reflection of the general discontent of the population. Boston and New York had especially active groups. In support of their actions to promote self-government, they engaged in extralegal activities: tarring and feathering officials and intimidation of British officials. They raised funds through rallies and dinners where they denounced the British, sang revolutionary songs, and hanged officials in effigy.

tea, subject to a duty as aforesaid, he shall be deemed an enemy to the liberties of America.

3d. Resolved, that whoever shall sell, or buy, or in any manner contribute to the sale, or purchase of tea, subject to a duty as aforesaid, or shall aid, or abet, in transporting such tea, by land or water, from this city, until the seventh year of the reign of George III, chap. 46, of Parliamentary resolutions, shall be totally and clearly repealed, he shall be deemed an enemy to the liberties of America.

4th. Resolved, that whether the duties on tea, imposed by this Act, be paid in Great Britain or in America, our liberties are equally affected.

5th. Resolved, that whoever shall transgress any of these resolutions, we will not deal with, or employ, or have any connection with him.[3]

[3]The membership of the New York Sons of Liberty consisted of the most prominent and influential merchants and lawyers of the city. These resolutions were widely distributed in order to give people from all classes of society the opportunity to "sign on" to the document. Those who refused were excluded from the ranks of association with leadership, with the attendant ostracization that naturally would follow.

Source: H. Niles, *Principles and Acts of the Revolution in America*. (Baltimore: Printed by W.O. Niles, 1822).

Three Accounts of the Boston Tea Party
(1773)

INTRODUCTION

In opposition to Parliament's imposition of port duties and the establishment of a virtual monopoly in the tea trade in favor of the ailing East India Company, Samuel Adams broke up the Boston Town meeting of December 16, 1773, by declaring that since the colonial governor Hutchinson refused to allow three tea ships to return to England without paying the duty, there was nothing more a peaceful meeting could accomplish. It was then that the "Sons of Liberty," in disguise, boarded the tea ships and threw 342 chests of tea into Boston harbor. That night the harbor became a giant tea pot and the colonials adopted violence as a technique of dealing with British oppression.

Account Told by George Hewes[1]

[1]Hewes was a participant in the Boston Tea Party, an eyewitness to the events.

On the day preceding the seventeenth, there was a meeting of the citizens of the county of Suffolk, convened at one of the churches in Boston, for the purpose of consulting on what measures might be considered expedient to prevent the landing of the tea, or secure the people from the collection of the duty. At that meeting a committee was appointed to wait on Governor Hutchinson . . .

When the committee returned and informed the meeting of the absence of the Governor, there was a confused murmur among the members, and the meeting was immediately dissolved, many of them crying out, "Let every man do his duty, and be true to his country"; and there was a general huzza for Griffin's wharf.

It was now evening, and I immediately dressed myself in the costume of an Indian, equipped with a small hatchet, which I and my associates denominated the tomahawk, with which, and a club, after having painted my face and hands with coal dust in the shop of a blacksmith, I repaired to Griffin's wharf, where the ships lay that contained the tea. When I fell in with many who were dressed, equipped and painted as I was, and who fell in with me and marched ignored to the place of our destination.

When we arrived at the wharf, there were three of our number who assumed an authority to direct our operations, to which we readily submitted.[2] They divided us into three parties, for the purpose of boarding the three ships which contained the tea. . .

We were immediately ordered by the respective commanders to board all the ships at the same time, which we promptly obeyed. The commander of the division to which I belonged as soon as we were on board the ship appointed me boatswain, and ordered me to go to the captain and demand of him the keys to the hatches and a dozen candles. I made the demand accordingly and the captain promptly replied and delivered the articles; but requested me at the same time to do no damage to the ship or rigging.

Source: James Hawkes, *A Retrospect of the Boston Tea Party.* (New York, 1834), 36–41.

[3]The letters of John Andrews, a prominent Boston merchant and active "Whig," are an important source of our knowledge of everyday life during the British occupation. Andrews remained in Boston to protect his property during the period immediately preceding armed hostilities. His correspondence with William Barrett, a Philadelphia merchant, is rife with reports of conflict between citizens and redcoats. This account is a secondhand but contemporary report by an observer not a participant.

[4]*Hall*, *Bruce*, and *Coffin* were the names of the tea ships involved in the Boston Tea Party. Here Andrews remarks the ships have arrived in harbor.

[5]Castle William was a place of refuge for those consigners who refused to resign their positions. Supported by the royal government and protected by British soldiers, they lived insulated from the storms of colonial conflict in the streets of Boston. They spent their time drinking toasts to the Crown and partying with army officers.

Letters of John Andrews[3]

December 1st

Hall and Bruce arrived Saturday evening with each an hundred and odd chests of the detested tea.[4] What will be done with it, can't say: but I tremble for ye consequences should your consignees still persist in their obstinacy and not consent to reship it . . .

December 1st . . .

The consignees have all taken their residence at the Castle,[5] as they still persist in their refusal to take the tea back. Its not only ye town, but the country are unanimous against the landing it . . .

December 18th

However precarious our situation may be, yet such is the present calm composure of the people that a stranger would hardly think that ten thousand pounds sterling of the East India Company's tea was destroy'd the night, or rather evening before last, yet its a serious truth . . . when a general muster was assembled, from this and ye neighboring towns, to the number of five or six thousand, at 10 o'clock Thursday morning in the Old South Meeting house, where they pass'd a unanimous vote that the Tea should go out of the harbour that afternoon, and sent a committee with Mr Ratch to ye Custom house to demand a clearance, which the collector told 'em was not in his power to give, without the duties first paid . . .[6]

They muster'd, I'm told, upon Fort Hill, to the number of about two hundred, and proceeded, two by two, to Griffins wharf, where Hall, Bruce, and Coffin lay, each with 114 chests of the ill fated article on board; the two former with only that article, but ye latter arrived at ye wharf only ye day before, was freighted with a large quantity of other goods; which they took the greatest care not to injure in the least, and before nine o'clock in ye evening, every chest from on board the three vessels was knock'd to pieces and flung over ye sides. They say the actors were Indians from Narragansett.[7] Whether they were or not, to a transient observer they appear'd as such, being clothed in Blankets with the heads muffled, and copper color'd countenances, being each arm'd with a hatchet or axe, and pair pistols, nor was their dialect different from what I conceive these geniuses to speak, as their jargon was unintelligible to all but themselves . . .

Source: John Andrews, *Letters of John Andrews, esq, of Boston*. (Massachusetts Historical Society, Proceedings, edited by Winthrop Sargent, 1866).

An Account from the *Boston Gazetteer* and *New Daily Advertiser*[8]

There have been some doubts concerning the destruction of the tea on the 16th of December, 1773. The number of the ships, and the place where they were situated is not quite certain . . . The number of chests destroyed was, according to the newspapers of the time, 342. There was a body meeting on the 16th of December, 1773. This matter of the tea was the occasion of the meeting . . . The meeting began at Faneuil Hall but it was adjourned to the Old South and even that place could not contain all who came . . . among the spectators was John Rowe[9] who, among other things, said, "Who knows how tea will mingle with salt water"[10] and this suggestion was received with great applause . . . A committee was sent from the meeting, to request Gov Hutchinson to order the ships to depart . . . The committee returned about sunset with his answer, that he could not interfere. At this moment the Indian yell was heard from the street . . . the people rushed out, and accompanied the "Indians" to the ships. The number of persons

[6]Captain Ratch was the commander of the guard at the Customs House where imported merchandise was stored pending payment of import duties. He stated that he would attempt to land the tea himself if ordered to do so by "the proper officers." It was that inflammatory statement that set off the attack on the tea ships.

[7]The "Indians" have been described as both Mohawks and Narragansets. The colonists disguised themselves in order to protect their identities in case they were arrested for treason. It worked; the attorney general of Massachusetts was unable to identify any of the culprits. Only one colonist, of the hundreds who witnessed the tea party, was willing to testify.

[8]This reflects the political slant of a "middle of the road" publication. Neither Tory nor Whig, it presents a colorful account of the meeting that led to the action of December 16, 1773.

[9]John Rowe was a resident of Pond Street in Boston, near the wharfs where the tea ships were tied up. He owned one of the tea ships in the harbor (the *Eleanor*).

[10]Rowe's diary for December 16 says, "I being a little unwell staid at home all day and all the evening," which may have been meant to give cover for his attendance, and this inflammatory comment, at this meeting.

disguised as Indians is variously stated . . . none put it lower than 60, none higher than 80. It is said by persons who were present, that nothing was destroyed but tea . . . the destruction was effected by disguised persons, and some young men who volunteered . . . The contrivers of this measure, and those who carried it into effect, will never be known as some few persons have been mentioned as being among the disguised; but there are many and obvious reasons why secrecy then, and concealment since, were necessary . . . Mr Samuel Adams is thought to have been in the counseling of this exploit, and many other men who were leaders in the political affairs of the times . . .

Source: Hezekiah Niles, *Principles and Acts of the American Revolution.* (Baltimore: Printed by W.O. Niles, 1822), 485–486.

Maryland's Reaction to the Intolerable Acts

(1773–1774)

INTRODUCTION

Lord North, prime minister of Great Britain, reacted to the Boston Tea Party by causing Parliament to pass a series of so-called Intolerable Acts to punish the colonies, especially Massachusetts, for their disloyalties. The first of them, the Boston Port Act, closed the port of Boston until the colonists paid for the damages caused to the East India Company by the loss of their property. The Boston Port Act soon became a cause célèbre for the colonies, uniting them in support of Boston, and saw the beginnings of a formal movement of resistance, including the call for meetings and the formation of Committees of Correspondence to coordinate that resistance.

Maryland's declaration (May 30, 1774) was soon followed by resolutions from Pennsylvania (June 20, 1774), New York (July 6, 1774), and Virginia (July 26, 1774). By September 1774, the First Continental Congress was in session and the die was cast.

Action of the People of Maryland upon the Subject of the Boston Port-Bill

Queen Anne's County, May 30, 1774

At a meeting of a considerable number of the magistrates, and other of the most respectable inhabitants of Queen-Anne's county, at Queen's town, on the thirtieth day of May, 1774, in order to deliberate upon the tendency and effect of the act of parliament for blocking up the port and harbor of Boston. Duly considering and deeply affected with the prospect of the unhappy situation of Great Britain and British America, under any kind of disunion, this meeting think themselves obliged, by all the ties which ever ought to preserve a firm union among Americans, as speedily as possible to make known their sentiments to their distressed brethren of Boston;. . .

That they look upon the cause of Boston in its consequences to be the common cause of America. That the act of parliament for blocking up the port and harbor of Boston, appears to them a cruel and

This was an attempt to gain relief from British anticolonial actions by promoting a refusal to purchase British commodities. It became a sign of patriotism to support such action to use pressure to injure the British economy.

oppressive invasion of their natural rights, as men, and constitutional rights as English subjects, and if not repealed, will be a foundation for the utter destruction of American freedom. That all legal and constitutional means ought to be used by all America, for procuring a repeal of the said act of parliament. That the only effectual means of obtaining such repeal, they are at present of opinion, is an association, under the strongest ties, for breaking off all commercial connections with Great Britain,[1] until the said act of parliament be repealed, and the right assumed by parliament for taxing America, in all cases whatsoever, be given up, and American freedom ascertained and settled upon a permanent constitutional foundation.

That the most practicable mode of forming such an effectual association, they conceive to be a general meeting of the gentlemen, who are already or shall be appointed committees, to form an American intercourse and correspondence upon this most interesting occasion. That in the mean time they will form such particular associations as to them shall seem effectual; yet professing themselves ready to join in any reasonable general one that may be devised as aforesaid. That these sentiments be immediately forwarded to be printed in the Maryland and Pennsylvania Gazettes . . .

Source: H. Niles, *Principles and Acts of the Revolution in America.* (Baltimore: Printed by W.O. Niles, 1822), 172.

The Committee of Correspondence
(May 31, 1774)

INTRODUCTION

Committees of Correspondence were committees organized to support the patriot cause. The earliest Committee of Correspondence was organized in Massachusetts by Samuel Adams in 1772, but the idea quickly spread to other colonies, most notably to Virginia. There were three types: local committees such as those in Massachusetts organized in 1772 by Samuel Adams; colony committees that became parts of legislatures (Virginia 1773); and, most important, county committees that directed public opinion and exercised executive, judicial, and legislative function. The Baltimore Committee is an example of the third type. The purpose of the committee was to spread pro-revolutionary propaganda. At times the committee acted as both local court and legislature laying the groundwork for local governments.

Baltimore County, May 31, 1774.

At a general meeting of the freeholders, gentlemen, merchants, tradesmen, and other inhabitants of Baltimore county, held at the court house of the said county, on Tuesday the 31st of May 1774, Captain Charles Ridgely, Chairman . . .

I. Resolved. That it is the opinion of this meeting, that the town of Boston is now suffering in the common cause of America, and that it is the duty of every colony in America to unite in the most effectual means to obtain a repeal of the late act of parliament for blocking up the harbor of Boston . . .

II. That it is the opinion of this meeting, that if the colonies come into a joint resolution to stop importations from, and exportations to Great Britain and the West-Indies, until the act for blocking up the harbor of Boston be repealed, the same may be the means of preserving North America in her liberties.

III. That therefore the inhabitants of this county will join in an association with the several counties in this province and the principal colonies in America, to put a stop to exports to Great Britain and the West-Indies, after the first day of October next, or such other day as may be agreed on, and to put a stop to the imports from Great Britain after the first day of December next, or such other day as may be agreed upon, until the said act shall be repealed, and that such association shall be upon oath.

IV. Unanimously. That it is the opinion of this meeting, that as the most effectual means of uniting all parts of this province in such association, as proposed, a general congress of deputies from each county be held at Annapolis at such times as may be agreed upon and that if agreeable to the sense of our sister colonies, delegates shall be appointed from this province to attend a general congress of delegates from the colonies, at such time and place as shall be agreed on, in order to settle and establish a general plan of conduct for the important purposes aforementioned.

V. Unanimously. That the inhabitants of this county will, and it is the opinion of this meeting, that this province ought to break off all trade and dealings with that colony, province or town, which all decline or refuse to come into similar resolutions with a majority of the colonies.

VI. That Capt. Charles Ridgely, [et al] . . be a committee to attend a general meeting at Annapolis.[1] And that the same gentlemen . . . be a committee of correspondence to receive and answer all letters, and on any emergency, to call a general meeting, and that any six of the number have power to act.

VII. That a copy of the proceedings be transmitted to the several counties of this province, directed to their committee of correspondence, and be also published in the Maryland Gazette, to evince to all the world the sense they entertain of the invasion of their constitutional rights and liberties.

VIII. That the chairman be desired to return the thanks of this meeting to the gentlemen of the committee of correspondence

[1]This call for united action shows that Annapolis had long been an advocate for organized resistance. After the revolution (1786), a convention was held to discuss changes in the Articles of Confederation. This meeting was moved to Philadelphia at the urging of Hamilton and Madison where, as the Constitutional Convention, the founding document of the American polity was framed (1789).

from Annapolis, for their polite personal attendance in consequence of an invitation by the committee of correspondence for Baltimore town.

Signed per order,
William Lux, Clerk.

> **Source:** H. Niles, *Principles and Acts of the Revolution in America*. (Baltimore: Printed by W.O. Niles, 1822), 172.

The Suffolk Resolves

(1774)

INTRODUCTION

In the spring and summer of 1774, Parliament took action in retaliation for the Boston Tea Party. It closed Boston Harbor to all shipping until the city had paid the East India Company for the losses it suffered because of the destruction of its property. Other measures canceled Massachusetts's right to select its own judges and provided for the billeting of British troops in private homes throughout the colony. These actions, known as the Coercive Acts, resulted in a pushback by the citizens of Suffolk County, the area that included Boston and the surrounding towns.

A meeting was held in Milton, just south of Boston, where Dr. Joseph Warren, a leading patriot, presented these Resolves, denouncing the acts of Parliament and proposing, among other things, that they be ignored, that a militia be established, and that from then on no taxes be paid to the mother country.

The meeting passed the resolutions unanimously and had Paul Revere carry them to the Continental Congress then meeting in Philadelphia. When Congress approved the resolves on September 9, the colonies took a major step toward independence.

At a meeting of the delegates of every town & district in the county of Suffolk . . . at the house of Mr. Richard Woodward, of Deadham, & by adjournment, at the house of Mr. [Daniel] Vose, of Milton, on Friday the 9th instant, Joseph Palmer, esq. being chosen moderator, and William Thompson, esq. clerk, a committee was chosen to bring in a report to the convention, and the following being several times read, and put paragraph by paragraph, was unanimously voted, viz.

Whereas the power but not the justice, the vengeance but not the wisdom of Great-Britain, which of old persecuted, scourged, and exiled our fugitive parents from their native shores, now pursues us, their guiltless children, with unrelenting severity: And whereas, this, then savage and uncultivated desart, was purchased by the toil and treasure, or acquired by the blood and valor of those our venerable progenitors;

to us they bequeathed the dear bought inheritance, to our care and protection they consigned it, and the most sacred obligations are upon us to transmit the glorious purchase, unfettered by power, unclogged with shackles, to our innocent and beloved offspring. On the fortitude, on the wisdom and on the exertions of this important day, is suspended the fate of this new world, and of unborn millions. If a boundless extent of continent, swarming with millions, will tamely submit to live, move and have their being at the arbitrary will of a licentious minister,[1] they basely yield to voluntary slavery,[2] and future generations shall load their memories with incessant execrations.[3]— On the other hand, if we arrest the hand which would ransack our pockets, if we disarm the parricide[4] which points the dagger to our bosoms, if we nobly defeat that fatal edict which proclaims a power to frame laws for us in all cases whatsoever, thereby entailing the endless and numberless curses of slavery upon us, our heirs and their heirs forever; if we successfully resist that unparalleled usurpation[5] of unconstitutional power, whereby our capital is robbed of the means of life; whereby the streets of Boston are thronged with military executioners;[6] whereby our coasts are lined and harbours crowded with ships of war; whereby the charter of the colony, that sacred barrier against the encroachments of tyranny, is mutilated[7] and, in effect, annihilated; whereby a murderous law is framed to shelter villains from the hands of justice;[8] whereby the unalienable and inestimable inheritance, which we derived from nature,[9] the constitution of Britain, and the privileges warranted to us in the charter of the province, is totally wrecked, annulled, and vacated, posterity will acknowledge that virtue which preserved them free and happy; and while we enjoy the rewards and blessings of the faithful, the torrent of panegyrists will roll our reputations to that latest period, when the streams of time shall be absorbed in the abyss of eternity.[10]—Therefore, we have resolved, and do resolve,

1. That whereas his majesty, George the Third, is the rightful successor to the throne of Great-Britain, and justly entitled to the allegiance of the British realm, and agreeable to compact, of the English colonies in America—therefore, we, the heirs and successors of the first planters of this colony, do cheerfully acknowledge the said George the Third to be our rightful sovereign, and that said covenant is the tenure and claim on which are founded our allegiance and submission.[11]

2. That it is an indispensable duty which we owe to God, our country, ourselves and posterity, by all lawful ways and means in our power

[1] Lord North, prime minister of Britain, is accused of acting in an immoral and illegal manner.

[2] History loves irony. It is ironic that the diction of the Suffolk Resolves, which protests against the enslavement of the colonies by king and Parliament, was written at a time when the enslavement of blacks was an accepted fact. The year 1619 that witnessed the first cargo of slaves brought to Virginia also witnessed the establishment of the first representative assembly on American soil, the Virginia House of Burgesses. When that assembly passed statutes restraining the slave trade, King George vetoed the measures because they limited the heavy profits that the English realized from that shameful business. This action added to the growing friction between the colonies and the mother country. Slavery was introduced into Massachusetts in 1636 and given legal status five years later. By the end of the 17th century, slavery was legal in all the English colonies. Massachusetts, Rhode Island, Connecticut, and New Hampshire grew rich from the trade and by 1771, 192 English slave ships were active. By the time of the Suffolk Resolves, the attitude against slavery in the northern colonies was morally based; but it soon died out because of the huge profits that the trade produced. By 1776, the black population has been estimated at one half million. By 1774, antislavery feeling was strong among the founders. Jefferson condemned the slave trade in the original text of the Declaration of Independence, but New England traders joined with southern planters to force him to remove the clause. The authors of the resolves were consistent in their abhorrence of physical and political slavery. But their concerns were overwhelmed by mercantile political interests.

[3] Future generations shall denounce them harshly.

[4] A parricide occurs when a person kills a close relative. Here, Britain (the "mother" country) is murdering her own child (the Massachusetts colony).

[5] This means to seize by force illegally.

[6] This is a reference to the Boston Massacre.

[7]The Massachusetts Government Act repealed the Royal Charter granted to the founders of the Massachusetts Bay Colony.

[8]"An Act for the Administration of Justice" in March 1774 said that any judge or official indicted for murder had to be tried in England.

[9]This statement anticipates Jefferson's phrase in the Declaration of Independence. It reflects the doctrine of natural rights of man that are "inalienable" and not transferred to another.

[10]So long as we remain faithful to the causes of freedom, we will be highly praised forever.

[11]This opening statement frames the document with an expression of loyalty to the king. Many colonists still hoped for some agreement with the Crown. Many of the delegates agreed with John Adams when he remarked, "There is not a man among us who would not be happy to see accommodation with Britain." John Adams of Massachusetts was a distant relative of Samuel Adams. He was a fearless leader of the patriot cause and succeeded to the presidency on the retirement of George Washington. Educated as a lawyer, he had a fierce sense of justice and even represented the soldiers accused of murder in the Boston Massacre trial. He was a great speaker and a leader of the deliberations of the Continental Congress, where his powers of persuasion, apt reasoning, and sense of humor drove and shaped the deliberations.

[12]This is a recurring theme of many revolutionary documents: fighting to preserve freedom and concern with preserving that freedom for future generations.

[13]This refers to the law that officials indicted for murder had to be tried in Britain, since colonial magistrates had been delegitimized.

[14]This phrase states that colonial law enforcement officers will not obey orders of courts run by judges appointed by Britain.

[15]Here the focus is narrowed to a specific: not just freedom but preserving it by constructing a legal framework for settling disputes and avoiding recourse to British courts.

[16]Officers are told to refuse to transmit tax money to British officials.

to maintain, defend and preserve those civil and religious rights and liberties, for which many of our fathers fought, bled and died, and to hand them down entire to future generations.[12]

3. That the late acts of the British parliament for blocking up the harbour of Boston, for altering the established form of government in this colony, and for screening the most flagitious violators of the laws of the province from a legal trial,[13] are gross infractions of those rights to which we are justly entitled by the laws of nature, the British constitution, and the charter of the province.

4. That no obedience is due from this province to either or any part of the acts above-mentioned, but that they be rejected as the attempts of a wicked administration to enslave America.

5. That so long as the justices of our superior court of judicature, court of assize, &c. and inferior court of common pleas in this county are appointed, or hold their places, by any other tenure than that which the charter and the laws of the province direct, they must be considered as under undue influence, and are therefore unconstitutional officers, and, as such, no regard ought to be paid to them by the people of this county.

6. That if the justices of the superior court of judicature, assize, &c. justices of the court of common pleas, or of the general sessions of the peace, shall sit and act during their present disqualified state, this county will support, and bear harmless, all sheriffs and their deputies, constables, jurors and other officers who shall refuse to carry into execution the orders of said courts;[14] and, as far as possible, to prevent the many inconveniences which must be occasioned by a suspension of the courts of justice, we do most earnestly recommend it to all creditors, that they shew all reasonable and even generous forbearance to their debtors; and to all debtors, to pay their just debts with all possible speed, and if any disputes relative to debts or trespasses shall arise, which cannot be settled by the parties, we recommend it to them to submit all such causes to arbitration;[15] and it is our opinion that the contending parties or either of them, who shall refuse so to do, ought to be considered as co-operating with the enemies of this country.

7. That it be recommended to the collectors of taxes, constables, and all other officers, who have public monies in their hands, to retain the same, and not to make any payment thereof to the provincial county treasurer[16] until the civil government of the province is placed upon a constitutional foundation, or until it shall otherwise be ordered by the proposed provincial Congress.

8. That the persons who have accepted seats at the council board, by virtue of a mandamus from the King,[17] in conformity to the late act of the British parliament, entitled, an act for the regulating the government of the Massachusetts-Bay, have acted in direct violation of the duty they owe to their county, and have thereby given great and just offence to this people; therefore, resolved, that this county do recommend it to all persons, who have so highly offended by accepting said departments, and have not already publicly resigned their seats at the council board, to make public resignations of their places at said board, on or before the 20th day of this instant, September; and that all persons refusing so to do, shall, from and after said day, be considered by this county as obstinate and incorrigible enemies to this country.[18]

9. That the fortifications begun and now carrying on upon Boston Neck,[19] are justly alarming to this county, and gives us reason to apprehend some hostile intention against that town, more especially as the commander in chief has, in a very extraordinary manner, removed the powder from the magazine at Charlestown, and has also forbidden the keeper of the magazine at Boston, to deliver out to the owners, the powder, which they had lodged in said magazine.

10. That the late act of parliament for establishing the Roman Catholic religion and the French laws in that extensive country, now called Canada, is dangerous in an extreme degree to the Protestant religion and to the civil rights and liberties of all America; and, therefore, as men and Protestant Christians, we are indispensably obliged to take all proper measures for our security.[20]

11. That whereas our enemies have flattered themselves that they shall make an easy prey of this numerous, brave and hardy people, from an apprehension that they are unacquainted with military discipline; we, therefore, for the honour, defence and security of this county and province, advise, as it has been recommended to take away all commissions from the officers of the militia, that those who now hold commissions, or such other persons, be elected in each town as officers in the militia, as shall be judged of sufficient capacity for that purpose, and who have evidenced themselves the inflexible friends to the rights of the people; and that the inhabitants of those towns and districts, who are qualified, do use their utmost diligence to acquaint themselves with the art of war as soon as possible, and do, for that purpose, appear under arms at least once every week.[21]

[17]A "mandamus" is an order from the king.

[18]Officials appointed by the Crown must resign by September 20 or be considered enemies of the county.

[19]The British built fortifications after the Battles of Lexington and Concord to "protect the city."

[20]The legitimization of the Roman Catholic religion in French Canada was seen as a hostile act to the Protestant colonists. It was one of the reasons for the colonial attack on Montreal and Quebec in the early period of revolution. For almost two centuries, the French and English colonies had been antagonists in the struggle for control of America. The French were Roman Catholic, accepting of the absolutism of the Bourbon dynasty; the British colonies were a Protestant self-governing people. In June 1774, Parliament passed the Quebec Act, which aroused the opposition in the colonies as much as the Stamp Act had. Under the act, Quebec was to be governed by a governor and council appointed by Parliament. The territory of Quebec was extended south to the Ohio River and west to the Mississippi; French civil law was to be regional and the Roman Catholic religion tolerated. The act was both a territorial, governmental, and religious act of aggression.

[21]This provides for the establishment of a colonial militia.

12. That during the present hostile appearances on the part of Great-Britain, notwithstanding the many insults and oppressions which we most sensibly resent, yet, nevertheless, from our affection to his majesty, which we have at all times evidenced, we are determined to act merely upon the defensive, so long as such conduct may be vindicated by reason and the principles of self-preservation, but no longer.[22]

13. That, as we understand it has been in contemplation to apprehend sundry persons of this county, who have rendered themselves conspicuous in contending for the violated rights and liberties of their countrymen; we do recommend, should such an audacious measure be put in practice, to seize and keep in safe custody, every servant of the present tyrannical and unconstitutional government throughout the county and province, until the persons so apprehended be liberated from the bands of our adversaries, and restored safe and uninjured to their respective friends and families.[23]

14. That until our rights are fully restored to us, we will, to the utmost of our power, and we recommend the same to the other counties, to withhold all commercial intercourse with Great-Britain, Ireland, and the West-Indies, and abstain from the consumption of British merchandise and manufactures, and especially of East-Indies, and piece goods, with such additions, alterations, and exceptions only, as the General Congress of the colonies may agree to.[24]

15. That under our present circumstances, it is incumbent on us to encourage arts and manufactures amongst us,[25] by all means in our power, and that be and are hereby appointed a committee, to consider of the best ways and means to promote and establish the same, and to report to this convention as soon as may be.

16. That the exigencies of our public affairs, demand that a provincial Congress be called to consult such measures as may be adopted, and vigorously executed by the whole people; and we do recommend it to the several towns in this county, to chuse members for such a provincial Congress,[26] to be holden at Concord, on the second Tuesday of October, next ensuing.

17. That this county, confiding in the wisdom and integrity of the continental Congress, now sitting at Philadelphia, pay all due respect and submission to such measures as may be recommended by them to the colonies, for the restoration and establishment of our just rights, civil and religious, and for renewing that harmony

and union between Great-Britain and the colonies, so earnestly wished for by all good men.

18. That whereas the universal uneasiness which prevails among all orders of men, arising from the wicked and oppressive measures of the present administration, may influence some unthinking persons to commit outrage upon private property; we would heartily recommend to all persons of this community, not to engage in any routs, riots, or licentious attacks upon the properties of any person whatsoever, as being subversive of all order and government; but, by a steady, manly, uniform, and persevering opposition, to convince our enemies, that in a contest so important, in a cause so solemn, our conduct shall be such as to merit the approbation of the wise, and the admiration of the brave and free of every age and of every country.

19. That should our enemies, by any sudden manoeuvres, render it necessary to ask the aid and assistance of our brethren in the country, some one of the committee of correspondence, or a select man of such town, or the town adjoining, where such hostilities shall commence, or shall be expected to commence, shall despatch couriers with written messages to the select men, or committees of correspondence, of the several towns in the vicinity, with a written account of such matter, who shall despatch others to committees more remote, until proper and sufficient assistance be obtained, and that the expense of said couriers be defrayed by the county, until it shall be otherwise ordered by the provincial Congress.

Source: *Journal of the Proceedings of the Congress.* (London: J. Almon, 1775), 24–32.

Thomas Jefferson's Summary View of the Rights of British America

(August 1774)

Thomas Jefferson, the scion of an aristocratic Virginia family, intellectual giant, lawyer, member of the Virginia Assembly, slave owner, and main author of the Declaration of Independence, was outraged when news arrived in Virginia that Parliament had closed the port of Boston in reprisal for the Boston Tea Party.

Jefferson urged action by the assembly to support the citizens of Boston. A day of fasting and mourning was proclaimed for June 11, 1774, whereupon the British governor of Virginia dissolved the assembly. The members then met at Williamsburg to form a revolutionary convention to act. Jefferson was one of those chosen to represent Virginia at the First Continental Congress.

This document constitutes a list of grievances against the Crown destined to guide the deliberation of the Congress. It is invaluable as a key to the Declaration of Independence. Most notable is its discussion of the evils of the institution of slavery, which Jefferson sees as supported by the Crown for commercial purposes. Although in his will Jefferson freed five of his slaves, he remained a slaveholder all his life; after his death the 200-odd slaves he still owned were sold at auction to pay some of his debts.

[1] Notice that at this point Jefferson was not an advocate of separation from Great Britain. The document is written as an acknowledgment of the king's power. It is a list of grievances and an appeal to the monarch's sense of history and justice.

Resolved, that it be an instruction to the said deputies, when assembled in general congress with the deputies from the other states of British America, to propose to the said congress that an humble and dutiful address[1] be presented to his majesty, begging leave to lay before him, as chief magistrate of the British empire, the united complaints of his majesty's subjects in America; complaints which are excited by many unwarrantable incroachments and usurpations attempted to be made by the legislature of one part of the empire, upon those rights which God and the laws have given equally and independently to all. To represent to his majesty that these his states have often individually made humble application to his imperial throne to obtain, through its intervention, some redress of their injured rights,[2] to none of which was ever even an answer condescended . . . shall obtain from his majesty a more respectful acceptance . . .

[2]To ask for redress is to ask for relief from some wrong.

. . . to remind him that our ancestors, before their emigration to America, were the free inhabitants of the British dominions in Europe, and possessed a right which nature has given to all men . . . of going in quest of new habitations, and of their establishing new societies, under such laws and regulations as to them shall seem most likely to promote public happiness . . .

America was conquered, and her settlements made, and firmly established, at the expence of individuals, and not of the British public. Their own blood was spilt in acquiring lands for their settlement, their own fortunes expended in making that settlement effectual; for themselves they fought, for themselves they conquered, and for themselves alone they have right to hold. Not a shilling was ever issued from the public treasuries of his majesty, or his ancestors, for their assistance, till of very late times, after the colonies had become established on a firm and permanent footing. That then, indeed, having become valuable to Great Britain for her commercial purposes, his parliament was pleased to lend them assistance . . .

We do not, however, mean to under-rate those aids, which to us were doubtless valuable . . . but we would shew that they cannot give a title to that authority[3] which the British parliament would arrogate over us . . . That settlements having been thus effected in the wilds of America, the emigrants thought proper to adopt that system of laws under which they had hitherto lived in the mother country, and to continue their union with her by submitting themselves to the same common sovereign, who was thereby made the central link connecting the several parts of the empire thus newly multiplied. But that not long were they permitted . . . to hold undisturbed the rights thus acquired, at the hazard of their lives, and loss of their fortunes . . .

[3]They cannot give title, meaning they cannot give the right.

That the exercise of a free trade with all parts of the world, possessed by the American colonists, as of natural right, and which no law of their own had taken away or abridged, was next the object of unjust encroachment . . . the parliament for the commonwealth . . . assumed upon themselves the power of prohibiting their trade with all other parts of the world, except the island of Great Britain. This arbitrary

[4]The Navigation Acts were a series of laws passed and revised between 1649 and 1696. The purpose of the acts was to support the policy of mercantilism, that is, controlling trade in favor of the interests of the mother country. The mechanism was to protect British shipping against competition from Dutch vessels. No goods could be imported or exported from any British colony except in British ships. American colonists were thus limited in their trade by the British monopoly created by the Navigation Acts.

[5]The revolution was not just a fight for political freedom. Economic colonial interests in conflict with those of Britain lay at the heart of the cause. Every act of Parliament was meant to preserve Britain's domination of the American colonies, but the ones that finally brought out the arms were economic restrictions on American prosperity.

[6]In 1612, John Rolfe, one of the leaders of the first Virginia colony, discovered a method of curing tobacco that made it a profitable commodity for export to the mother country. As tobacco culture became more profitable, the demand for slaves increased and slavery was given legal recognition. Tobacco was easy to raise, requiring little investment and unskilled labor to produce it. Many Englishmen, including King Charles I, found the "cursed weed" objectionable; still the colonists continued to raise it. The demand in England was huge; it was still in every tavern and ale house. By the late 18th century, it brought annual profit of over 200,000 pounds.

[7]The year 1776 was famous for more than revolution. That year saw the publication of Adam Smith's *An Inquiry into the Source of the Wealth of Nations*, the founding document of free market capitalism. Britain was enjoying the benefits of the Industrial Revolution. It had become "the workshop of the world." Its machines, powered by James Watt's steam engine, were the glory of Britain and the wonder of the world. The colonists were, they felt, the natural heirs to such prosperity. They were not ready to be cut out of the mother country's will.

[8]Having none of the properties that endow something with value.

act, however, they soon recalled, and by solemn treaty, entered into on the 12th day of March, 1651, between the said commonwealth by their commissioners, and the colony of Virginia by their house of burgesses, it was expressly stipulated, by the 8th article of the said treaty, that they should have "free trade as the people of England do enjoy to all places and with all nations, according to the laws of that commonwealth". . .[4]

History has informed us that bodies of men, as well as individuals, are susceptible of the spirit of tyranny. A view of these acts of parliament for regulation, as it has been affectedly (falsely) called, of the American trade . . . would undeniably evince the truth of this observation. Besides the duties they impose on our articles of export and import, they prohibit our going to any markets . . . for the sale of commodities which Great Britain will not take from us, and for the purchase of others, with which she cannot supply us . . .[5]

That these acts prohibit us from carrying in quest of other purchasers the surplus of our tobaccos remaining after the consumption of Great Britain is supplied; so that we must leave them with the British merchant for whatever he will please to allow us,[6] to be by him reshipped to foreign markets, where he will reap the benefits of making sale of them for full value . . . we take leave to mention to his majesty certain other acts of British parliament, by which they would prohibit us from manufacturing for our own use the articles we raise on our own lands with our own labour . . . an American subject is forbidden to make a hat for himself of the fur which he has taken perhaps on his own soil; an instance of despotism to which no parallel can be produced in the most arbitrary ages of British history . . . the iron which we make we are forbidden to manufacture . . . we are to pay freight for it to Great Britain, and freight for it back again, for the purpose of supporting not men, but machines, in the island of Great Britain.[7] In the same spirit of equal and impartial legislation is to be viewed the act of parliament. . . by which American lands are made subject to the demands of British creditors, while their own lands were still continued unanswerable for their debts; from which one of these conclusions must necessarily follow, either that justice is not the same in America as in Britain, or else that the British parliament pay less regard to it here than there . . . we do not point out to his majesty the injustice of these acts, with intent to rest on that principle the cause of their nullity;[8] but to shew that experience confirms the propriety of those political principles which exempt us from the jurisdiction of the British parliament. The true ground on which we declare these acts void is, that the British parliament has no right to exercise authority over us . . . they have also intermeddled with the regulation of the internal affairs of the colonies. The act of . . . establishing a post office in America seems to have had little connection with British convenience, except that of accommodating his majesty's ministers and favourites with the sale of a lucrative and easy office . . . [9]

Single acts of tyranny may be ascribed to the accidental opinion of a day; but a series of oppressions,[10] begun at a distinguished period, and pursued unalterably through every change of ministers, too plainly prove a deliberate and systematical plan of reducing us to slavery . . .

"An act for granting certain duties in the British colonies and plantations in America, &c."

"An act for granting and applying certain stamp duties and other duties in the British colonies and plantations in America, &c."

"An act for the better securing the dependency of his majesty's dominions in America upon the crown and parliament of Great Britain;"

"An act for granting duties on paper, tea, &c." form that connected chain of parliamentary usurpation, which has already been the subject of frequent applications to his majesty, and the houses of lords and commons of Great Britain; and no answers having yet been condescended to any of these, we shall not trouble his majesty with a repetition of the matters they contained . . .

"An act for suspending the legislature of New York."[11] One free and independent legislature hereby takes upon itself to suspend the powers of another, free and independent as itself; thus exhibiting a phenomenon unknown in nature, the creator and creature of its own power. Not only the principles of common sense, but the common feelings of human nature, must be surrendered up before his majesty's subjects here can be persuaded to believe that they hold their political existence at the will of a British parliament. Shall these governments be dissolved, their property annihilated, and their people reduced to a state of nature,[12] at the imperious

[9] Jefferson's position reflects the colonial argument most famously summarized in the phrase, "no taxation without representation." Parliament's position was that the colonials were Englishmen and therefore had virtual representation. The colonists demanded actual representation in legislative bodies that had power over them. The post-office comment is a reference to the practice of establishing British officers throughout the colonies, nominally to provide services but actually to spy out and report on revolutionary sentiment in the colonies.

[10] Jefferson refers to the Sugar Act and the Stamp Act.

[11] With the tensions between the Crown and the colonies increasing, the British had two choices: negotiation or aggressive repression. King George and his prime minister chose the latter. New York had been an advocate of cooperation, but the British unwisely determined to deal with all colonies in an equally repressive fashion. When the authorities suspended the New York Legislature, the action forced the colony firmly into the camp of rebellion.

[12] Here he means reduced to a society without self-government.

breath of a body of men, whom they never saw, in whom they never confided, and over whom they have no powers of punishment or removal, let their crimes against the American public be ever so great? Can any one reason be assigned why 160,000 electors in the island of Great Britain should give law to four millions in the states of America, every individual of whom is equal to every individual of them, in virtue, in understanding, and in bodily strength? Were this to be admitted, instead of being a free people, as we have hitherto supposed, and mean to continue ourselves, we should suddenly be found the slaves, not of one, but of 160,000 tyrants, distinguished too from all others by this singular circumstance, that they are removed from the reach of fear, the only restraining motive which may hold the hand of a tyrant.

"An act to discontinue in such manner and for such time as are therein mentioned the landing and discharging, lading or shipping, of goods, wares, and merchandize, at the town and within the harbour of Boston, in the province of Massachusetts Bay, in North America,"... a large and populous town, whose trade was their sole subsistence, was deprived of that trade, and involved in utter ruin.[13] Let us for a while suppose the question of right suspended, in order to examine this act on principles of justice: An act of parliament had been passed imposing duties on teas,[14] to be paid in America, against which act the Americans had protested as inauthoritative. The East India company, who till that time had never sent a pound of tea to America on their own account, step forth on that occasion the assertors of parliamentary right, and send hither many ship loads of that obnoxious commodity. The masters of their several vessels, however, on their arrival in America, wisely attended to admonition, and returned with their cargoes. In the province of New England alone the remonstrances of the people were disregarded, and a compliance, after being many days waited for, was flatly refused. Whether in this the master of the vessel was governed by his obstinancy, or his instructions, let those who know, say. There are extraordinary situations which require extraordinary interposition. An exasperated people, who feel that they possess power, are not easily restrained within limits strictly regular. A number of them assembled in the town of Boston, threw the tea into the ocean, and dispersed without doing any other act of violence. If in this they did wrong, they were known and were amenable to the laws of the land, against which it could not be objected that they had ever, in any instance, been obstructed or diverted from their regular course in favour of popular

[13] Jefferson is referring to the Boston Port Act of March 1774, passed by Parliament to punish Boston for the Tea Party. The act closed the port until the colonists paid for the tea destroyed on December 16, 1773. All the colonies saw the act as an attack on American liberties. The result was the establishment of the Continental Congress to coordinate colonial opposition to the Crown.

[14] The East India Company was losing revenue because of the huge amount of Dutch tea being smuggled into the colonies (duty free) after British tea had been taxed to raise revenue for the Crown: 12,000 pounds per year. The tax was retained as part of a program of Parliament to assert its right to curtail the colonial economy.

offenders. They should therefore not have been distrusted on this occasion. But that ill fated colony had formerly been bold in their enmities against the house of Stuart, and were now devoted to ruin by that unseen hand *[George III]* which governs the momentous affairs of this great empire.[15] On the partial representations of a few worthless ministerial dependents, whose constant office it has been to keep that government embroiled, and who, by their treacheries, hope to obtain the dignity of the British knighthood,[16] without calling for a party accused, without asking a proof, without attempting a distinction between the guilty and the innocent, the whole of that antient and wealthy town is in a moment reduced from opulence to beggary. Men who had spent their lives in extending the British commerce, who had invested in that place the wealth their honest endeavours had merited, found themselves and their families thrown at once on the world for subsistence by its charities. Not the hundredth part of the inhabitants of that town had been concerned in the act complained of;[17] many of them were in Great Britain and in other parts beyond sea; yet all were involved in one indiscriminate ruin, by a new executive power, unheard of till then, that of a British parliament. A property, of the value of many millions of money, was sacrificed to revenge, not repay, the loss of a few thousands. This is administering justice with a heavy hand indeed! and when is this tempest to be arrested in its course? Two wharfs are to be opened again when his majesty shall think proper. The residue which lined the extensive shores of the bay of Boston are forever interdicted the exercise of commerce.[18] This little exception seems to have been thrown in for no other purpose than that of setting a precedent for investing his majesty with legislative powers. If the pulse of his people shall beat calmly under this experiment, another and another will be tried, till the measure of despotism be filled up. It would be an insult on common sense to pretend that this exception was made in order to restore its commerce to that great town . . .

By the act for the suppression of riots and tumults in the town of Boston . . . a murder committed there is, if the governor pleases, to be tried in the court of King's Bench, in the island of Great Britain . . .[19] That these are the acts of power, assumed by a body of men, foreign to our constitutions, and unacknowledged by our laws, against which we do, on behalf of the inhabitants of British America, enter this our solemn and determined protest; and we do earnestly entreat his majesty . . . to recommend to his parliament of Great Britain the total revocation of these acts . . .

[15]The "House of Stuart" was the ruling family of England in the 17th century, the period when Britain rose to prominence in commercial affairs. The "House of Tudor" immediately preceded it. Most famously, Henry VIII and Elizabeth I were Tudors. George III, British monarch during the American Revolution, was a member of the "House of Hanover," a German dynasty. This was succeeded by the current "House of Windsor." The present queen, Elizabeth II, is a Windsor.

[16]The reference is to sycophantic courtiers who hoped to win knighthood by supporting the policies of George III.

[17]The Boston Tea Party.

[18]Forbidden to engage in commerce.

[19]"A murder committed there" is a reference to the Boston Massacre.

[20]The king had an absolute veto power over acts of Parliament. Here he is urged to use it to correct unjust laws.

[21]This passage presents one of the greatest of ironic statements. These Virginia statesmen, Jefferson among them, denounce the "infamous practice" of slavery while owning slaves themselves. Later, at the Constitutional Convention, the delegates debated the future of slavery in the new nation but, with the exception of ending the importation of new slaves after 1808, did nothing. The African corsairs referenced were pirates who profited by the slave trade.

That we next proceed to consider the conduct of his majesty . . . and mark out his deviations from the line of duty: By the constitution of Great Britain, as well as of the several American states, his majesty possesses the power of refusing to pass into a law any bill which has already passed the other two branches of legislature.[20] His majesty, however, and his ancestors . . . have modestly declined the exercise of this power . . . But by change of circumstances, other principles than those of justice simply have obtained an influence on their determinations; the addition of new states to the British empire has produced an addition of new, and sometimes opposite interests. It is now, therefore, the great office of his majesty, to resume the exercise of his negative power, and to prevent the passage of laws by any one legislature of the empire, which might bear injuriously on the rights and interests of another. Yet this will not excuse the wanton exercise of this power which we have seen his majesty practise on the laws of the American legislatures. For the most trifling reasons, and sometimes for no conceivable reason at all, his majesty has rejected laws of the most salutary tendency. The abolition of domestic slavery is the great object of desire in those colonies, where it was unhappily introduced in their infant state. But previous to the enfranchisement of the slaves we have, it is necessary to exclude all further importations from Africa; yet our repeated attempts to effect this by prohibitions, and by imposing duties which might amount to a prohibition, have been hitherto defeated by his majesty's negative: Thus preferring the immediate advantages of a few African corsairs to the lasting interests of the American states, and to the rights of human nature, deeply wounded by this infamous practice . . .[21]

With equal inattention to the necessities of his people here has his majesty permitted our laws to lie neglected in England for years . . . so that such of them as have no suspending clause we hold on the most precarious of all tenures, his majesty's will, and such of them as suspend themselves till his majesty's assent be obtained, we have feared, might be called into existence at some future and distant period, when time, and change of circumstances, shall have rendered them destructive to his people here. And to render this grievance still more oppressive, his majesty by his instructions has laid his governors under such restrictions that they can pass no law of any moment unless it have such suspending clause; so that, however immediate may be the call for legislative interposition, the law cannot be executed till it has twice crossed the atlantic, by which time the evil may have spent its whole force.

But in what terms, reconcileable to majesty, and at the same time to truth, shall we speak of a late instruction to his majesty's governor of the colony of Virginia, by which he is forbidden to assent to any law for the division of a county, unless the new county will consent to have no representative in assembly? . . .

Since the establishment . . . of the British constitution, at the glorious revolution . . .[22] neither his majesty, nor his ancestors, have exercised such a power of dissolution in the island of Great Britain; and when his majesty was petitioned, by the united voice of his people there, to dissolve the present parliament, who had become obnoxious to them, his ministers were heard to declare, in open parliament, that his majesty possessed no such power by the constitution. But how different their language and his practice here! To declare, as their duty required, the known rights of their country, to oppose the usurpations of every foreign judicature, to disregard the imperious mandates of a minister or governor, have been the avowed causes of dissolving houses of representatives in America. But if such powers be really vested in his majesty, can he suppose they are there placed to awe the members from such purposes as these? When the representative body have lost the confidence of their constituents, when they have notoriously made sale of their most valuable rights, when they have assumed to themselves powers which the people never put into their hands, then indeed their continuing in office becomes dangerous to the state, and calls for an exercise of the power of dissolution. Such being the causes for which the representative body should, and should not, be dissolved, will it not appear strange to an unbiased observer, that that of Great Britain was not dissolved, while those of the colonies have repeatedly incurred that sentence? . . .

But your majesty, or your governors, have carried this power beyond every limit known, or provided for, by the laws: After dissolving one house of representatives, they have refused to call another, so that, for a great length of time, the legislature provided by the laws has been out of existence.[23] From the nature of things, every society must at all times possess within itself the sovereign powers of legislation . . . While those bodies are in existence to whom the people have delegated the powers of legislation, they alone possess and may exercise those powers; but when they are dissolved by the lopping off one or more of their branches, the power reverts to the people, who may exercise it to unlimited extent, either assembling

[22]In the 17th and 18th centuries, the word "revolution" originally meant restoration. The word was first used in 1660 after the overthrow of the Rump Parliament and on the occasion of the restoration of the monarchy. In 1688, when the Stuart dynasty was replaced and royal power given to William and Mary, the "Glorious Revolution" was not thought of as a revolution at all but as a restoration of royal power. It was in connection with Cromwell's activity that "revolution" first received the political meaning that we associate with it today. When King Charles I refused to preserve the freedoms guaranteed to Britain by the Magna Carta, there was a "glorious revolution" against his rule led by Oliver Cromwell, a Puritan leader of Parliament. The king was beheaded and Cromwell then ruled as "Lord Protector of the Commonwealth." Cromwell increased England's power by developing colonies in America and India and by making it ruler of the seas. That tradition of the people's right to overthrow unjust rule is referenced in these passages and expressed in Locke's *Second Treatise on Government.*

[23]King George III by decree dissolved the colonial legislatures in Massachusetts and Virginia.

together in person, sending deputies, or in any other way they may think proper . . .

His majesty has from time to time sent among us large bodies of armed forces, not made up of the people here, nor raised by the authority of our laws: Did his majesty possess such a right as this, it might swallow up all our other rights whenever he should think proper. But his majesty has no right to land a single armed man on our shores, and those whom he sends here are liable to our laws made for the suppression and punishment of riots, routs, and unlawful assemblies; or are hostile bodies, invading us in defiance of law . . .

Every state must judge for itself the number of armed men which they may safely trust among them, of whom they are to consist, and under what restrictions they shall be laid . . . To render these proceedings still more criminal against our laws, instead of subjecting the military to the civil powers, his majesty has expressly made the civil subordinate to the military . . .[24]

That these are our grievances which we have thus laid before his majesty, with that freedom of language and sentiment which becomes a free people claiming their rights, as derived from the laws of nature, and not as the gift of their chief magistrate: Let those flatter who fear; it is not an American art.[25] To give praise which is not due might be well from the venal, but would ill beseem those who are asserting the rights of human nature. They know, and will therefore say, that kings are the servants, not the proprietors of the people. Open your breast, sire, to liberal and expanded thought. Let not the name of George the Third be a blot in the page of history. You are surrounded by British counsellors, but remember that they are parties. You have no ministers for American affairs, because you have none taken from among us, nor amenable to the laws on which they are to give you advice.[26] It behoves you, therefore, to think and to act for yourself and your people. The great principles of right and wrong are legible to every reader; to pursue them requires not the aid of many counsellors. The whole art of government consists in the art of being honest. Only aim to do your duty, and mankind will give you credit where you fail. No longer persevere in sacrificing the rights of one part of the empire to the inordinate desires of another; but deal out to all equal and impartial right. Let no act be passed by any one legislature which may infringe on the rights and liberties of another.

[25]Let those who live in fear see these things in a favorable way: It is not the American way!

[26]The issue was one of representation. Parliament's view was that all English subjects, wherever they lived, were automatically "represented," since British law applied to all. The colonial view demanded actual representation by elected spokesmen for colonial interests.

This is the important post in which fortune has placed you, holding the balance of a great, if a well poised empire. This, sire, is the advice of your great American council, on the observance of which may perhaps depend your felicity and future fame, and the preservation of that harmony which alone can continue both to Great Britain and America the reciprocal advantages of their connection. It is neither our wish, nor our interest, to separate from her. We are willing, on our part, to sacrifice every thing which reason can ask to the restoration of that tranquillity for which all must wish. On their part, let them be ready to establish union and a generous plan. Let them name their terms, but let them be just. Accept of every commercial preference it is in our power to give for such things as we can raise for their use, or they make for ours. But let them not think to exclude us from going to other markets to dispose of those commodities which they cannot use, or to supply those wants which they cannot supply. Still less let it be proposed that our properties within our own territories shall be taxed or regulated by any power on earth but our own. The God who gave us life gave us liberty at the same time; the hand of force may destroy, but cannot disjoin them. This, sire, is our last, our determined resolution; and that you will be pleased to interpose with that efficacy which your earnest endeavours may ensure to procure redress of these our great grievances, to quiet the minds of your subjects in British America, against any apprehensions of future encroachment, to establish fraternal love and harmony through the whole empire, and that these may continue to the latest ages of time, is the fervent prayer of all British America!

Source: H.A. Washington, *The Writings of Thomas Jefferson*, Volume 1. (Washington, DC: Taylor & Maury, 1853), 124–142.

Patrick Henry's Speech to the Virginia House of Burgesses

(March 23, 1775)

INTRODUCTION

Patrick Henry was a man of the frontier west. This distinguishes him from many of the revolutionary leaders from the more sober New England colonies. He was a young, brilliant lawyer, a fiery advocate for the revolutionary cause. His Fairfax Resolutions in support of colonial liberties and privileges paved the way for an increased radicalization of the colony. This speech is probably the most famous call to arms in American history. It is the watchword of the revolution. Expressing both the principles on which rebellion was based and the aim of the conflict, it was widely circulated throughout the colonies and, along with Paine's *Common Sense*, brought many who were on the fence to the point of active participation in armed conflict.

I shall speak forth my sentiments freely and without reserve. This is no time for ceremony. The question before the house is one of awful moment to this country. For my own part, I consider it as nothing less than a question of freedom or slavery . . . Mr. President, it is natural to man to indulge in the illusions of hope. We are apt to shut our eyes against a painful truth . . . Is this the part of wise men, engaged in a great and arduous struggle for liberty? . . . For my part, whatever anguish of spirit it may cost, I am willing to know the whole truth, to know the worst and to provide for it . . . I ask gentlemen, sir, what means this martial array, if its purpose be not to force us to submission?[1] Can gentlemen assign any other possible motive for it? Has Great Britain any enemy, in this quarter of the world, to call for all this accumulation of navies and armies? No, sir, she has none. They are sent over to bind and rivet upon us those chains which the British ministry have been so long forging . . .

Let us not, I beseech you, sir, deceive ourselves. Sir, we have done everything that could be done to avert the storm which is now coming on. We have petitioned; we have remonstrated; we have supplicated; we have prostrated ourselves before the throne, and have

[1] When some of Henry's resolutions were declared too radical (he had advocated organization of a militia for defense of the colony), he rose to defend his position.

implored its interposition to rest the tyrannical hands of the ministry and Parliament. Our petitions have been slighted; our supplications have been disregarded; and we have been spurned, with contempt, from the foot of the throne![2] In vain, after these things, may we indulge the fond hope of peace and reconciliation. There is no longer any room for hope. If we wish to be free . . . we must fight! I repeat it, sir, we must fight! . . .

They tell us, sir, that we are weak; unable to cope with so formidable an adversary. But when shall we be stronger? Will it be the next week, or the next year? Will it be when we are totally disarmed, and when a British guard shall be stationed in every house? Shall we gather strength by irresolution and inaction? . . . Sir, we are not weak if we make a proper use of those means which the God of nature hath placed in our power. The millions of people, armed in the holy cause of liberty, and in such a country as that which we possess, are invincible by any force which our enemy can send against us. Besides, sir, we shall not fight our battles alone. There is a God who presides over the destinies of nations, and who will raise up friends to fight our battles for us. The battle, sir, is not to the strong alone; it is to the vigilant, the active, the brave. Besides, sir, we have no election. If we were base enough to desire it, it is now too late to retire from the contest.[3] There is no retreat but in submission and slavery! Our chains are forged! Their clanking may be heard on the plains of Boston! The war is inevitable . . . and let it come! I repeat it, sir, let it come . . .

Gentlemen may cry, 'Peace, Peace . . . but there is no peace.'[4] The war is actually begun! The next gale that sweeps from the north will bring to our ears the clash of resounding arms! Our brethren are already in the field![5] Why stand we here idle? What is it that gentlemen wish? What would they have? Is life so dear, or peace so sweet, as to be purchased at the price of chains and slavery? Forbid it, Almighty God! I know not what course others may take; but as for me, give me liberty or give me death!

Source: Selim H. Peabody, *American Patriotism; Speeches, Letters and Other Papers Which Illustrate the Foundation, the Development, the Preservation of the United States of America.* (New York: American Book Exchange, 1880), 108–110.

[2]Henry recounts the history of colonial attempts to reach an accommodation with the king, and summarizes Jefferson's argument in the previous document.

[3]When he uses the word "election," he means choice. Even if the colonists wanted peace, it is now too late to go back.

[4]Henry quotes the Old Testament: Jeremiah Chapter VI verse 14. Jeremiah, known as the "prophet of doom," railed against the existing government and predicted its downfall.
[5]In another portion of his speech, Henry refers to the agitation in Boston. "Our chains are forged: their clanking may be heard on the plains of Boston. The war is inevitable. Let it come!"

Letter from Thomas Jefferson to Dr. Small

(May 7, 1775)

INTRODUCTION

Of all the founding fathers of the American Republic, only Jefferson possessed a universal genius, one perhaps even greater than Benjamin Franklin's. He distinguished himself not only in the political realm but also in literature, music, mathematics, architecture, education, and philosophy. Dr. William Small had been a professor at the College of William and Mary and had moved to Birmingham, England, to use his scientific expertise to improve manufacturing processes then developing in the industrial centers of the Industrial Revolution. Jefferson attempts to show that the movement for independence was a reaction to the abusive actions of Parliament and not a plot long contemplated by colonial leaders.

[1]On the evening of April 18, 1775, the British sent troops to destroy an ammunition depot at Concord. Paul Revere warned the minutemen of the plan and the first battle of the revolution was fought on Lexington Green. After another skirmish at North Bridge, the redcoats retreated to Boston, but their withdrawal was harassed by the colonials with great effect. The battle proved to the colonials that by their own tactical "hit and run" methods, they could defeat the British.

[2]Lord North, prime minister and former chancellor of the exchequer (secretary of the Treasury), strongly resented the Boston Tea Party. He was an architect of Britain's anticolonial policy. He refused to repeal the tax on tea, closed the port of Boston in retaliation for the Boston Tea Party, and attempted to reform the Massachusetts constitution. His policies served to enflame colonial opposition to the crisis.

Within this week we have received the unhappy news of an action of considerable magnitude, between the King's troops and our brethren of Boston, in which it is said five hundred of the former, with the Earl of Percy, are slain.[1] That such an action has occurred, is undoubted, though perhaps the circumstances may not have reached us with truth. This accident has cut off our last hope of reconciliation, and a frenzy of revenge seems to have seized all ranks of people. It is a lamentable circumstance, that the only mediatory power, acknowledged by both parties, instead of leading to a reconciliation of his divided people, should pursue the incendiary purpose of still blowing up the flames, as we find him constantly doing, in every speech and public declaration.[2] This may, perhaps, be intended to intimidate into acquiescence, but the effect has been most unfortunately otherwise. A little knowledge of human nature, and attention to its ordinary workings, might have foreseen that the spirits of the people here were in a state, in which they were more likely to be provoked, than frightened, by haughty deportment. And to fill up the measure of irritation, a proscription of individuals has been substituted in the room of just trial. Can it be believed, that a grateful people will suffer those to be consigned to execution, whose sole crime has been the developing and asserting their rights? Had the Parliament possessed the power of reflection, they would have avoided a measure as

48

impotent, as it was inflammatory. When I saw Lord Chatham's bill, I entertained high hope that a reconciliation could have been brought about.[3] The difference between his terms, and those offered by our Congress, might have been accommodated, if entered on, by both parties, with a disposition to accommodate. But the dignity of Parliament, it seems, can brook no opposition to its power.

Strange, that a set of men, who have made sale of their virtue to the Minister, should yet talk of retaining dignity! . . .[4]

[3]Lord Chatham (William Pitt) was a friend of the colonists and an advocate for peace. He advocated the removal of British troops from Massachusetts and was asked to form a ministry by George III. The Americans saw Pitt as a welcome hero, as he had advocated repeal of the Stamp Act, defining it as a tyranny. He declared that the colonists had a right to tax themselves. He was called the "great commoner" and even "the American Moses." But when he accepted a peerage, and with his increasing infirmity, both his influence and his popularity in the colonies declined. He was eventually replaced by Charles Townsend, whose restrictive anti-colonial policies inflamed the colonies even more.

[4]Parliament is compared to a prostitute whose favors are for sale to the highest bidder. In this case, the legislature switching its support from Pitt to Townsend, from a friend of the colonies to an enemy.

Source: H. Niles, *Principles and Acts of the Revolution in America*. (Baltimore: Printed by W.O. Niles, 1822), 311–312.

Congress Grants Washington Command
of the Continental Army
(July 3, 1775)

INTRODUCTION

Less than a month after the Battles of Lexington and Concord, the Second Continental Congress met in Philadelphia (May 10, 1775). With the consent of all the colonies, it assumed the powers of a regular government and organized the several militias around Boston into a Continental Army under George Washington, who was appointed commander in chief of the Continental Army. Washington was a member of the Virginia aristocracy who had distinguished himself during colonial wars. He was a member of the Congress, and later first president of the United States. Washington, accompanied by a troop of Philadelphia cavalry, set out for New York where they were joined by companies of New York militia. Before their departure for Cambridge, Massachusetts, the Provincial Congress of New York presented Washington with this address to which, after declaring his gratitude, he added his reply.

"May it please your excellency": At a time when the most loyal of his majesty's subjects, from a regard to the laws and constitution, by which he sits on the throne, feel themselves reduced to the unhappy necessity of taking up arms to defend their dearest rights and privileges; while we deplore the calamities of this divided empire, we rejoice in the appointment of a gentleman, from whose abilities and virtue, we are taught to expect both security and peace.[1]

"Confiding in you, sir, and in the worthy generals immediately under your command, we have the most flattering hopes of success in the glorious struggle for American liberty, and the fullest assurances, that whenever this important contest shall be decided, by that fondest wish of each American soul, an accommodation with our mother country, you will cheerfully resign the important deposit committed into your hands, and reassume the character of our worthiest citizen."

"Gentlemen: At the same time that with you I deplore the unhappy necessity of such an appointment, as that with which I am now

1And from this derives his description as "first in war; first in peace; first in the hearts of his countrymen."

honored, I cannot but feel sentiments of the highest gratitude for this affecting instance of distinction and regard.

May your warmest wishes be realized in the success of America, at this important and interesting period; and be assured, that every exertion of my worthy colleagues and myself, will be equally extended to the re-establishment of peace and harmony, between the mother country and these colonies: as to the fatal but necessary operations of war, when we assumed the soldier, we did not lay aside the citizen, and we shall most sincerely rejoice, with you, in that happy hour, when the establishment of American liberty, on the most firm and solid foundations, shall enable us to return to our private stations, in the bosom of a free, peaceful and happy country."

G. Washington

Source: H. Niles, *Principles and Acts of the Revolution in America.* (Baltimore: Printed by W.O. Niles, 1822), 441.

Declaration of the Causes and Necessity of Taking Up Arms

(July 6, 1775)

INTRODUCTION

Even in the aftermath of the Battles of Lexington and Concord, there was still division among the members of the Second Continental Congress as to what the proper action should be. On July 8, 1775, the Congress sent a petition to the king known as the "Olive Branch" petition seeking reconciliation. King George rejected the petition and issued a proclamation that the colonies were in rebellion. Thereupon, the Congress appointed Benjamin Franklin, William Livingston, Thomas Jefferson, John Rutledge, and John Jay to prepare a statement that Washington, newly appointed "generalissimo" of the army, could read to the troops. This Declaration was a statement of grievances and a justification for rebellion.

A declaration by the representatives of the united colonies of North America, now met in Congress at Philadelphia, setting forth the causes and necessity of their taking up arms.

If it was possible for men, who exercise their reason to believe, that the divine Author of our existence intended a part of the human race to hold an absolute property in, and an unbounded power over others,[1] marked out by His infinite goodness and wisdom, as the objects of a legal domination never rightfully resistible, however severe and oppressive, the inhabitants of these colonies might at least require from the parliament of Great-Britain some evidence, that this dreadful authority over them, has been granted to that body. But a reverence for our Creator, principles of humanity, and the dictates of common sense, must convince all those who reflect upon the subject, that government was instituted to promote the welfare of mankind, and ought to be administered for the attainment of that end. The legislature of Great-Britain, however, stimulated by an inordinate passion for a power not only unjustifiable, but which they know to be peculiarly reprobated by the very constitution of that kingdom, and desperate of success in any mode of contest, where regard

[1] Notice the irony of slave owners objecting to themselves being treated as property.

should be had to truth, law, or right, have at length, deserting those, attempted to effect their cruel and impolitic purpose of enslaving these colonies by violence, and have thereby rendered it necessary for us to close with their last appeal from reason to arms. Yet, however blinded that assembly may be, by their intemperate rage for unlimited domination, so to sight justice and the opinion of mankind, we esteem ourselves bound by obligations of respect to the rest of the world, to make known the justice of our cause.[2] Our forefathers, inhabitants of the island of Great-Britain, left their native land, to seek on these shores a residence for civil and religious freedom. At the expense of their blood, at the hazard of their fortunes, without the least charge to the country from which they removed, by unceasing labour, and an unconquerable spirit, they effected settlements in the distant and unhospitable wilds of America, then filled with numerous and warlike barbarians.—Societies or governments, vested with perfect legislatures, were formed under charters from the crown, and an harmonious intercourse was established between the colonies and the kingdom from which they derived their origin. The mutual benefits of this union became in a short time so extraordinary, as to excite astonishment. It is universally confessed, that the amazing increase of the wealth, strength, and navigation of the realm, arose from this source; and the minister, who so wisely and successfully directed the measures of Great-Britain in the late war, publicly declared, that these colonies enabled her to triumph over her enemies.[3]—Towards the conclusion of that war, it pleased our sovereign to make a change in his counsels.—From that fatal movement, the affairs of the British empire began to fall into confusion, and gradually sliding from the summit of glorious prosperity, to which they had been advanced by the virtues and abilities of one man, are at length distracted by the convulsions, that now shake it to its deepest foundations.—The new ministry finding the brave foes of Britain, though frequently defeated, yet still contending, took up the unfortunate idea of granting them a hasty peace, and then subduing her faithful friends.[4]

These colonies were judged to be in such a state, as to present victories without bloodshed . . . The uninterrupted tenor of their peaceable and respectful behaviour from the beginning of colonization, their dutiful, zealous, and useful services during the war, though so recently and amply acknowledged in the most honourable manner by his majesty, by the late king, and by parliament, could not save them from the meditated innovations.—Parliament was influenced

[2]Here Jefferson anticipates his passage in the Declaration of Independence: "A decent respect to the opinion of mankind requires that they should declare the causes which impel them to the separation."

[3]The minister was William Pitt, the greatest English statesman of the 18th century. He was confident that England's destiny was to defeat the French in the New World and beyond that to become a supreme world power. He raised an army of 56,000 in the colonies; inspired by his energy and leadership, the colonial forces conquered the French line of forts and established a settlement at what was named "Pittsburgh" in his honor.

[4]Making peace with France and dominating its colonies.

[5]The reference to 11 years is the period between the Peace of Paris (1763–1764) that ended the French and Indian War and the first hostilities in the colonies, the Battles of Lexington and Concord (1775).

[6]Laws were passed providing for colonists to be tried in naval courts.

[7]This is a reference to the Boston Port Act.

[8]Here he means Canada.

[9]In 1774, Parliament passed an act that provided that when there were no barracks for troops in Boston, the governor could take over inns or uninhabited buildings for lodging. The whole purpose was to punish Boston for the Tea Party by placing British troops in their midst. The colonists resisted and did not allow repairs on the buildings, forcing the British to camp out on the Boston Common.

[10]The issue is the objection to Parliament's passage of a series of "intolerable acts" to punish the colonies that had no actual representation in the legislature.

[11]American taxes were used to pay imperial costs.

[12]Parliament anticipated how free men would react to such laws.

[13]The First "Continental" Congress met from September 5 to October 26, 1774. It was known simply as "the Congress" but was soon called "Continental" to distinguish it from the several provincial congresses organized at the time.

to adopt the pernicious project, and assuming a new power over them, have in the course of eleven years,[5] given such decisive specimens of the spirit and consequences attending this power, as to leave no doubt concerning the effects of acquiescence under it. They have undertaken to give and grant our money without our consent, though we have ever exercised an exclusive right to dispose of our own property; statutes have been passed for extending the jurisdiction of courts of admiralty and vice-admiralty beyond their ancient limits;[6] for depriving us of the accustomed and inestimable privilege of trial by jury, in cases affecting both life and property; for suspending the legislature of one of the colonies; for interdicting all commerce to the capital of another;[7] and for altering fundamentally the form of government established by charter, and secured by acts of its own legislature solemnly confirmed by the crown; for exempting the "murderers" of colonists from legal trial, and in effect, from punishment; for erecting in a neighbouring province,[8] acquired by the joint arms of Great-Britain and America, a despotism dangerous to our very existence; and for quartering soldiers[9] upon the colonists in time of profound peace. It has also been resolved in parliament, that colonists charged with committing certain offences, shall be transported to England to be tried. But why should we enumerate our injuries in detail? By one statute it is declared, that parliament can "of right make laws to bind us in all cases whatsoever." What is to defend us against so enormous, so unlimited a power? Not a single man of those who assume it, is chosen by us;[10] or is subject to our control or influence; but, on the contrary, they are all of them exempt from the operation of such laws, and an American revenue, if not diverted from the ostensible purposes for which it is raised, would actually lighten their own burdens in proportion, as they increase ours.[11] We saw the misery to which such despotism would reduce us. We for ten years incessantly and ineffectually besieged the throne as supplicants; we reasoned, we remonstrated with parliament, in the most mild and decent language.

Administration sensible that we should regard these oppressive measures as freemen ought to do,[12] sent over fleets and armies to enforce them. The indignation of the Americans was roused, it is true; but it was the indignation of a virtuous, loyal, and affectionate people. A Congress of delegates from the United Colonies was assembled at Philadelphia, on the fifth day of last September.[13] We resolved again to offer a humble and dutiful petition to the King, and also addressed our fellow-subjects of Great-Britain. We have pursued every temperate, every respectful measure; we have even proceeded to break off our commercial intercourse with our fellow-subjects, as the last peaceable admonition, that our attachment to no nation upon earth should supplant our attachment to liberty.—This, we flattered ourselves, was the ultimate step of the controversy: but subsequent events have shewn, how vain was this hope of finding moderation in our enemies.

Several threatening expressions against the colonies were inserted in his majesty's speech;[14] our petition, tho' we were told it was a decent one, and that his majesty had been pleased to receive it graciously, and to promise laying it before his parliament, was huddled into both houses among a bundle of American papers, and there neglected. The lords and commons in their address, in the month of February, said, that "a rebellion at that time actually existed within the province of Massachusetts-Bay; and that those concerned with it, had been countenanced and encouraged by unlawful combinations and engagements, entered into by his majesty's subjects in several of the other colonies; and therefore they besought his majesty, that he would take the most effectual measures to inforce due obedience to the laws and authority of the supreme legislature."—Soon after, the commercial intercourse of whole colonies, with foreign countries, and with each other, was cut off by an act of parliament;[15] by another several of them were entirely prohibited from the fisheries in the seas near their coasts, on which they always depended for their sustenance; and large reinforcements of ships and troops were immediately sent over to General Gage.[16]

Fruitless were all the entreaties, arguments, and eloquence of an illustrious band of the most distinguished peers, and commoners, who nobly and strenuously asserted the justice of our cause,[17] to stay, or even to mitigate the heedless fury with which these accumulated and unexampled outrages were hurried on.—equally fruitless was the interference of the city of London, of Bristol, and many other respectable towns in our favor. Parliament adopted an insidious manouevre calculated to divide us, to establish a perpetual auction of taxations where colony should bid against colony, all of them uninformed what ransom would redeem their lives; and thus to extort from us, at the point of the bayonet, the unknown sums that should be sufficient to gratify, if possible to gratify, ministerial rapacity with the miserable indulgence left to us of raising, in our own mode, the prescribed tribute. What terms more rigid and humiliating could

[14]King George III expressed his view of Boston as follows: "The capital of Massachusetts is a center of vulgar sedition, strewn with brickbats and broken glass, where our enemies go about clothed in homespun and our friends in tar and feathers."

[15]The Boston Port Act was passed by Parliament in 1774 to punish the citizens of Boston for the tea party. It closed the port to all commerce until the people paid for the tea that was destroyed. Lord North, the prime minister, miscalculated the effect on the colonies. He thought since it was directed only at Boston it would have limited effect. The event became a rallying point for all the colonies and led to the formation of the First Continental Congress.

[16]General Gage was the governor of Massachusetts (1774) who tried to destroy the power of the colonial legislature.

[17]There were members of Parliament, led by the Earl of Chatham, William Pitt, and Edmund Burke, who opposed the Boston Port Bill. They were friends of the colonies but had little practical effect on the course of history. Despite their eloquence and their vision of a British "Commonwealth of Nations," every motion they made in favor of comity was regularly shot down.

have been dictated by remorseless victors to conquered enemies? In our circumstances to accept them, would be to deserve them.

Soon after the intelligence of these proceedings arrived on this continent; General Gage, who in the course of the last year had taken possession of the town of Boston, in the province of Massachusetts-Bay, and still occupied it, a garrison, on the 19th day of April, sent out from that place a large detachment of his army, who made an unprovoked assault on the inhabitants of the said province, at the town of Lexington, as appears by the affidavits of a great number of persons, some of whom were officers and soldiers of that detachment, murdered eight of the inhabitants, and wounded many others. From thence the troops proceeded in warlike array to the town of Concord,[18] where they set upon another party of the inhabitants . . . killing several and wounding more, until compelled to retreat by the country people suddenly assembled to repel this cruel aggression. Hostilities, thus commenced by the British troops, have been since prosecuted by them without regard to faith or reputation.—The inhabitants of Boston being confined within that town by the general their governor, and having, in order to procure their dismission, entered into a treaty with him, it was stipulated that the said inhabitants having deposited their arms with their own magistrate, should have liberty to depart, taking with them their other effects. They accordingly delivered up their arms, but in open violation of honour, in defiance of the obligation of treaties, which even savage nations esteemed sacred, the governor ordered the arms deposited as aforesaid, that they might be preserved for their owners, to be seized by a body of soldiers; detained the greatest part of the inhabitants in the town, and compelled the few who were permitted to retire, to leave their most valuable effects behind.[19]

By these perfidies wives are separated from their husbands, children from their parents, the aged and the sick from their relations and friends, who wish to attend and comfort them; and those who have been used to live in plenty and even elegance, are reduced to deplorable distress.

The general, further emulating his ministerial masters, by a proclamation bearing date on the 12th day of June, after venting the grossest falsehoods and calumnies against the good people of these colonies, proceeds to "declare them all, either by name or description,

[18]Lexington and Concord were the first battles, though really skirmishes, of the revolution.

[19]General Gage, governor of Massachusetts, was not a wise or aggressive leader. His instincts were always in favor of a peaceful settlement of affairs. After Lexington, Concord, and Bunker's Hill, he might have defeated the Continentals who were weakened and without stores or organization. But the redcoats, confined to Boston proper, had little taste for aggressive action. Gage arranged for a peaceful relaxation of tensions by agreeing to allow colonials who wished to leave Boston to do so with their possessions so long as they agreed to give up their arms. Once the arms were delivered up, Gage went back on his agreement and fired up the spirit of resistance even more. Within a year he had been replaced.

to be rebels and traitors, to supercede the course of the common law, and instead thereof to publish and order the use and exercise of the law martial."—His troops have butchered our countrymen, have wantonly burnt Charlestown,[20] besides a considerable number of houses in other places; our ships and vessels are seized; the necessary supplies of provisions are intercepted, and he is exerting his utmost power to spread destruction and devastation around him.

We have received certain intelligence, that general Carleton, the governor of Canada,[21] is instigating the people of that province and the Indians to fall upon us; and we have but too much reason to apprehend, that schemes have been formed to excite domestic enemies against us. In brief, a part of these colonies now feel, and all of them are sure of feeling, as far as the vengeance of administration can inflict them, the complicated calamities of fire, sword and famine. We are reduced to the alternative of chusing an unconditional submission to the tyranny of irritated ministers, or resistance by force.—The latter is our choice.—We have counted the cost of this contest, and find nothing so dreadful as voluntary slavery.—Honour, justice, and humanity, forbid us tamely to surrender that freedom which we received from our gallant ancestors, and which our innocent posterity have a right to receive from us. We cannot endure the infamy and guilt of resigning succeeding generations to that wretchedness which inevitably awaits them, if we basely entail hereditary bondage upon them.

Our cause is just. Our union is perfect. Our internal resources are great, and, if necessary, foreign assistance is undoubtedly attainable.— We gratefully acknowledge, as signal instances of the Divine favour towards us, that his Providence would not permit us to be called into this severe controversy, until we were grown up to our present strength, had been previously exercised in warlike operation, and possessed of the means of defending ourselves. With hearts fortified with these animating reflections, we most solemnly, before God and the world, declare, that, exerting the utmost energy of those powers, which our beneficent Creator hath graciously bestowed upon us, the arms we have been compelled by our enemies to assume, we will, in defiance of every hazard, with unabating firmness and perseverance, employ for the preservation of our liberties; being with one mind resolved to die freemen rather than to live slaves.

Lest this declaration should disquiet the minds of our friends and fellow-subjects in any part of the empire, we assure them that we

[20]In June 1775, General Gage's troops fought the Battle of Bunker Hill, in the course of which the adjacent town of Charleston was burned to the ground.

[21]War involving Native Americans was a constant feature of the revolution. Many of the tribes were hostile to the colonials and fought on the side of the British. The British had articles for trade and supplies, and they seemed to be the defender of Indian interests against the colonials who were invading their hunting grounds. In Canada, General Carleton made good use of them. Both sides attempted to enlist the Indians on their side and the Continental Congress financially supported this policy. But because of the fierceness with which the natives fought, both sides found them an embarrassment.

mean not to dissolve that union which has so long and so happily subsisted between us, and which we sincerely wish to see restored.— Necessity has not yet driven us into that desperate measure, or induced us to excite any other nation to war against them.—We have not raised armies with ambitious designs of separating from Great-Britain, and establishing independent states. We fight not for glory or for conquest. We exhibit to mankind the remarkable spectacle of a people attacked by unprovoked enemies, without any imputation or even suspicion of offence. They boast of their privileges and civilization, and yet proffer no milder conditions than servitude or death.

In our own native land, in defence of the freedom that is our birthright, and which we ever enjoyed till the late violation of it—for the protection of our property, acquired solely by the honest industry of our fore-fathers and ourselves, against violence actually offered, we have taken up arms. We shall lay them down when hostilities shall cease on the part of the aggressors, and all danger of their being renewed shall be removed, and not before.

With an humble confidence in the mercies of the supreme and impartial Judge and Ruler of the Universe, we most devoutly implore His divine goodness to protect us happily through this great conflict, to dispose our adversaries to reconciliation on reasonable terms, and thereby to relieve the empire from the calamities of civil war.

Source: Charles C. Tansill, *Documents Illustrative of the Formation of the Union of the American States.* (Washington, DC: Government Printing Office, 1927).

Letter from Thomas Jefferson Hoping for Reconciliation with Britain

(August 25, 1775)

INTRODUCTION

The recipient of this letter, John Randolph, was a kinsman to Thomas Jefferson and a distinguished Virginian. He served as attorney general of the colony as well as an admiralty judge. As a member of the House of Burgesses, he had voted against Patrick Henry's resolves and had been a strong supporter of reconciliation. Though Jefferson held out the hope that Parliament's mistaken views of the colonial situation might be corrected by the actions of men such as Randolph, who had chosen to emigrate to Britain, by November 1775, Jefferson had given up that hope. As he wrote to Randolph, "There is not a man in the Empire who more cordially loves a union then I do. But I will cease to exist before I yield to a connection on such terms as the British Parliament proposes."

. . . I am sorry the situation of our country should render it not eligible to you to remain longer in it. I hope the returning wisdom of Great Britain will, ere long, put an end to this unnatural contest. There may be people to whose tempers and dispositions contention is pleasing, and who, therefore, wish a continuance of confusion, but to me it is of all states but one, the most horrid. My first wish is a restoration of our just rights; my second, a return of the happy period, when, consistently with duty, I may withdraw myself totally from the public stage, and pass the rest of my days in domestic ease and tranquility, banishing every desire of ever hearing what passes in the world. Perhaps (for the latter adds considerably to the warmth of the former wish), looking with fondness towards a reconciliation with Great Britain, I cannot help hoping you may be able to contribute towards expediting this good work. I think it must be evident to yourself, that the Ministry have been deceived by their officers on this side of the water, who (for what purpose I cannot tell) have constantly represented the American opposition as that of a small faction, in which the body of the people took little part. This, you can inform them, of your own knowledge, is untrue. They have taken it into their heads, too, that we are cowards, and shall surrender at discretion to an armed force. The past and future operations of the war must confirm or undeceive them on that head. I wish they were thoroughly and minutely acquainted with every circumstance relative to America, as it exists in truth. I am persuaded, this would go far towards disposing them to reconciliation.[1] Even those in Parliament who are called friends to America, seem to know nothing of our real determinations. I observe, they pronounced in the last Parliament, that the Congress of 1774[2] did not mean to insist rigorously on the terms they held out, but kept something in reserve, to give up; and, in fact, that they would give up everything but the article of taxation. Now, the truth is far from this, as I can affirm, and put my honor to the assertion. Their continuance in this error may, perhaps, produce very ill consequences. The Congress stated the lowest terms they thought possible to be accepted, in order to convince the world, they were not unreasonable. They gave up the monopoly and regulation of trade, and all acts of Parliament prior to 1764, leaving to British generosity to render these, at some future time, as easy to America as the interest of Britain would admit. But this was before blood was spilt. I cannot affirm, but have reason to think, these terms would not now be accepted. I wish no false sense of honor, no ignorance of our real intentions, no vain hope that partial concessions of right will be accepted, may induce the Ministry to trifle with accommodation, till it shall be out of their power ever to accommodate. If, indeed, Great Britain, disjointed from her colonies, be a match for the most potent nations of Europe, with the colonies thrown into their scale, they may go on securely. But if they are not assured of this, it would be certainly unwise, by trying the event of another campaign, to risk our accepting a foreign aid, which, perhaps, may not be attainable, but on condition of everlasting avulsion from Great Britain.[3] This would be thought a hard condition, to those who still wish for reunion with their parent country. I am sincerely one of those, and would rather be in dependence on Great Britain, properly limited, than on any other nation on earth, or than on no nation. But I am one of those, too, who, rather than submit to the rights of legislating for us, assumed by the British Parliament, and which late experience has shown they will so cruelly exercise,[4] would lend my hand to sink the whole Island in the ocean . . .

Source: H. Niles, *Principles and Acts of the Revolution in America.* (Baltimore: Printed by W.O. Niles, 1822), 312.

Thomas Paine: *Common Sense*

(1776)

INTRODUCTION

In the intellectual run up to the revolution, no document was more influential than Thomas Paine's *Common Sense*. Published in January 1776, it effectively destroyed the arguments of those who opposed British tyranny but still supported loyalty to the Crown. The job that Paine began with this essay, Jefferson finished with the Declaration of Independence.

Paine was an Englishman who had personally suffered under British tyranny in London. He had worked as a minor government official as an employee of the taxing authority. He believed that his salary was too low and attempted to organize his fellow employees to win a raise in pay. He was branded a troublemaker and was fired. He immediately emigrated to America with his liberal ideas intact.

In *Common Sense*, Paine urges the inhabitants of America to realize that they were the nucleus of a great American nation destined to cover the continent and to be an example to the world of a people free from royal tyranny. George Washington said of the essay, "I find Common Sense is working a powerful change in the minds of men."

IN the following pages I offer nothing more than simple facts, plain arguments, and common sense . . .[1] Volumes have been written on the subject of the struggle between England and America. Men of all ranks have embarked in the controversy, from different motives, and with various designs; but all have been ineffectual, and the period of debate is closed. Arms as the last resource decide the contest; the appeal was the choice of the King, and the Continent has accepted the challenge . . . The Sun never shined on a cause of greater worth. 'Tis not the affair of a City, a County, a Province, or a Kingdom; but of a Continent . . . 'Tis not the concern of a day, a year, or an age; posterity are virtually involved in the contest, and will be more or less affected even to the end of time, by the proceedings now. Now is the seed-time of Continental union, faith and honor . . .

By referring the matter from argument to arms, a new era for politics is struck—a new method of thinking hath arisen. All plans,

[1] Paine addresses a wide audience. His purpose is to persuade those "on the fence" through simple direct argument.

proposals, &c. prior to the nineteenth of April,[2] i.e. to the commencement of hostilities, are like the almanacks of the last year; which tho' proper then, are superseded and useless now. Whatever was advanced by the advocates on either side of the question then, terminated in one and the same point, viz. a union with Great Britain; the only difference between the parties was the method of effecting it; the one proposing force, the other friendship; but it hath so far happened that the first hath failed, and the second hath withdrawn her influence.

As much hath been said of the advantages of reconciliation, which, like an agreeable dream, hath passed away and left us as we were, it is but right that we should examine the contrary side of the argument, and enquire into some of the many material injuries which these Colonies sustain, and always will sustain, by being connected with and dependent on Great Britain. To examine that connection and dependence, on the principles of nature and common sense, to see what we have to trust to, if separated, and what we are to expect, if dependent. I have heard it asserted by some, that as America has flourished under her former connection with Great Britain, the same connection is necessary towards her future happiness . . . Nothing can be more fallacious than this kind of argument . . . I answer roundly that America would have flourished as much, and probably much more, had no European power taken any notice of her. The commerce by which she hath enriched herself are the necessaries of life, and will always have a market while eating is the custom of Europe.[3]

[3]Paine's popularity with the general public is based, in part, on his ability to use humor to lighten the most serious of subjects. Here, America's prosperity is based on European taste for its exports (tobacco, for example) and foodstuffs. His point is simply that colonial prosperity is not based on a connection with Britain.

[4]Britain has monopolized our trade.

But she has protected us, say some. That she hath engrossed us is true,[4] and defended the Continent at our expense as well as her own, is admitted; and she would have defended Turkey from the same motive, viz.—for the sake of trade and dominion . . . We have boasted the protection of Great Britain, without considering, that her motive was interest not attachment; and that she did not protect us from our enemies on our account; but from her enemies on her own account, from those who had no quarrel with us on any other account, and who will always be our enemies on the same account. Let Britain waive her pretensions to the Continent . . . and we should be at peace with France and Spain . . .[5]

[5]America's problems arise because of its continued connection with Britain. America shares Britain's enemies, who are basically not ours.

It hath lately been asserted in parliament, that the Colonies have no relation to each other but through the Parent Country . . . this is certainly a very roundabout way of proving relationship, but it is the nearest and only true way of proving enmity (or enemyship, if I may so call it.) France and Spain never were, nor perhaps ever will be, our enemies as Americans, but as our being the subjects of Great Britain.

But Britain is the parent country, say some. Then the more shame upon her conduct. Even brutes do not devour their young, nor savages make war upon their families. Wherefore, the assertion, if true, turns to her reproach; but it happens not to be true, or only partly so, and the phrase Parent or Mother country hath been jesuitically[6] adopted by the King and his parasites, with a low papistical[7] design of gaining an unfair bias on the credulous weakness of our minds. Europe, and not England, is the parent country of America. This new world hath been the asylum for the persecuted lovers of civil and religious liberty from every part of Europe. Hither have they fled, not from the tender embraces of the mother, but from the cruelty of the monster; and it is so far true of England, that the same tyranny which drove the first emigrants from home, pursues their descendants still . . . [8]

But, admitting that we were all of English descent, what does it amount to? Nothing. Britain, being now an open enemy, extinguishes every other name and title: and to say that reconciliation is our duty, is truly farcical . . . Much hath been said of the united strength of Britain and the Colonies, that in conjunction they might bid defiance to the world. But this is mere presumption; the fate of war is uncertain . . . for this continent would never suffer itself to be drained of inhabitants, to support the British arms in either Asia, Africa, or Europe . . .

Our plan is commerce, and that, well attended to, will secure us the peace and friendship of all Europe; because it is the interest of all Europe to have America a free port.[9] Her trade will always be a protection, and her barrenness of gold and silver secure her from invaders.

I challenge the warmest advocate for reconciliation to show a single advantage that this continent can reap by being connected with Great Britain. I repeat the challenge; not a single advantage is derived . . .

[6]This term refers to Jesuit priests and means subtle or sly reasoning.
[7]This is a disparaging reference to the pope, and by extension, to Roman Catholics.

[8]The pilgrims and puritans suffered from a tyrannical regime of Parliament and the Anglican Church. This is correct when applied to the northern colonies. The southern planters were in step with Great Britain at first.

[9]An argument in support of free trade. This argument has persisted through American history to the present.

But the injuries and disadvantages which we sustain by that connection, are without number; and our duty to mankind at large, as well as to ourselves, instruct us to renounce the alliance: because, any submission to, or dependence on, Great Britain, tends directly to involve this Continent in European wars and quarrels, and set us at variance with nations who would otherwise seek our friendship,[10] and against whom we have neither anger nor complaint. As Europe is our market for trade, we ought to form no partial connection with any part of it. It is the true interest of America to steer clear of European contentions which she never can do, while, by her dependence on Britain, she is made the makeweight[11] in the scale of British politics.

But the injuries and disadvantages which we sustain by that connection, are without number; and our duty to mankind at large, as well as to ourselves, instruct us to renounce the alliance: because, any submission to, or dependence on, Great Britain, tends directly to involve this Continent in European wars and quarrels, and set us at variance with nations who would otherwise seek our friendship,[10] and against whom we have neither anger nor complaint. As Europe is our market for trade, we ought to form no partial connection with any part of it. It is the true interest of America to steer clear of European contentions which she never can do, while, by her dependence on Britain, she is made the makeweight[11] in the scale of British politics.

Europe is too thickly planted with Kingdoms to be long at peace, and whenever a war breaks out between England and any foreign power, the trade of America goes to ruin, because of her connection with Britain. The next war may not turn out like the last,[12] and should it not, the advocates for reconciliation now will be wishing for separation then, because neutrality in that case would be a safer convoy than a man of war. Everything that is right or reasonable pleads for separation. The blood of the slain, the weeping voice of nature cries, 'Tis time to part. Even the distance at which the Almighty hath placed England and America is a strong and natural proof that the authority of the one over the other, was never the design of Heaven . . .

Though I would carefully avoid giving unnecessary offence yet I am inclined to believe, that all those who espouse the doctrine of reconciliation, may be included within the following descriptions. Interested men, who are not to be trusted, weak men who cannot see, prejudiced men who will not see, and a certain set of moderate men who think better of the European world than it deserves; and this last class, by an ill-judged deliberation, will be the cause of more calamities to this Continent than all the other three . . .

Men of passive tempers look somewhat lightly over the offences of Great Britain, and, still hoping for the best, are apt to call out, "Come, come, we shall be friends again for all this." . . . bring the doctrine of reconciliation to the touchstone of nature,[13] and then tell me whether you can hereafter love, honour, and faithfully serve the power that hath carried fire and sword into your land? If you

[10]The theme of avoidance of alliances with European countries is a recurring refrain that is sounded throughout American history. It is most famously reflected in Washington's farewell address to the nation in 1796. "Why forego the advantages of so peculiar a situation? [America's geography separating her from Europe] Why quit our own to stand upon foreign ground? Why, by interweaving our destiny with that of any part of Europe, entangle our peace and prosperity in the toils of European ambition, interest, humor or caprice? It is our true policy to steer clear of permanent alliance with any portion of the foreign world."

[11]A makeweight is something added to achieve an advantage.

[12]The French and Indian War, which Britain won.

[13]Test the validity of the argument in favor of reconciliation against the natural law.

cannot do all these, then are you only deceiving yourselves, and by your delay bringing ruin upon posterity . . . But if you say, you can still pass the violations over, then I ask, hath your house been burnt? Hath your property been destroyed before your face? Are your wife and children destitute of a bed to lie on, or bread to live on? Have you lost a parent or a child by their hands, and yourself the ruined and wretched survivor? If you have not, then are you not a judge of those who have. But if you have, and can still shake hands with the murderers, then are you unworthy the name of husband, father, friend or lover, and whatever may be your rank or title in life, you have the heart of a coward, and the spirit of a sycophant . . .[14]

[14]A self-seeker who seeks fame by flattering influential people.

I mean not to exhibit horror for the purpose of provoking revenge, but to awaken us from fatal and unmanly slumbers, that we may pursue determinately some fixed object. It is not in the power of Britain or of Europe to conquer America, if she do not conquer herself by delay and timidity . . .

It is repugnant to reason, to the universal order of things to all examples from former ages, to suppose, that this continent can longer remain subject to any external power . . . The utmost stretch of human wisdom cannot, at this time, compass a plan short of separation, which can promise the continent even a year's security. Reconciliation is now a falacious dream . .[15]

[15]Meaning it is based on a mistaken belief.

Every quiet method for peace hath been ineffectual. Our prayers have been rejected with disdain; and only tended to convince us, that nothing flatters vanity, or confirms obstinacy in Kings more than repeated petitioning . . . Wherefore, since nothing but blows will do, for God's sake, let us come to a final separation . . .

As to government matters, it is not in the power of Britain to do this continent justice: The business of it will soon be too weighty, and intricate, to be managed with any tolerable degree of convenience, by a power, so distant from us . . . for if they cannot conquer us, they cannot govern us. To be always running three or four thousand miles with a tale or a petition, waiting four or five months for an answer, which when obtained requires five or six more to explain it in, will in a few years be looked upon as folly and childishness—There was a time when it was proper, and there is a proper time for it to cease.

The laws of planetary motion, developed by Copernicus (using logic), Kepler (using mathematics), and Galileo (using observation), are seen as natural truth—laws of "nature and nature's god." In the same way, Paine implies that satellites invariably are smaller and thus independent of the larger bodies with which they are associated. Thus, it would be a violation of natural law for a smaller political entity (Britain) to control a more substantial polity (the American colonies).

. . . there is something very absurd, in supposing a continent to be perpetually governed by an island. In no instance hath nature made the satellite larger than its primary planet, and as England and America, with respect to each other, reverses the common order of nature, it is evident they belong to different systems: England to Europe, America to itself.[16]

I am not induced by motives of pride, party, or resentment to espouse the doctrine of separation and independence; I am clearly, positively, and conscientiously persuaded that it is the true interest of this continent to be so; that every thing short of that is mere patchwork, that it can afford no lasting felicity . . .

As Britain hath not manifested the least inclination towards a compromise, we may be assured that no terms can be obtained worthy the acceptance . . .

As I have always considered the independency of this continent, as an event, which sooner or later must arrive, so from the late rapid progress of the continent to maturity, the event could not be far off. Wherefore, on the breaking out of hostilities, it was not worth the while to have disputed a matter, which time would have finally redressed, unless we meant to be in earnest . . . No man was a warmer wisher for reconciliation than myself, before the fatal nineteenth of April 1775, but the moment the event of that day was made known, I rejected the hardened, sullen tempered Pharaoh of England forever; and disdain the wretch, that with the pretended title of Father of His People, can unfeelingly hear of their slaughter, and composedly sleep with their blood upon his soul.[17] But admitting that matters were now made up, what would be the event? I answer, the ruin of the continent. And that for several reasons.

[17]Revolutionary documents contain many biblical references, a reflection of the fact that the founding fathers were well-versed in biblical literature. Here George III is compared with the king of Egypt, Rameses II, who kept the Hebrews in slavery until they were led to freedom by Moses.

First. The powers of governing still remaining in the hands of the king, he will have a negative over the whole legislation of this continent. And as he hath shewn himself such an inveterate enemy to liberty . . . is he, or is he not, a proper man to say to these colonies, "You shall make no laws but what I please." And is there any inhabitant in America so ignorant, as not to know, that according to what is called the present constitution, that this continent can make no laws but what the king gives it leave to; and is there any man so unwise, as not to see, that (considering what has happened) he will suffer no law to be made here, but such as suit his purpose . . . can there be any doubt, but the whole power of the crown will be exerted, to keep this continent as low and humble as possible? Instead of going forward we shall go backward ... We are already greater than the king wishes us to be, and will he not hereafter endeavour to make us less? To bring the matter to one point. Is the power who is jealous of our prosperity, a proper power to govern us? ...

America is only a secondary object in the system of British politics, England consults the good of this country, no farther than it answers her own purpose.[18] Wherefore, her own interest leads her to suppress the growth of ours in every case which doth not promote her advantage ...

Secondly. That as even the best terms, which we can expect to obtain, can amount to no more than a temporary expedient, or a kind of government by guardianship, which can last no longer than till the colonies come of age, so the general face and state of things, in the interim, will be unsettled and unpromising. Emigrants of property will not choose to come to a country whose form of government hangs but by a thread, and who is every day tottering on the brink of commotion and disturbance; and numbers of the present inhabitants would lay hold of the interval, to dispose of their effects, and quit the continent.

But the most powerful of all arguments, is, that nothing but independence, i.e. a continental form of government, can keep the peace of the continent and preserve it inviolate from civil wars. I dread the event of a reconciliation with Britain now, as it is more than probable, that it will be followed by a revolt somewhere or other, the consequences of which may be far more fatal than all the malice of Britain.[19]

Thousands are already ruined by British barbarity; (thousands more will probably suffer the same fate.) Those men have other feelings than us who have nothing suffered. All they now possess is liberty, what they before enjoyed is sacrificed to its service, and having nothing more to lose, they disdain submission ... a government which cannot preserve the peace, is no government at all ... what is it that Britain can do, whose power will be wholly on paper, should a civil tumult break out the very day after reconciliation? I have heard some men say ... that they dreaded an independence, fearing that it would produce civil wars ... for there are ten times more to dread from a patched up connexion than from independence ...

[18]A reference to the economic doctrine of mercantilism characteristic of European countries in the 17th or 18th centuries. But this statement is an unfair one, for although mercantilist doctrine promoted control of colonial trade for the benefit of the European country, this was only partly true in the case of England. England engaged in what may be called "enlightened" mercantilism, a system where both England and its colonies shared the benefits of trade regulations. Colonial manufacture that competed with goods produced in the home country was discouraged; still, the colonies were given protection of certain products such as tobacco, molasses, hemp, tar, and other naval stores.

[19]Paine correctly anticipates the fact that a continental government (i.e., a government recognized and accepted by all sections of a polity) is a prerequisite for a peaceful society. When in the mid-19th century sectional interests refused to accept the authority of the central government, the revolt was the American Civil War.

[20]Two Continental Congresses met, the first in September 1774 and the second in May 1775. The purposes of those congresses were to secure colonial rights and liberties seen as violated by the actions of Parliament. The colonies resolved to employ economic pressure against Britain (limiting both imports and exports). When the events in Massachusetts deteriorated into war, the Congress raised an army and chose Washington to lead it. At that point (June 15, 1775), the Congress assumed power over the united cause of the colonies. In early 1775, the main focus of activity was still protection of colonial rights without separation from Britain, but it soon became clear that it was common sense to accept the fact that independence was the only route to redress of grievances. To this point, it had not become evident that an effective organization of the state was needed to achieve colonial objectives. Paine's suppositions were an outline for creating such an organization. Confederation was an attempt to form a formal government (November 15, 1777). When the articles proved less than successful, a Continental Congress was called (1787).

[21]Once again, the recurring theme of "a government of laws, not men."

If there is any true cause of fear respecting independence, it is because no plan is yet laid down . . . Wherefore, as an opening into that business, I offer the following hints . . . Let each colony be divided into six, eight, or ten, convenient districts, each district to send a proper number of delegates to Congress, so that each colony send at least thirty. The whole number in Congress will be least 390. Each Congress to sit and to choose a president . . . in order that nothing may pass into a law but what is satisfactorily just, not less than three fifths of the Congress to be called a majority . . . But as there is a peculiar delicacy, from whom, or in what manner, this business must first arise . . . let a Continental Conference be held . . . for the following purpose . . . The conferring members being met, let their business be to frame a Continental Charter, or Charter of the United Colonies . . . fixing the number and manner of choosing members of Congress, members of Assembly . . .[20] drawing the line of business and jurisdiction between them: (Always remembering, that our strength is continental, not provincial:) Securing freedom and property to all men, and above all things, the free exercise of religion, according to the dictates of conscience; with such other matter as is necessary for a charter to contain. Immediately after which, the said Conference to dissolve, and the bodies which shall be chosen comfortable to the said charter, to be the legislators and governors of this continent for the time being: Whose peace and happiness, may God preserve, Amen . . .

But where says some is the King of America? I'll tell you Friend, he reigns above, and doth not make havoc of mankind like the Royal Brute of Britain. Yet that we may not appear to be defective even in earthly honors, let a day be solemnly set apart for proclaiming the charter; let it be brought forth placed on the divine law, the word of God; let a crown be placed thereon, by which the world may know, that so far as we approve as monarchy, that in America the law is king.[21] For as in absolute governments the King is law, so in free countries the law ought to be King; and there ought to be no other. But lest any ill use should afterwards arise, let the crown at the conclusion of the ceremony be demolished, and scattered among the people whose right it is.

A government of our own is our natural right: And when a man seriously reflects on the precariousness of human affairs, he will become convinced, that it is infinitely wiser and safer, to form a constitution of our own in a cool deliberate manner . . . than to trust such an interesting event to time and chance. If we omit it now, some, Massanello[22] may hereafter arise, who laying hold of popular disquietudes, may collect together the desperate and discontented, and by assuming to themselves the powers of government, may sweep away the liberties of the continent like a deluge. Should the government of America return again into the hands of Britain, the tottering situation of things, will be a temptation for some desperate adventurer to try his fortune; and in such a case, what relief can Britain give? Ere she could hear the news, the fatal business might be done; and ourselves suffering like the wretched Britons under the oppression of the Conqueror.[23] Ye that oppose independence now, ye know not what ye do; ye are opening a door to eternal tyranny, by keeping vacant the seat of government. There are thousands, and tens of thousands, who would think it glorious to expel from the continent, that barbarous and hellish power, which hath stirred up the Indians and Negroes to destroy us, the cruelty hath a double guilt,[24] it is dealing brutally by us, and treacherously by them.

To talk of friendship with those in whom our reason forbids us to have faith, and our affections wounded through a thousand pores instruct us to detest, is madness and folly. Every day wears out the little remains of kindred between us and them, and can there be any reason to hope, that as the relationship expires, the affection will increase, or that we shall agree better, when we have ten times more and greater concerns to quarrel over than ever?

Ye that tell us of harmony and reconciliation, can ye restore to us the time that is past? Can ye give to prostitution its former innocence? Neither can ye reconcile Britain and America. The last cord now is broken . . . There are injuries which nature cannot forgive; she would cease to be nature if she did. As well can the lover forgive the ravisher of his mistress, as the continent forgive the murderers of Britain . . .

O ye that love mankind! Ye that dare oppose, not only the tyranny, but the tyrant, stand forth! Every spot of the old world is overrun with oppression. Freedom hath been hunted round the globe. Asia, and Africa, have long expelled her.—Europe regards her like a stranger, and England hath given her warning to depart. O! receive the fugitive, and prepare in time an asylum for mankind.

[22]"Massanello" [actually Massaniélo] was the leader of an unsuccessful popular revolt against Spanish rule in the Kingdom of Naples (1647). Spain had ruled the territory for years and represented the established order. Massaniélo was a populist demagogue who created turmoil in the society.

[23]William I, known as "the Conqueror," was French, born in Normandy in 1027. He invaded Saxon England and was crowned king on Christmas Day 1066. He suppressed rebellions throughout the realm and levied the first tax on property in all of Europe. He was a rigid ruler, demanding fealty from his vassals. Historically, his most important contribution was the creation of the Domesday Book, a survey of the landholdings of the English nobility.

[24]In March 1775, the Stockbridge, Massachusetts Indians offered to join the patriot cause as minutemen. When this became known, the secretary of state for the colonies attempted to convince the Indians to support the British cause. Early in 1775, the royal governor of Virginia, in a desperate move to control the armaments stored at Williamsburg, called on black slaves to support his cause by promising them emancipation: the white Virginians called this attempt to attract black support to the British a "hellish plot" and a call for a race war. The governor also was said to be intriguing with Indians to attack white settlements and to be holding nightly meetings with blacks "for the glorious purpose of enticing them to cut their master's throats while they are asleep" (*Virginia Gazette*, October 27, 1775).

Of the Present Ability of America: With Some Miscellaneous Reflections

. . . let us . . . take a general survey of things . . . 'Tis not in numbers but in unity that our great strength lies: yet our present numbers are sufficient to repel the force of all the world. The Continent hath at this time the largest body of armed and disciplined men of any power under Heaven . . . Our land force is more than sufficient, and as to Naval affairs, we cannot be insensible that Britain would never suffer an American man of war to be built, while the Continent remained in her hands . . . Were the Continent crowded with inhabitants, her sufferings under the present circumstances would be intolerable. The more seaport-towns we had, the more should we have both to defend and to lose. Our present numbers are so happily proportioned to our wants, that no man need be idle . . . Debts we have none . . .

Can we but leave posterity with a settled form of government, an independent constitution of its own, the purchase at any price will be cheap. But to expend millions for the sake of getting a few vile acts repealed, and routing the present ministry only, is unworthy the charge, and is using posterity with the utmost cruelty; because it is leaving them the great work to do, and a debt upon their backs from which they derive no advantage. Such a thought is unworthy a man of honour, and is the true characteristic of a narrow heart and a piddling politician.

The debt we may contract doth not deserve our regard if the work be but accomplished. No nation ought to be without a debt. A national debt is a national bond; and when it bears no interest, is in no case a grievance. Britain is oppressed with a debt of upwards of one hundred and forty millions sterling, for which she pays upwards of four millions interest. And as a compensation for her debt, she has a large navy; America is without a debt, and without a navy; yet for the twentieth part of the English national debt, could have a navy as large again . . .[25] No country on the globe is so happily situated, or so internally capable of raising a fleet as America. Tar, timber, iron, and cordage are her natural produce. We need go abroad for nothing . . . We ought to view the building a fleet as an article of commerce, it being the natural manufactory of this country. 'Tis the best money we can lay out. A navy when finished is worth more than it cost: and is that nice point in national

[25] John Adams gives us an apt evaluation of the power of the British Navy in September 1775. "The navy of Great Britain is now mistress of the seas, all over the globe. The navy of France almost annihilated . . . all her dominion . . . lay at the mercy of Great Britain."

policy, in which commerce and protection are united. Let us build; if we want them not, we can sell; and by that means replace our paper currency with ready gold and silver . . . we never can be more capable of beginning on maritime matters than now, while our timber is standing, our fisheries blocked up, and our sailors and shipwrights out of employ. Men of war . . . were built forty years ago in New England, and why not the same now? Ship building is America's greatest pride, and in which she will, in time, excel the whole world . . . In point of safety, ought we to be without a fleet? We are not the little people now which we were sixty years ago; at that time, we might have trusted our property in the streets, or fields rather, and slept securely without locks or bolts to our doors and windows. The case is now altered, and our methods of defense ought to improve with our increase of property . . . Some perhaps will say, that after we have made it up with Britain, she will protect us. Can they be so unwise as to mean that she will keep a navy in our harbors for that purpose? Common sense will tell us that the power which hath endeavoured to subdue us, is of all others the most improper to defend us . . . A navy three or four thousand miles off can be of little use, and on sudden emergencies, none at all. Wherefore if we must hereafter protect ourselves, why not do it for ourselves? . . .

Nothing can be further from truth than this; for if America had only a twentieth part of the naval force of Britain, she would be by far an over-match for her; because, as we neither have, nor claim any foreign dominion, our whole force would be employed on our own coast, where we should, in the long run, have two to one the advantage of those who had three or four thousand miles to sail over before they could attack us, and the same distance to return in order to refit and recruit. And although Britain, by her fleet, hath a check over our trade to Europe, we have as large a one over her trade to the West Indies, which, by laying in the neighborhood of the Continent, lies entirely at its mercy . . .[26]

To unite the sinews of commerce and defense is sound policy;[27] or when our strength and our riches play into each other's hand, we need fear no external enemy. In almost every article of defense we abound. Hemp flourishes even to rankness so that we need not want cordage. Our iron is superior to that of other countries. Our small arms equal to any in the world. Cannon we can cast at pleasure.

[26]The American Navy was founded by Congress on October 13, 1775, with 27 frigate ships. The frigate was a midsized man-of-war ship. It would typically have 3 masts and carry between 24 and 40 guns. Only three survived the revolution.

[27]This is one of the earliest statements in favor of promoting what has been called, in the 20th century, the "military-industrial complex." Eisenhower warned against it in his farewell TV address to the nation, but most mid-century Americans saw the alliance of private industry with the needs of national defense as a source of jobs and prosperity. In this they were closer to Paine than to Eisenhower.

Saltpetre and gunpowder we are every day producing. Our knowledge is hourly improving. Resolution is our inherent character, and courage hath never yet forsaken us. Wherefore, what is it that we want? Why is it that we hesitate? From Britain we can expect nothing but ruin. If she is once admitted to the government of America again, this Continent will not be worth living in. Jealousies will be always arising; insurrections will be constantly happening; and who will go forth to quell them? Who will venture his life to reduce his own countrymen to a foreign obedience? . . . nothing but Continental authority can regulate Continental matters . . . the fewer our numbers are, the more land there is yet unoccupied, which, instead of being lavished by the king on his worthless dependents, may be hereafter applied, not only to the discharge of the present debt, but to the constant support of government. No nation under Heaven hath such an advantage as this.

The infant state of the Colonies . . . so far from being against, is an argument in favour of independence. We are sufficiently numerous, and were we more so we might be less united . . . the more a country is peopled, the smaller their armies are . . . and the reason is evident, for trade being the consequence of population, men became too much absorbed thereby to attend to anything else. Commerce diminishes the spirit both of patriotism and military defence. And history sufficiently informs us that the bravest achievements were always accomplished in the non-age of a nation . . . The more men have to lose, the less willing are they to venture. The rich are in general slaves to fear, and submit to courtly power with the trembling duplicity of a spaniel.

Youth is the seed-time of good habits as well in nations as in individuals. It might be difficult, if not impossible, to form the Continent into one government half a century hence. The vast variety of interests . . . would create confusion. Colony would be against colony . . . and while the proud and foolish gloried in their little distinctions the wise would lament that the union had not been formed before. Wherefore the present time is the true time for establishing it. The intimacy which is contracted in infancy, and the friendship which is formed in misfortune, are of all others the most lasting and unalterable. Our present union is marked with both these characters; we are young, and we have been distressed; but our concord hath withstood our troubles, and fixes a memorable era for posterity to glory in.

The present time, likewise, is that peculiar time which never happens to a nation but once . . . the time of forming itself into a government. Most nations have let slip the opportunity, and by that means have been compelled to receive laws from their conquerors, instead of making laws for themselves . . .

When William the Conqueror subdued England, he gave them law at the point of the sword; and, until we consent that the seat of government in America be legally and authoritatively occupied, we shall be in danger of having it filled by some fortunate ruffian, who may treat us in the same manner, and then, where will be our freedom? Where our property?

As to religion, I hold it to be the indispensable duty of government to protect all conscientious professors thereof, and I know of no other business which government hath to do therewith . . .

For myself, I fully and conscientiously believe that it is the will of the Almighty that there should be a diversity of religious opinions among us.[28] It affords a larger field for our Christian kindness; were we all of one way of thinking, our religious dispositions would want matter for probation; and on this liberal principle I look on the various denominations among us to be like children of the same family, differing only in what is called their Christian names . . .

[28] A call for freedom of religion later reflected in Article 1 of the Constitution: "Congress shall make no law respecting an establishment of religion, or prohibiting the free excise thereof."

I threw out a few thoughts on the propriety of a Continental Charter . . . and in this place I take the liberty of re-mentioning the subject, by observing that a charter is to be understood as a bond of solemn obligation, which the whole enters into, to support the right of every separate part, whether of religion, professional freedom, or property. A firm bargain and a right reckoning make long friends.

I have heretofore likewise mentioned the necessity of a large and equal representation; and there is no political matter which more deserves our attention. A small number of electors, or a small number of representatives, are equally dangerous. But if the number of the representatives be not only small, but unequal, the danger is increased . . .

Immediate necessity makes many things convenient, which if continued would grow into oppressions. Expedience and right are different things. When the calamities of America required a consultation, there was no method so ready, or at that time so proper, as to appoint persons from the several houses of assembly for that purpose; and the wisdom with which they have proceeded hath preserved this Continent from ruin. But as it is more than probable that we shall never be without a Congress, every well wisher to good order must own that the mode for choosing members of that body deserves consideration . . . I put it as a question to those who make a study of mankind, whether representation and election is not too great a power for one and the same body of men to possess? When we are planning for posterity, we ought to remember that virtue is not hereditary . . .

To conclude, however strange it may appear to some . . . many strong and striking reasons may be given to show that nothing can settle our affairs so expeditiously as an open and determined declaration for independence.[29] Some of which are,

First.—It is the custom of Nations, when any two are at war, for some other powers, not engaged in the quarrel, to step in as mediators, and bring about the preliminaries of a peace; But while America calls herself the subject of Great Britain, no power, however well disposed she may be, can offer her mediation. Wherefore, in our present state we may quarrel on for ever.

Secondly.—It is unreasonable to suppose that France or Spain will give us any kind of assistance, if we mean only to make use of that assistance for the purpose of repairing the breach, and strengthening the connection between Britain and America; because, those powers would be sufferers by the consequences.

Thirdly.—While we profess ourselves the subjects of Britain, we must, in the eyes of foreign nations, be considered as Rebels. The precedent is somewhat dangerous to their peace, for men to be in arms under the name of subjects; we, on the spot, can solve the paradox; but to unite resistance and subjection requires an idea much too refined for common understanding.

Fourthly.—Were a manifesto to be published, and dispatched to foreign Courts, setting forth the miseries we have endured, and the peaceful methods which we have ineffectually used for redress; declaring at the same time that not being able longer to live happily or safely under the cruel disposition of the British Court, we had been driven to the necessity of breaking off all connections with her;[30] at the same time, assuring all such Courts of our peaceable disposition towards them, and of our desire of entering

29*Common Sense*, published in January 1776, represents an epochal change in the thinking of the leadership of the colonies. Previously the thinking was characterized by a policy of demanding the rights of British subjects within the empire. By 1776, the colonists adopted a policy of separation. It was this policy, enunciated by Paine, that found expression in the Declaration of Independence.

30This is essentially an outline for the Declaration of Independence.

into trade with them; such a memorial would produce more good effects to this Continent than if a ship were freighted with petitions to Britain.

Under our present denomination of British subjects, we can neither be received nor heard abroad; the custom of all Courts is against us, and will be so, until by an independence we take rank with other nations.

These proceedings may at first seem strange and difficult, but like all other steps which we have already passed over, will in a little time become familiar and agreeable; and until an independence is declared, the Continent will feel itself like a man who continues putting off some unpleasant business from day to day, yet knows it must be done, hates to set about it, wishes it over, and is continually haunted with the thoughts of its necessity.

Source: Thomas Paine (1737–1809), *Common Sense*. (Philadelphia: R. Bell, 1776). American Imprint Collection, Rare Book and Special Collections Division, Library of Congress.

John Adams: "Thoughts on Government"

(April 1776)

INTRODUCTION

Adams, who later became the second president of the United States, was one of the intellectual fathers of both the Declaration of Independence and the Constitution. He was a leader in the deliberation of the Continental Congress. "Thoughts on Government" was published in April 1776. His idea, in favor of the formation of republican government, fell on fertile soil, soil that had been well prepared by *Common Sense*. His outline of what the new government should look like gave substance and form to ideas implied in *Common Sense*.

[1] John Adams's contemporaries were familiar with the political theories of Niccolo Machiavelli, author of *The Prince*, an examination of the techniques needed for successful leadership. Although written in 15th–16th-century Florence, his doctrines have had wide-ranging influence because of their clear-eyed realism. Machiavelli was a champion of "Virtù," or manly courage, as an indispensable quality of leadership. He also proclaimed that for a leader it is "better to be feared than to be loved"—a comment also reflected in Adams's comment on government formation.

. . . We ought to consider, what is the end of government, before we determine which is the best form. Upon this point all speculative politicians will agree, that the happiness of society is the end of government . . . From this principle it will follow, that the form of government, which communicates ease, comfort, security, or in one word happiness to the greatest number of persons, and in the greatest degree, is the best.

All sober enquiries after truth, ancient and modern, Pagan and Christian, have declared that the happiness of man, as well as his dignity consists in virtue . . . [1]

If there is a form of government then, whose principle and foundation is virtue, will not every sober man acknowledge it better calculated to promote the general happiness than any other form?

Fear is the foundation of most governments; but is so sordid and brutal a passion, and renders men, in whose breasts it predominates, so stupid, and miserable, that Americans will not be likely to approve of any political institution which is founded on it . . .

The foundation of every government is some principle or passion in the minds of the people. The noblest principles . . . in our nature . . .

have the fairest chance to support the noblest and most generous models of government.[2] . . . there is no good government but what is Republican . . . the very definition of a Republic, is an Empire of Laws, and not of men.[3] That, as a Republic is the best of governments, so that particular arrangement of the powers of society, or in other words that form of government, which is best contrived to secure an impartial and exact execution of the laws, is the best of Republics . . .

As good government, is an empire of laws, how shall your laws be made? In a large society, inhabiting an extensive country, it is impossible that the whole should assemble, to make laws: The first necessary step then, is, to depute power from the many, to a few of the most wise and good. But by what rules shall you chuse your Representatives? Agree upon the number and qualifications of persons, who shall have the benefit of choosing, or annex this privilege to the inhabitants of a certain extent of ground.[4] The principal difficulty lies, and the greatest care should be employed in constituting this Representative Assembly. It should be in miniature, an exact portrait of the people at large. It should think, feel, reason, and act like them . . . equal interest among the people should have equal interest in it. Great care should be taken to effect this, and to prevent unfair, partial, and corrupt elections . . .

But shall the whole power of legislation rest in one Assembly?[5] . . . the legislative power ought to be more complex . . . if the legislative power is wholly in one Assembly, and the executive in another, or in a single person, these two powers will oppose and enervate upon each other, until the contest shall end in war, and the whole power, legislative and executive, be usurped by the strongest.

The judicial power, in such case, could not mediate, or hold the balance between the two contending powers, because the legislative would undermine it. And this shows the necessity too, of giving the executive power a negative upon the legislative, otherwise this will be continually encroaching upon that.

To avoid these dangers let a [distinct] Assembly be constituted, as a mediator between the two extreme branches of the legislature, that which represents the people and that which is vested with the executive power.[6]

[2]This statement reflects the political philosophy of Thomas Hobbes (1588–1679) who, in his treatise *Leviathan*, expressed his opinion that because human beings were essentially evil, a government needed to use fear to preserve order in society.

[3]Adams's definition is loosely based on the Latin origin of the word "republic": *res publicae*, the thing (*res*) of the people (*publicae*)—that is, "the peoples' thing" or in Lincoln's phrase, government "of, by, and for the people."

[4]Adams is discussing the problem of forming a representative assembly. He feels the easy part of the process is deciding how many representatives there shall be and what qualifications they shall have. He recognizes that representation in the British Parliament was limited to men of property. Indeed, property requirements for office-holding were common prerequisites typical of colonial assemblies. He is also raising the question of voting qualifications and whether representation should be geographically limited or determined by population. He seems to recognize that in Britain certain so-called rotten boroughs with few inhabitants had equal representation with more populous areas.

[5]Adams begins to sketch out the three modern branches of American government (executive, judicial, and legislative) with checks on each other's powers.

[6]Adams's outline for the structure of a government bears some resemblance to the format developed under the Constitution. The "two extreme branches" he mentions are the executive and legislative.

[7]When he mentions an assembly, he first refers to what we would call our House of Representatives. But he then calls for the formation of a council independent of the House, which we would recognize as our Senate.

[8]Then he provides for the election by both Houses of a governor, that is, a president. He also calls for annual elections.

[9]Although his rough outline is far from what the Constitutional Convention developed, his contribution was the underlying principle of each locus of power having a check on the other. As for the choice of "governor" by the legislature, in the early years of the republic candidates were selected by party caucuses in Congress. About 1830, as natural political parties were organized, party conventions nominated candidates. The quotation "where annual elections end there slavery begins" is from Cicero in *De Republicae I* (concerning republics).

[10]At the beginning of the 18th century, all British colonies established by royal charter were obliged to send their laws for approval to Parliament. The exceptions were private colonies, that is, self-governing communities.

[11]Or, in our terms the president and the Senate. This is expressed in Article 2, section 2 of the Constitution: power of the executive.

Let the Representative Assembly then elect by ballot, from among themselves or their constituents, or both, a distinct Assembly, which for the sake of perspicuity we will call a Council . . . and should have a free and independent exercise of its judgment, and consequently a negative voice in the legislature.[7]

These two bodies thus constituted, and made integral parts of the legislature, let them unite, and by joint ballot choose a Governor, who, after being stripped of most of those badges of domination called prerogatives, should have a free and independent exercise of his judgment, and be made also an integral part of the legislature . . . as the Governor is to be invested with the executive power, with consent of Council, I think he ought to have a negative upon the legislative. If he is annually elective, as he ought to be, he will always have so much reverence and affection for the People, their Representatives and Councillors, that although you give him an independent exercise of his judgment, he will seldom use it in opposition to the two Houses[8] . . . these and all other elections, especially of Representatives, and Councillors, should be annual . . . "Where annual elections end, there slavery begins."[9]

. . . This will teach them the great political virtues of humility, patience, and moderation, without which every man in power becomes a ravenous beast of prey.

This mode of constituting the great offices of state will answer very well for the present, but if, by experiment, it should be found inconvenient, the legislature may at its leisure devise other methods of creating them, by elections of the people at large, as in Connecticut,[10] or it may enlarge the term for which they shall be chosen to seven years, or three years, or for life, or make any other alterations which the society shall find productive of its ease, its safety, its freedom, or in one word, its happiness . . .

The Governor should have the command of the militia, and of all your armies. The power of pardons should be with the Governor and Council. Judges, Justices and all other officers, civil and military, should be nominated and appointed by the Governor, with the advice and consent of Council . . .[11] the judicial power ought to be distinct from both the legislative and executive, and independent upon both, that so it may be a check upon both, as both should be checks upon that. The Judges therefore should always be men of learning and experience in the laws, of exemplary morals, great patience, calmness, coolness and attention. Their minds should not be distracted with jarring interests; they should not be dependant upon any man or body of men. To these ends they should hold estates for life in their offices . . . Laws for the liberal education of youth, especially of the lower class of people, are so extremely wise and useful, that to a humane and generous mind, no expence for this purpose would be thought extravagant . . .

A Constitution, founded on these principles, introduces knowledge among the People, and inspires them with a conscious dignity, becoming Freemen. A general emulation takes place, which causes good humour, sociability, good manners, and good morals to be general. That elevation of sentiment, inspired by such a government, makes the common people brave and enterprising. That ambition which is inspired by it makes them sober, industrious and frugal. You will find among them some elegance, perhaps, but more solidity; a little pleasure, but a great deal of business—some politeness, but more civility. If you compare such a country with the regions of domination, whether Monarchial or Aristocratical, you will fancy yourself in Arcadia or Elisium . . .[12]

[12]Arcadia was home to the Greek god Pan; it also meant an unspoiled, harmonious wilderness; Elysium was the Greek conception of Heaven.

If a Continental Constitution should be formed, it should be a Congress, containing a fair and adequate Representation of the Colonies, and its authority should sacredly be confined to these cases, viz. war, trade, disputes between Colony and Colony, the Post-Office, and the unappropriated lands of the Crown, as they used to be called . . .

You and I, my dear Friend, have been sent into life, at a time when the greatest law-givers of antiquity would have wished to have lived. How few of the human race have ever enjoyed an opportunity of making an election of government more than of air, soil, or climate, for themselves or their children. When! Before the present epocha,[13] had three millions of people full power and a fair opportunity to form and establish the wisest and happiest government that human wisdom can contrive? . . .

[13]Epoch: an event or a time that begins a new period of development.

Source: C. F. Adams, *The Works of John Adams.* (Boston: Little, Brown & Co., 1850).

The Virginia Declaration of Rights

(June 12, 1776)

INTRODUCTION

This document with its statement in support of individual liberties is the forerunner of the first 10 amendments for the Constitution (the Bill of Rights). It was largely written by George Mason, a political philosopher who claimed "nothing but the liberty and privileges of Englishmen." Mason was an advocate of political freedom and, like many, was not yet an advocate for independence. But once his statement was adopted by the Virginia Convention on June 12, 1776, it was soon followed by the adoption of a constitution that declared Virginia to be an independent state.

A DECLARATION OF RIGHTS made by the representatives of the good people of Virginia, assembled in full and free convention which rights do pertain to them and their posterity, as the basis and foundation of government.

[1]This paragraph is the model for Jefferson's statement in the Declaration of Independence that "all men are created equal"; that they have rights to "life, liberty, and the pursuit of happiness."

1. That all men are by nature equally free and independent and have certain inherent rights, of which, when they enter into a state of society, they cannot, by any compact deprive or divest their posterity; namely, the enjoyment of life and liberty, with the means of acquiring and possessing property, and pursuing and obtaining happiness and safety.[1]

[2]This paragraph is the model for the preamble to the Constitution: "We the people . . . ordain and establish this Constitution."

2. That all power is vested in, and consequently derived from, the people; that magistrates are their trustees and servants and at all times amenable to them.[2]

[3]In his *Second Treatise on Government*, the British political philosopher John Locke expresses the idea that government derives its power from the people, and that when it does not prove equal to its job of promoting the well-being of the people, the people have a right to change it. This idea is also reflected in the Declaration of Independence.

3. That government is, or ought to be instituted for the common benefit, protection, and security of the people, nation, or community; of all the various modes and forms of government, that is best which is capable of producing the greatest degree of happiness and safety and is most effectually secured against the danger of maladministration; and that when any government shall be found inadequate or contrary to these purposes, a majority of the community has an indubitable, unalienable, and indefeasible right to reform, alter or abolish it, in such manner as shall be judged most conducive to the public weal.[3]

4. That no man, or set of men, are entitled to exclusive or separate emoluments[4] or privileges from the community, but in consideration of public services; which, not being descendible, neither ought the offices of magistrate, legislator or judge to be hereditary.

5. That the legislative and executive powers of the state should be separate and distinct from the judiciary; and that the members of the two first may be restrained from oppression, by feeling and participating the burdens of the people, they should, at fixed periods, be reduced to a private station, return into that body from which they were originally taken, and the vacancies be supplied by frequent, certain, and regular elections, in which all, or any part of the former members to be again eligible, or ineligible, as the laws shall direct.[5]

6. That elections of members to serve as representatives of the people in assembly, ought to be free; and that all men, having sufficient evidence of permanent common interest with, and attachment to the community, have the right of suffrage, and cannot be taxed or deprived of their property for public uses, without their own consent, or that of their representatives so elected, nor bound by any law to which they have not, in like manner, assented for the public good.[6]

7. That all power of suspending laws, or the execution of laws, by any authority without consent of the representatives of the people, is injurious to their rights, and ought not to be exercised.[7]

8. That in all capital or criminal prosecutions a man has a right to demand the cause and nature of his accusation, to be confronted with the accusers and witnesses, to call for evidence in his favor, and to a speedy trial by an impartial jury of his vicinage, without whose unanimous consent he cannot be found guilty; nor can he be compelled to give evidence against himself; that no man be deprived of his liberty, except by the law of the land or the judgment of his peers.[8]

9. That excessive bail ought not to be required, nor excessive fines imposed, nor cruel and unusual punishments inflicted.[9]

10. That general warrants, whereby an officer or messenger may be commanded to search suspected places without evidence of a fact committed, or to seize any person or persons not named, or whose offense is not particularly described and supported by evidence, are grievous and oppressive, and ought not to be granted.[10]

11. That in controversies respecting property, and in suits between man and man, the ancient trial by jury is preferable to any other, and ought to be held sacred.[11]

[4]Salary for government services.

[5]This statement is reflected in the structure of the national government provided by the Constitution, providing for separation of powers and regular elections.

[6]This paragraph reflects a reaction to one of the great abuses, which led to the revolution: taxation without representation.

[7]This paragraph reflects the idea of a government of limited powers.

[8]This paragraph is reflected in the Fifth and Sixth Amendments to the Constitution.

[9]This paragraph has been taken in whole into the Constitution.

[10]This paragraph is reflected in the Fourth Amendment's protection of citizens from "unreasonable searches and seizures."

[11]This paragraph is reflected in the Sixth Amendment, which guarantees the right to trial by jury.

[12]This is reflected in the First Amendment, which guarantees freedom from an official state religion, and guarantees freedoms of speech, press, assembly, and the right to petition the government for redress of grievances.

[13]This paragraph is reflected in the Second Amendment: "The right of the people to keep and bear arms shall not be infringed."

[14]This paragraph is reflected in the preamble to the Constitution. "We the people of the United States . . . do ordain and establish this constitution for a United States of America."

[15]This paragraph is the basis of the First Amendment.

12. That the freedom of the press is one of the great bulwarks of liberty, and can never be restrained but by despotic governments.[12]

13. That a well-regulated militia, composed of the body of the people trained to arms, is the proper, natural, and safe defense of a free state; that standing armies in time of peace should be avoided as dangerous to liberty; and that in all cases the military should be under strict subordination to, and governed by, the civil power.[13]

14. That the people have a right to uniform government; and, therefore, that no government separate from or independent of the government of Virginia, ought to be erected or established within the limits thereof.[14]

15. That no free government, or the blessings of liberty, can be preserved to any people, but by a firm adherence to justice, moderation, temperance, frugality, and virtue, and by frequent recurrence to fundamental principles.[15]

16. That religion, or the duty which we owe to our Creator, and the manner of discharging it, can be directed only by reason and conviction, not by force or violence; and therefore all men are equally entitled to the free exercise of religion, according to the dictates of conscience; and that it is the mutual duty of all to practise Christian forbearance, love, and charity toward each other.

Source: Proceedings and Debates of the Virginia State Convention. (Richmond: Samuel Shepherd & Co., 1830), 895–896.

The Unanimous Declaration of the Thirteen United States of America

(July 4, 1776)

INTRODUCTION

On June 7, 1776, Richard Henry Lee, chairman of the Virginia delegation to the Continental Congress, submitted a resolution stating that "these united colonies are, and of right ought to be free and independent states." Congress voted to support this official declaration of independence on July 2. A committee composed of Jefferson, Adams, Franklin, Robert Sherman, and Robert Livingston was appointed to prepare a declaration in support of Lee's resolution. This document, "A Declaration by the Representatives of the United States of America in Congress Assembled," was adopted on July 4, 1776. It is this document that is commonly called the "Declaration of Independence."

Jefferson is the main author, although Adams and Franklin added some changes. During the congressional debate, more changes were made including the omission of a paragraph on the slave trade.

In Congress, July 4, 1776,

The Unanimous Declaration of the Thirteen United States of America[1]

When in the Course of human events, it becomes necessary for one people to dissolve the political bands which have connected them with another, and to assume, among the Powers of the earth, the separate and equal station to which the Laws of Nature and of Nature's God entitle them, a decent respect to the opinions of mankind requires that they should declare the causes which impel them to the separation.[2]

We hold these truths to be self-evident, that all men are created equal, that they are endowed by their Creator with certain unalienable Rights, that among these are Life, Liberty, and the pursuit of

[1] This is the final name of the Declaration. So the common title "Declaration of Independence" is a mistaken designation; Lee's resolution, approved on July 2, was the act by which independence was declared.

[2] The purpose of the Declaration is stated in this paragraph—it is a document proclaiming to the world the reasons for proclaiming independence.

[3] This paragraph is a summary of the theory of "natural rights" and supports the idea that the colonials were a free people, not part of the British people, and that their governments were separate polities and not creations of Parliament. The Declaration goes on to present a theory of government that supports the action of the colonies as legitimate.

[4] The main text of the document is a list of grievances that legitimized separation.

Happiness. That, to secure these rights, Governments are instituted among Men, deriving their just Powers from the consent of the governed. That, whenever any Form of Government becomes destructive of these ends, it is the Right of the People to alter or to abolish it, and to institute new Government, laying its foundation on such Principles and organizing its Powers in such form, as to them shall seem most likely to effect their Safety and Happiness . . .[3]

. . . [W]hen a long train of abuses and usurpations, pursuing invariably the same Object, evinces a design to reduce them under absolute Despotism, it is their right, it is their duty, to throw off such Government, and to provide new Guards for their future security. Such has been the patient sufferance of these Colonies; and such is now the necessity which constrains them to alter their former Systems of Government. The history of the present King of Great Britain is a history of repeated injuries and usurpations, all having in direct object the establishment of an absolute Tyranny over these States. To prove this, let Facts be submitted to a candid world . . .[4]

We, therefore, the Representatives of the United States of America, in General Congress assembled, appealing to the Supreme Judge of the World for the rectitude of our intentions, do, in the Name, and by Authority of the good People of these Colonies, solemnly publish and declare, That these United Colonies are, and of Right, ought to be free and Independent States; that they are Absolved from all Allegiance to the British Crown, and that all political connection between them and the State of Great Britain, is and ought to be totally dissolved; and that, as free and independent states, they have full Power to levy War, conclude Peace, contract Alliances, establish Commerce, and to do all other Acts and Things which independent states may of right do. And for the support of this Declaration, with a firm reliance on the protection of divine Providence, we mutually pledge to each other our Lives, our Fortunes and our sacred Honor.

Source: America's Founding Documents, National Archives.

The American Crisis Papers #1

(December 19, 1776)

INTRODUCTION

Thomas Paine, author of *Common Sense*, was an active supporter of the revolution. He joined Washington's army and experienced the demoralizing retreat from New York across New Jersey. At Newark, he wrote the first of a series of pamphlets that are known as the "Crisis Papers." It was published on December 19, 1776, and, because of its eloquent expression, was read to the troops on Washington's orders.

THESE are the times that try men's souls. The summer soldier and the sunshine patriot will, in this crisis, shrink from the service of their country; but he that stands by it now, deserves the love and thanks of man and woman. Tyranny, like hell, is not easily conquered; yet we have this consolation with us, that the harder the conflict, the more glorious the triumph. What we obtain too cheap, we esteem too lightly: it is dearness only that gives every thing its value. Heaven knows how to put a proper price upon its goods; and it would be strange indeed if so celestial an article as freedom should not be highly rated. Britain, with an army to enforce her tyranny, has declared that she has a right (not only to tax) but "to bind us in all cases whatsoever" and if being bound in that manner, is not slavery, then is there not such a thing as slavery upon earth. Even the expression is impious for so unlimited a power can belong only to God.[1]

[1] The reference is to the Declaratory Act (March 4, 1766). Parliament had agreed to repeal the Stamp Act but, in order to preserve its authority over the colonies, passed this act on the same day of the repeal. The act asserted that the colonies were subordinate to the king and Parliament and stated that both "had, hath, and of right ought to have full power and authority to make laws and statutes of sufficient force and validity to bind the colonies and people of America, subjects of the crown of Great Britain, in all cases whatsoever." The act was seen as a threat to colonial self-government. Paine's quote is an inexact reference to this passage.

Source: The American crisis (No. 1) by the author of *Common Sense* [Boston]. Sold opposite the court house Queen Street [1776]. Courtesy of an American Time Capsule: Three Centuries of Broadsides and Other Printed Ephemera, Rare Book and Special Collections Division, Library of Congress.

Paul Revere's Account of His Ride

(1783)

INTRODUCTION

Paul Revere was a member of the colonial upper class and a patriot member of the Boston Committee of Safety. Late on the evening of April 18, 1775, he heard that the British were planning a march to destroy the military arsenal at Concord. He raced on horseback to Concord to sound the alarm. He arrived at Lexington in time to warn John Hancock and Samuel Adams of their imminent arrests; they made their escapes. Revere was not so lucky; he was stopped by a British patrol and arrested. When it became clear that the whole countryside was up in arms, he was released. He returned to Lexington in time to witness the first shots fired on Lexington Green.

I, PAUL REVERE, of Boston . . . do testify and say; that I was sent for by Dr. Joseph Warren . . . on the evening of the 18th of April, about 10 o'clock; when he desired me, "to go to Lexington, and inform Mr. Samuel Adams, and the Hon. John Hancock Esq. that there was a number of soldiers . . . it was supposed that they were going to Lexington, by the way of Cambridge River, to take them, or go to Concord, to destroy the colony stores." . . .

I set off, it was then about 11 o'clock, the moon shone bright. I had got almost over Charlestown Common . . . when I saw two officers on horse-back, standing under the shade of a tree . . . One of them started his horse towards me, the other up the road, as I supposed, to head me, should I escape the first. I turned my horse short about, and rode upon a full gallop for Mistick Road. He followed me about 300 yards, and finding he could not catch me, returned. I proceeded to Lexington, through Mistick, and alarmed Mr. Adams and Col. Hancock.

After I had been there about half an hour Mr. Daws arrived . . . We set off for Concord . . . I saw two officers . . . In an instant I saw four of them, who rode up to me with their pistols in their bands, said "G——d d——n you, stop. If you go an inch further, you are a dead man." . . . They forced us in . . . He took to the left, I to the

86

right towards a wood at the bottom of the pasture, intending, when I gained that, to jump my horse and run afoot. Just as I reached it, out started six officers, seized my bridle, put their pistols to my breast, ordered me to dismount, which I did. One of them . . . said "Sir, may I crave your name?" I answered "My name is Revere." "What" said he, "Paul Revere"? I answered "Yes.". . . He told me not to be afraid, no one should hurt me . . . He said . . . they were only waiting for some deserters they expected down the road. I told him I knew better, I knew what they were after; that I had alarmed the country all the way up . . . and I should have 500 men there soon. One of them said they had 1500 coming . . .

He then ordered me to mount my horse, they first searched me for pistols. When I was mounted, the Major took the reins out of my hand, and said "By G—-d Sir, you are not to ride with reins I assure you"; and gave them to an officer on my right, to lead me . . . He said to me, "We are now going towards your friends, and if you attempt to run, or we are insulted, we will blow your brains out." . . .

We rode towards Lexington at a quick pace; they very often insulted me calling me rebel, etc., etc . . .

When we got within sight of the Meeting House, we heard a volley of guns fired, as I supposed at the tavern, as an alarm; the Major ordered us to halt, he asked me how far it was to Cambridge . . . He then asked the sergeant, if his horse was tired, he said yes; he ordered him to take my horse. I dismounted, and the sergeant mounted my horse; they cut the bridle and saddle of the sergeant's horse, and rode off down the road. I then went to the house where I left Messrs. Adams and Hancock, and told them what had happened; their friends advised them to go out of the way; I went with them, about two miles across road.

Source: Paul Revere's deposition, fair copy, circa 1775. Accounts of his famous ride, 1775–1798. https://www.masshist.org/database/98. Massachusetts Historical Society. Used by permission.

SECTION II

Battles of Liberty

Introduction

The Duke of Wellington, the military genius who defeated Napoleon at the Battle of Waterloo, famously remarked, "You can no more write the history of a battle than you can describe every dance at a ball." And yet it was in battle that the fate of the revolution was decided.

Throughout history, war has been the constant determinant of the fate of men and nations. The actors in the revolution were diverse: there were professionals, British and Hessian, and Washington's Continentals schooled by the Prussian von Steuben in the arts of European maneuvers; militias who fought as irregulars and whose improvised tactics easily confused regiments trained in the orthodoxy of battle; and there were the Native Americans who fought both against and in support of the British. This hodge-podge of fighters could no more enter battle confident of victory than they could be sure of the next day's weather.

Along the coasts of America, the war was characterized by major battles. In the West and interior, it was largely a matter of skirmishes involving Indians, loyalists, and rebels. Today, since the concept

of "total war" was established in the 20th century where no one is safe, where every locality is fair game and susceptible to destruction, where every citizen is a soldier and every soldier a citizen, it is not easy to understand the military actions of the 18th century. The very concept of a "battlefield" seems foreign to us—a place reserved for fighting, and fighting constrained by rigid rules of warfare.

Washington's victory at Trenton on Christmas night of 1776 was a violation of such rules. Gentlemen did not attack at 5:00 a.m. and certainly not at Christmas! But still, "all remains fair in love and war," and his victory over the sleeping Hessians was a badly needed morale booster for his troops.

To aid our understanding of these battles, we must have some familiarity with the conventions of 18th-century warfare. Infantry (foot soldiers) were arranged either in "line" or "square," the latter an order that was resistant to cavalry charges since horses refused to run into lines of bayonets. Those militiamen in the rear of the square were well positioned to take out cavalrymen.

Cannon were used to break up the square formation, but since it took time to reload the cannon between shots, the troops were vulnerable to cavalry charge.

Line soldiers had the advantage of maximum fire power and fusillades, where series of shots were aimed at the enemy from one end of the line to the other.

These were the formations, the rules of the game understood by all. But it was the genius and flexibility of the commanders like Washington who bent the rules and observed the conventions that as much as fate determined the outcome of the American Revolution.

Letters on Lexington and Concord

(1775)

INTRODUCTION

Lexington: The first fighting began in Massachusetts. General Thomas Gage was commander of the redcoats. Colonists were collecting and storing armaments at Concord. Gage sent a detachment to destroy the weapons. The Americans were warned that the British were on the march; they gathered on the Lexington Green to await the arrival of the redcoats. There was an exchange of fire and the American militia retreated (8 were dead; 10 were wounded).

Concord: The British marched to Concord and destroyed the magazine (arsenal). On their return march to Boston, they were attacked by groups of "Minute Men," patriotic irregulars. There were hundreds of British casualties. Troops from many colonies came to the aid of Massachusetts. The British were surrounded, and the city was soon under a blockade. The situation became a standoff. The Americans did not have artillery with which to bombard Boston as the British waited for reinforcements to arrive by sea. When the fresh troops arrived, led by Generals Howe, Clinton, and Burgoyne, they planned to free themselves by taking control of Charles Town, across the harbor from Boston. The Americans heard of the plan, took control of Charles Town, and set up a small fort on Breed's Hill.

These first battles of the revolution began on April 18, 1775. Rebellion, a spirit of defiance, until then largely expressed in words, now found its manifestation in armed conflict. The importance of these battles is impossible to overestimate. There are many eyewitness accounts of these events. They do not agree on the details. But these details are relatively unimportant. The Battles of Lexington and Concord proved that the rebels could defeat the British regulars. It was a psychological as well as a military victory.

Diary of an Anonymous British Officer, April 20, 1775[1]

[1]This extract from a letter of an officer to a friend in London reflects the British attitude toward the colonials.

General Gage detached a party of the troops, under the command of Lieut. Col. Smith, to destroy a magazine of military stores, which the Provincials had formed at Concord, about 18 miles from this town. It was my lot to be one of the party. We were soon discovered upon our march, and the Country raised an alarm. Nothing material happened till we were within six miles of the object of our destination;

but here a body of the rebels opposed us, and gave the first fire, which was immediately returned, with some effect, by the troops, and the rebels dispersed. When we came to Concord, the commanding officer assured the Inhabitants that they need be under no apprehensions of injury to their persons and properties, and the troops behaved with the utmost lenity, though the people were very sulky . . . One fellow had the impudence to strike Major Pitcairne, of the Marines, while searching for the stores according to his orders.[2] We demolished and destroyed everything of that sort we could find. Upon our return we were fired upon from every house, barn, ditch, hill, and place that afforded cover . . . When our ammunition was nearly exhausted, Lord Percy came up with his Brigade and two pieces of cannon very opportunely to our relief. These showered them, and kept them more at a distance. The rebels fought like the savages of the country . . . We got to Boston in the evening, much fatigued with the march and duty of the day, and with as little loss as could have been expected . . . The troops conducted themselves throughout with the greatest coolness and intrepidity.

Source: *Farley's Bristol Journal*, London, June 17, 1775.

[2]An equal mixture of arrogance and surprise, this attitude is a clue to the reason for the eventual British defeat: they underestimated the enemy.

[3]This account by Lieutenant John Barker fills in the details of the incidents at Lexington and Concord. It gives a full account of the tactics the colonials adopted.

Account by Lieutenant John Barker of the King's Own, April 19, 1775[3]

Last night between 10 and 11 o'clock all the Grenadiers and Light Infantry of the army . . . embarked and were landed upon the opposite shore on Cambridge Marsh . . . At 2 o'clock we began our march . . . About 5 miles on this side of a town called Lexington . . . we heard there were some hundreds of people collected together intending to oppose us and stop our going on. At 5 o'clock we arrived there and saw a number of people . . . formed in a common in the middle of the town . . . on our coming near them they fired one or two shots, upon which our men without any orders rushed in upon them, fired and put 'em to flight. Several of them were killed . . . We . . . at length proceeded on our way to Concord . . . in order to destroy a magazine[4] of stores collected there . . . we marched into the town after taking possession of a hill with a Liberty Pole[5] on it and a flag flying, which was cut down . . . While the grenadiers remained in the town, destroying 3 pieces of cannon, several gun carriages and about 200 barrels of flour with harness and other things. The Light companies were detached beyond the river to examine some houses for more stores . . . During this time the people were

[4]A magazine is a storehouse for ammunition.
[5]A Liberty Pole was a flagstaff with a liberty cap at the top. A liberty cap was also a close-fitting cone-shaped hat worn during this period. It was a symbol of liberty during the American Revolution and, later, during the French Revolution. Freed slaves wore them in ancient Rome.

gathering together in great numbers and, taking advantage of our scattered disposition,[6] seemed as if they were going to cut off the communication . . . In the meantime the Rebels marched into the road and were coming down upon us . . . The Rebels when they got near the bridge halted and fronted, filling the road from the top to the bottom. The fire soon began . . . the whole were forced to quit the bridge and return toward Concord . . . . We set out upon our return. Before the whole had quitted the town we were fired on from houses and behind trees, and before we had gone 1/2 a mile we were fired on from all sides, but mostly from the rear, where people had hid themselves in houses till we had passed, and then fired. The country was an amazing strong one, full of hills, woods, stone walls, etc., which the Rebels did not fail to take advantage of, for they were all lined with people who kept an incessant fire upon us, as we did too upon them, but not with the same advantage, for they were so well concealed there was hardly any seeing them.[7] In this way we marched between 9 and 10 miles, their numbers increasing from all parts, while ours was reduced by deaths, wounds and fatigue; and we were totally surrounded with such an incessant fire as it's impossible to conceive; our ammunition was likewise near expended.

When we got to Menotomy there was a very heavy fire; after that we took the short cut into the Charles Town Road, very luckily for us too, for the Rebels, thinking we should endeavor to return by Cambridge, had broken down the bridge and had a great number of men to line the road and to receive us there. However, we threw them and went on to Charles Town without any great interruption . . . Thus ended the expedition.

Source: "Diary of a British Officer." *Atlantic Monthly* 39, no. 234 (April 1877).

An Account of the Battles Written for Public Consumption as Propaganda[8]

General Gage, having received intelligence of a large quantity of military stores being collected at Concord, for the avowed purpose of supplying a body of troops to act in opposition to his Majesty's government, detached, on the 18th of April, at night, the grenadiers of his army and the light infantry, under the command of Lieut. Colonel Smith . . . with orders to destroy to said stores . . . Lieut. Col. Smith, finding, after he had advanced some miles on his march, that the country had been alarmed by the firing of guns and the ringing

[6]He refers to their scattered locations.

[7]Unlike other British accounts, this record does not make excuses for their defeat.

[8]This report from General Thomas Gage, commander of British forces in the colonies to Lord Barrington, secretary of war, makes light of the whole engagement and brushes the affair off as a minor annoyance. Gage held the Americans to be contemptible cowards.

of bells, dispatched six companies of light infantry in order to secure two bridges on different roads beyond Concord, who, upon their arrival at Lexington, found a body of the country people drawn up under arms on a green close to the road; and upon the King's troops marching up to them, in order to enquire the reason of their being so assembled, they went off in great confusion, and several guns were fired upon the King's troops from behind a stone wall, and also from the meeting-house and other houses . . . The troops returned the fire and killed several of them; after which the detachment marched on to Concord, without any thing further happening, where they effected the purpose for which they were sent . . .[9]

[9] Only partly true. They had been sent to arrest Samuel Adams and John Hancock.

On the return of the troops from Concord, they were very much annoyed, and had several men killed and wounded, by the rebels firing from behind walls, ditches, trees, and other ambushes; but the brigade under the command of Lord Percy having joined them at Lexington, with two pieces of cannon, the rebels were for a while dispersed; but as soon as the troops resumed their march, they began again to fire upon them from behind stone walls and houses, and kept up in that manner a scattering fire during the whole of their march of 15 miles, by which means several were killed and wounded; and such was the cruelty and barbarity of the rebels, that they scalped, and cut off the ears of some of the wounded men, who fell into their hands.[10]

[10] A report calculated to outrage the public and demean the colonists by associating them with savage practice.

It is not known what number of the rebels were killed and wounded, but it is supposed, that their loss was very considerable.

Source: *The Gentleman's Magazine and Historical Chronicle*, Volume 45, for the year 1775. (London: Printed at St. John's Gate, 1775), 293.

John Crozier to Dr. Rogers on Board the Empress of Russia, Boston, April 23, 1775[11]

[11] John Crozier, master of the frigate "Empress of Russia" writes to his friend Dr. Rogers of the British Navy, April 23, 1775. His is one of the few British accounts that recognize the seriousness of the situation.

The enthusiastic zeal with which these people must have behaved must convince every reasonable man what a difficult and unpleasant task General Gage has before him. Even weamin had firelocks. One was seen to fire a blunderbus[12] between her father and husband, from their window; there the three with an infant child soon suffered the fury of the day. In another house which was long defended by 8 resolute fellows the Grenadiers at last got possession when, after

[12] A blunderbuss was a muzzle-loading firearm.

having run their bayonets into 7, the 8th continued to abuse them with all the most like rage of a true Cromwellian . . .[13]

Source: J.E. Tyler, "Account of Lexington." *William and Mary Quarterly*: 3rd Series, X, no. 1, 104–107. [Printed by courtesy of the Earl Fitzwilliam and his trustees of the Wentworth Estates Co.], 1775.

William Emerson Describes the Stand at Concord Bridge, April 19, 1775[14]

This morning, between 1 and 2 o'clock, we were alarmed by the ringing of the bell, and upon examination found that the troops . . . had stole their march from Boston . . . and were at Lexington Meeting-house, half an hour before sunrise, where they had fired upon a body of our men, and . . . confirmed the account of the regulars' arrival at Lexington, and that they were on their way to Concord . . . Capt. Minot, who commanded them, thought it proper to take possession of the hill above the meeting-house, as the most advantageous situation. No sooner had our men gained it than we were met by the companies that were sent out to meet the troops . . . We then retreated from the hill near the Liberty Pole and took a new post back of the town upon an eminence,[15] where we formed into two battalions and waited the arrival of the enemy. Scarcely had we formed before we saw the British troops at the distance of a quarter of a mile, glittering in arms, advancing towards us with the greatest celerity . . .[16] Accordingly we retreated over the bridge, when the troops came into the town, set fire to several carriages for the artillery, destroyed 60 barrels of flour, rifled several houses, took possession of the town-house, destroyed 500 lb. of balls, set a guard of 100 men at the North Bridge, and sent up a party to the house of Col. Barrett, where they were in expectation of finding a quantity of warlike stores. But these were happily secured just before their arrival, by transportation into the woods and other by-places. In the meantime, the guard set by the enemy to secure the pass at the North Bridge were alarmed by the approach of our people, who had retreated, as mentioned before, and were now advancing with special orders not to fire upon the troops unless fired upon . . . .the firing then soon became general for several minutes, in which skirmish two were killed on each side, and several of the enemy wounded . . . The three companies of troops soon quitted their post at the bridge and retreated in the greatest disorder and confusion to the main body, who were soon upon the march to meet them . . . till at length they quitted the town and retreated by the way

[13] Oliver Cromwell was the Puritan leader of the British "Glorious Revolution" in 1688.

[14] William Emerson, who here describes the stand at Concord bridge, was the grandfather of Ralph Waldo Emerson, poet, essayist, and founder (with Thoreau) of the Transcendentalist movement. His poem "Concord Hymn" gave posterity a phrase indelibly associated with the revolution. "By the rude bridge that arched the flood, Their flag to April's breeze unfurled, Here once the embattled farmers stood, And fired the shot heard around the world."

[15] An eminence is a piece of rising ground. This gave them a visual advantage in seeing the British troops as they approached.

[16] Meaning the British were moving swiftly toward them.

they came. In the meantime, a party of our men (150) took the back way through the Great Fields into the east quarter and had placed themselves to advantage, lying in ambush behind walls, fences and buildings, ready to fire upon the enemy on their retreat.

Source: William Emerson, "Diary" in *Complete Works*, Volume 11: Miscellanies. Edited by Ralph Waldo Emerson, 91–93. (Boston: Houghton Mifflin Co., 1883).

[17]Sylvanus Woods was a strong opponent of the British Royal power. He was one of the minutemen who stood the British fire on Lexington Green on April 19, 1775. He wrote these eyewitness accounts of his participation in the battle 50 years after the event.

A Minuteman's Account of the Battle of Lexington, June 17, 1826[17]

I, Sylvanus Wood, of Woburn . . . aged seventy-four years, do testify and say that on the morning of the 19th of April, 1775, that about an hour before the break of day . . . I heard the Lexington bell ring, and fearing there was difficulty there, I immediately arose, took my gun and . . . went in haste to Lexington . . . When I arrived there, I inquired of Captain Parker . . . what was the news . . . a messenger came up and told the captain that the British troops were within half a mile. Parker immediately turned to his drummer, William Diman, and ordered him to beat to arms, which was done . . . . By the time many of the company had gathered . . . at the hearing of the drum . . . Parker says to his men, "Every man of you, who is equipped, follow me; and those of you who are not equipped, go into the meeting house and furnish yourselves from the magazine, and immediately join the company." Parker led those of us who were equipped to the north end of Lexington Common, near the Bedford Road, and formed us in single file . . . I perceived the British troops had arrived . . . The British troops immediately wheeled so as to cut off those who had gone into the meeting-house. The British troops approached us rapidly in platoons, with a general officer on horseback at their head. The officer came up to within about three rods distant. They were halted. The officer then swung his sword and said, "Lay down your arms, you dammed rebels, or you are all dead men. Fire!" Some guns were fired by the British at us from the first platoon, but no person was killed or hurt.

On the nineteenth morn of April, 1775 I heard Lexington bell about one hour before day. We concluded that trouble was near. We waited for no man but hastened and joined Captain Parker's company at the breaking of the day. Douglass and myself stood together in the center of said company when the enemy first fired. The English soon were on their march for Concord. I helped carry six dead in the meetinghouse and then set out after the enemy . . . but before I arrived at Concord I see one of the grenadiers standing sentinel. I cocked my piece and run up to him, seized his gun with my left hand. He surrendered his armor, one gun and bayonet, a large cutlash and brass fender, one box over the shoulder with twenty-two rounds,[18] one box round the waist with eighteen rounds. This was the first prisoner that was known to be taken that day. I followed the enemy to Concord and to Bunker Hill that day.

On Tuesday, the Eighteenth instant, these troops were collected with the utmost secrecy and quietness . . . where about eleven o'clock at night they were ferried over, and marched for Lexington, where Messrs. Hancock and Adams[19] were lodged, and it was supposed they were to take these two gentlemen; . . . our people found means to get a hint of the design, and dispatched two expresses, which arrived in season, for Messr. Hancock and Adams to depart . . .[20] These troops between day-light and sun-rise, came up with a company of our minute men . . . There are different accounts of their numbers, some say 30, and the most I have heard 90; 'tis probable there might be 50. Colonel Smith, of the 10th regiment, who commanded the troops, immediately ordered the minute men to disperse, and lay down their arms; they replied, they . . . would not lay down their arms; upon which Colonel Smith declared them Rebels, and ordered his men to fire, which they did, and killed eight men. This is one account; another is, that the minute men, upon being ordered to disperse, were doing it, and jumped over a stone wall, when the regulars ran at them with their bayonets fixed,[21] and made a great noise; on which one of the minute men fired his gun through surprise, and then the regulars fired several times, and killed the eight men as before. But I think you may depend on this, that the regulars fired first, and the minute men not all . . . the troops proceeded to Concord . . . Upon their arrival at Concord, they found a party of 450 of our men upon a hill . . . the regulars sent 300 of their party to attack this hill, but before they got half up, our troops fired on them, and killed 18 on the spot; they retreated immediately . . . and were returning home, when those few irregulars determined to attack and drove them back to Lexington . . . the troops themselves acknowledge they must have been destroyed to a man, but for the arrival of Earl Percy with a brigade of 1200 men, and two field pieces. They then made a stand of about half an hour, when they also thought proper to retreat . . . and our people, who gathered fast, kept close to them, and pursued them, with the Yankee way of bush-fighting, until they came into

[18]He is referring to a cutlass, which is a sword; a brass fender, which is a protective cover or scabbard for a sword; and rounds, which are bullets for the musket.

[19]John Hancock and Samuel Adams were revolutionary leaders.

[20]The two expresses are Paul Revere and William Dawes, who arrived "in time" to save Hancock and Adams from arrest.

[21]"Bayonets fixed" means there was a blade adapted to fit the muzzle end of a rifle, and it was used as a weapon in close combat.

Charles-Town . . . and we have by this action got in reality the term Yankee, which is an Indian word, and was given our forefathers, signifying Conquerors,[22] which these ignoramuses give us by way of derision. Thus I have given you, I firmly believe, as true an account as is possible . . .

I would only ask, if in all your reading of history, you have found an instance of irregular troops, hurried together at a moment's warning, with half the number at first, attacking and driving veterans, pick'd men, 17 miles, and continually firing the whole way . . . I view the hand of Providence in our favor . . . I confess I am pleased with my countrymen; but if the sweet hope of liberty will not induce a free-born American to fight, what will? . . . Where this matter will end, I know not; but that the country will not give up, I think I am certain, therefore I expect great effusion of blood, which I hope and trust the God of heaven will avenge on the tyrants that have been the cause thereof.

I am, dear Sir, your most humble servant.

Middlesex, ss., June 17th, 1826. The above-named Sylvanus Wood personally appeared, and subscribed and made oath to the foregoing affidavit. Before me,

Nathan Brooks, Justice of the Peace.

Source: Henry B. Dawson, *Battles of the United States by Sea and Land: Embracing Those of the Revolutionary and Indian Wars, the War of 1812, and the Mexican War; with Official Documents, and Biographies of the Most Distinguished Military and Naval Commanders*, Volume 1. (New York: Johnson, Fly and Co., 1858), 22–23.

Extract of an Anonymous Letter from Boston, April 23, 1775[23]

On the 19th instant a brigade went to Concord . . . to destroy a magazine the Provincials had collected at that place, and were, contrary to their expectations, fired upon. Who began the attack first is matter of doubt, but the military say there was a premeditated design of opposition in the Provincials, and that it matters not who began the attack . . . they . . . marched till day-break, when they were diverted from their march by a company of seventy of what they call minute men . . . these men refused to ground their arms and disperse, and after repeated warnings that they would be fired upon, the King's troops fired and killed a number of them; after that, they proceeded to Concord, and destroyed the magazine and cannon . . . in that time a great number of the Provincials to the amount of some thousands, presented themselves, to oppose the retreat of the troops . . . and were annoyed from behind stone walls . . . and from every height, of which the provincials took the advantage, and made great havoc; they likewise fired upon the troops out of the houses, of which there are a great many on the road . . . the troops broke into every house, and put all the males to the sword, and plundered the houses.[24] The troops were so enraged with the fire from the hills, the walls, and the houses, and the prospect of plunder, that it was difficult to keep them in order. This march lasted twelve miles, when a second brigade arrived to reinforce them, or they would have been cut to pieces.

Source: *Boston Gazetteer* and *New Daily Advertiser*, Boston, June 16, 1775.

[24]These actions convinced many who were lukewarm to the cause of revolution to embrace rebellion.

Extract of a Letter from a Gentleman of Rank in New England, April 25, 1775[25]

All eyes are turned upon the tragical event of the 19th. On that day a party of Gen. Gage's Army . . . marched secretly to Lexington . . . their object there was to seize on Messrs. Hancock and Adams . . . They were alarmed just in time to escape. When the Troops reached Lexington, they found a small party of Militia assembled on the Green, whom they attacked with great shouts, and menaces. At their approach the Militia dispersed, yet the Troops fired upon them and killed several. After some outrages at Lexington they marched on to Concord . . . By this time a body of the Militia was assembled, and marched up to the Bridge, where the Regulars assembled and drove them from their post . . . the Troops retreated with all possible expedition to Lexington . . . The Militia pursued and harassed them in their retreat; but upon the junction they were so greatly outnumbered, and without cannon, that they could not venture a regular engagement. The reason why the Militia were never in a large body equal to that of the Regulars was, that the alarm being sudden, they ran in small parties with such weapons as they could first pick up, in their hurry, to different parts of the road. From Lexington the Army returned to Boston with such precipitation as to expose themselves to a continual fire from their Pursuers, and to leave many of their wounded to fall into hands of the Militia. Thus ended this affair, much more to their loss when we consider that with all their vaunts[26] of infinite superiority, our Militia, suddenly assembled,

[25]This extract of a letter from a gentleman of rank in New England and published in London is an example of the attempt by Americans to influence British public opinion in favor of the colonial cause.

[26]"Vaunts" is an archaic term meaning boasting or bragging.

without a plan or leader, and at no time equal to them in numbers, could force them to retreat with confusion and loss.

[27]The war was fought with more than weapons and tactics. Propaganda was an important element of the conflict.

The truth is, Sir, which we fight in a very different cause. We consider everything that is dear and valuable as depending upon our arms; and we are unanimous in the resolution, to die, or be free . . . .[27]

Such scenes of carnage and of blood are new and horrible here. I saw some houses that had been set on fire, and some old men, women and children that had been killed.

Source: *Lloyd's Evening Post* and *British Chronicle*, London, June 17–21, 1775.

[28]This letter is from a man originally from Boston, but taking refuge with his family in Philadelphia.

Extract of a Letter from a Gentleman of Boston, July 3, 1775[28]

On the Eighteenth of April General Gage sent out a party of soldiers from Boston, consisting of 12 or 1300, in order to destroy a provincial magazine at Concord . . . who, meeting with a small number of provincial troops at Lexington, first fired upon them, and thus brought on an engagement, which lasted till night; in which the regulars sustained a considerable loss, and retreated with great precipitation . . . on their return, while pursued by a small body of provincials, they made the greatest haste. In the first fire the British troops made on the poor people at Lexington, they killed eight men. The news of this inhuman action was soon spread, and in a few days brought together 20 or 30,000 men; who surrounded Boston, and shut in the British soldiers, and cut off all supplies of fresh provisions. Since which the Continental Congress have fixed a standing army, who are all enlisted, and paid by the continent, and are under strict military discipline. This army consists at present of about 17 or 20,000 men; besides which number, there are 20 or 30,000 farmers who hold themselves ready to march at a minute's warning to the assistance of the regular continental army. The standing army is composed of men from the different colonies. Besides these men, every province has a separate army for their own defence; which is paid by each government; who are to march where ordered . . . All the associated provinces are in arms; business gives way to military preparations. The Hon. George Washington, a gentleman of great fortune, and an amiable character, both private and public, and who behaved bravely and judiciously in the last war in this country, is appointed

Generalissimo of the American forces, and is now at the grand army round Boston . . . Two . . . gentlemen, who have been brought up in the British army, and behaved well, have accepted appointments in the American army. The manufacture of saltpetre[29] among us goes on fast, and the powder mills are daily at work. Nothing but war is talked of. Interest is thought little of, compared with freedom; and the thousands who inhabit this vast continent determine not to survive the loss of it. There cannot be less than an hundred and fifty thousand men this day in arms in America . . . The battle at Lexington, which begun by the British troops, their killing of our people . . . has made the very men who were called friends of government join the popular side . . . .

Thus, my dear Sir, have I given a history of the present state of affairs in this country . . .

Source: *Boston Gazette*, Boston, August 24, 1775.

Extract of a Letter Written by a Private Soldier in Boston, August 20, 1775[30]

Dear Brother and Sister . . .

I was present at the different periods. On the evening of the Eighteenth of April last, about half past ten o'clock, which is a soldier's hour to be in bed, the light infantry to which I belong, and grenadiers, and the whole light infantry and grenadiers in Boston, were ordered to rise out of their beds, and equip themselves immediately with their arms and 36 rounds of powder and ball, which was soon done, and that as silent as possible; when ready, we marched in small parties thro' the several parts of the town, on purpose to prevent the inhabitants from having any suspicion of our leaving the town. But all our precautions were in vain; for the inhabitants rose out of their beds, and set off into the country, and apprized the people there of our leaving the town. However we proceeded through the town in small parties till we all assembled at the west side of the town, where the men of war's boats were ready to receive us. In all haste we got into the boats, and crossed the river opposite to Cambridge; we then continued our march farther into the country, until about four o'clock in the morning of the 19th. As we continued our march we could perceive the inhabitants assembling in many parts. As we went along the road, about half past four o'clock, we came near a village called Lexington,

[29]Saltpeter is the key ingredient for gunpowder along with brimstone (sulfur) and coal. The knowledge on how to manufacture it was freely distributed during the revolution, and both states and individuals did their part in making it for the American cause.

[30]This account is important not only because it confirms the reports of others but also because it contains details of the activities of the common British line soldier. It was a "private's eye view" of the battle.

[31]A Liberty Pole was a flagstaff with a liberty cap at the top. A liberty cap was also a
close-fitting cone-shaped hat worn during
this period. It was a symbol of liberty during
the American Revolution and, later, during the
French Revolution. Freed slaves wore them
in ancient Rome.

[31]A Liberty Pole was a flagstaff with a liberty cap at the top. A liberty cap was also a
close-fitting cone-shaped hat worn during
this period. It was a symbol of liberty during
the American Revolution and, later, during the
French Revolution. Freed slaves wore them
in ancient Rome.

[32]Captured guns would be spiked if they
could not be hauled away and the gun's
recapture seemed likely. Spiking was also a
quick way to make the cannon unservice-
able so it couldn't be used against retreating
soldiers. Spiking a gun could be temporary
and done by hammering a barbed steel
spike into the touch-hole, which could be
removed only with great difficulty. If a special spike was unavailable, spiking could be
done by driving a bayonet into the touch-
hole and breaking it off, to leave the blade's
tip embedded.

where, through a bush, on one side of the road, a country fellow fired
a gun on sum of the light infantry . . . the poor fellow soon lost his
life by it. From that time the firing of small arms continued, till we
arrived near to the town called Concord . . . On a hill near Concord
there was assembled a number of people, about 700, at exercise; they
were ready prepared for us, being all loaded with powder and ball.
We halted and looked at them . . . But it was not our business to wait
long looking at them; so we fixed our bayonets till we entered the
town of Concord, where we cut down what they call their Liberty
Pole.[31] When we had done, we searched the town, where we found
some cannon, and a great many cartridges for cannon; the latter we
burnt, and threw the cannon into the river, after we had spiked them.[32]
On searching further, we found a great quantity of flour, which we
destroyed and threw into the river. Upon this, they assembled in great
bodies, and manning every hill around, spooked into the town upon us,
that we were forced to quit Concord. After this we began a retreat back
towards Boston; but we were but a poor handful of men, being only
about 756, and they were so numerous, that we were not able to withstand them. They manned the hills on every side, and lined the stone
walls by the roads in such a manner, and that it was almost impossible
for us to make a retreat; and in fact we never should have accomplished
it (they having such numbers, that they almost surrounded us) but, as
God would have it, General Gage took it into his head to send the
first brigade to our assistance, with field pieces; the cannon the rebels
did not like; but nevertheless they fired so constantly from the hills,
the back of stone walls, and out of the houses, so smart upon is, that
we were glad to retreat as fast as possible to Boston . . . we returned to
Boston about seven o'clock that evening, with the loss of many a brave
soldier . . . I got home again safe, without being even wounded.

Source: Margaret Wheeler Willard, *Letters on the Revolution, 1774–1776.* (Boston and New York:
Houghton Mifflin, 1925).

[33]This is a summary account of the action
from a British source.

A Circumstantial Account of an Attack on His Majesty's Troops, April 19, 1775[33]

On Tuesday the Eighteenth of April . . . Lieutenant Colonel Smith . . .
embarked from the common at Boston . . . and landed on the opposite side from whence he began his march towards Concord, where
he was ordered to destroy a magazine of military stores, deposited

there for the use of an Army to be assembled in order to act against His Majesty and His Government. The Colonel called his officers together, and gave orders that the Troops should not fire unless fired upon . . . Soon after, they heard many signal guns, and the ringing of alarm-bells . . . which convinced them that the country was rising to oppose them . . . About three o'clock the next morning, the Troops being advanced within two miles of Lexington, intelligence was received that about five hundred men in arms were assembled, and determined to oppose the King's Troops . . . two officers informed him that a man . . . had presented his musket and attempted to shoot them . . . the Major gave directions to the Troops to move forward, but on no account to fire, nor even to attempt it without orders. When they arrived at the end of the village, they observed about two hundred men drawn up on a green . . . The Major instantly called to the soldiers not to fire, but to surround and disarm them. Some of them who had jumped over the wall, then fired four or five shot at the Troops . . . Upon this, without any order or regularity, the Light-Infantry began a scattered fire, and killed several of the country people . . . the whole body proceeded to Concord . . . vast numbers of armed people were seen assembling on all the heights . . . The people still continued increasing on the heights, and in about an hour after, a large body of them began to move towards the bridge . . . The people continued to advance in great numbers, and fired upon the King's Troops; killed three men, wounded four officers, one sergeant, and four privates . . . (after returning the fire) Captain Laurie and his officers thought it prudent to retreat towards the main body at Concord[34] . . . Colonel Smith had executed his orders, without opposition, by destroying all the military stores he could find . . . no hostilities happened from the affair at Lexington, until the Troops began their march back. As soon as the Troops had got out of the Town of Concord, they received a heavy fire on them from all sides; from walls, fences, houses, trees, barns, andc., which continued, without intermission . . . Notwithstanding their numbers, they did not attack openly during the whole day, but kept under cover on all occasions . . . The Troops had above fifty killed, and many more wounded; reports are various about the loss sustained by the country people; some make it very considerable, others not as much.

[34]This account is remarkable for its balance and freedom from special pleading.

Source: Peter Force, *Containing a Documentary History of the English Colonies in N. America*. American Archives: 4th Series, Volume 6. (Washington: [s.n.], 1837–1846).

Female Reaction to the News of the Battle of Lexington[35]

[35]The manuscript of the following interesting letter was written immediately after the Battle of Lexington, and prior to the Declaration of Independence. It fully exhibits the feelings of these times.

I will tell you what I have done . . . I have retrenched every superfluous expense in my table and family; tea I have not drank since last Christmas, nor bought a new cap or gown since your last defeat at Lexington, and what I never did before, have learnt to knit, and am now making stockings of American wool for my servants, and this way do I throw in my mite to the public good.[36] I know this, that as free I can die but once, but as a slave I shall not be worthy of life. I have the pleasure to assure you that these are the sentiments of all my sister Americans. They have sacrificed both assemblies, parties of pleasure, tea drinking and finery to that great spirit of patriotism, that actuates all ranks and degrees of people throughout this extensive continent.

[36]She herself made a small contribution.

. . . All ranks of men amongst us are in arms. Nothing is heard now in our streets but the trumpet and drum; and the universal cry is "Americans to arms." . . . Every county in Pennsylvania, and the Delaware government, can send two thousand men to the field . . . but such is our attachment to Great Britain, that we sincerely wish for reconciliation,[37] and cannot bear the thoughts of throwing off all dependence on her[38] . . . The God of mercy will, I hope, open the eyes of our king that he may see, while in seeking our destruction, he will go near to complete his own. It is my ardent prayer that the effusion of blood may be stopped. We hope yet to see you in this city, a friend to the liberties of America, which will give infinite satisfaction to,

[37]Before the official Declaration of Independence, the colonials were conflicted. Even when the conflict turned bloody many still hoped for reconciliation.
[38]Although they were determined to defend their rights and liberties, they hesitated to achieve a complete break with Britain.

Your sincere friend, C.S.
To Captain S., in Boston.

Source: H. Niles, *Principles and Acts of the Revolution in America.* (Baltimore: Printed by W.O. Niles, 1822), 305–306.

The Massachusetts Committee of Safety Appeals for Help, April 28, 1775[39]

[39]In 1774, an association of all the colonies except Georgia was formed to put economic pressure on Britain by boycotting British goods. The Continental Congress authorized the formation of Committees of Safety to enforce non-importation. In February 1775, the Massachusetts Committee began to make preparations for war and after Lexington and Concord a new urgency characterized its action.

Gentlemen: The barbarous murders committed on our innocent brethren on Wednesday the 19th instant have made it absolutely necessary that we immediately raise an army to defend our wives and children from the butchering hands of an inhuman soldiery, who, incensed at the obstacles they met with in their bloody progress, and enraged at being repulsed from the field of slaughter, will, without doubt, take the first opportunity in their power to ravage this devoted country with fire and sword. We conjure, therefore, by all that is sacred, that you give all assistance possible in forming the army. Our all is at stake.[40] Death and devastation are the certain consequences of delay; every moment is infinitely precious; an hour lost may deluge your country in blood and entail perpetual slavery upon the few of your posterity who may survive the carnage. We beg and entreat, as you will answer it to your country, to your own conscience, and above all, to God himself, that you will hasten and encourage, by all possible means, the enlistment of men to form the army, and send them forward to headquarters at Cambridge, with that expedition which the vast importance and instant urgency of the affair demands.

[40]This appeal is couched in language meant to incite emotion. It is equal parts a call to arms and propaganda.

Source: Jedidiah Morse, *Annals of the American Revolution.* (Hartford: Oliver D. Cooke & Sons, 1824), 229–230.

Bunker's Hill

(1775)

Pyrrhus was a Greek king who defeated the Romans in a huge battle in 279 BC. But it was a victory achieved at tremendous cost. Ever since that event, a battle won at such a cost has been referred to as a Pyrrhic victory. Such was the situation with the Battle of Bunker Hill.

Technically, the British redcoats under General Gage defeated the Continental force. But it took three disastrous charges against the colonial entrenchments to win the day, and the casualty lists tell the story. Americans: 1,500 fighters, 400 dead; British: 2,500 fighters, 1,150 dead. This battle was the beginning of the end of the British Empire in America.

[1]Amos Farnsworth was a corporal in the Massachusetts militia from the town of Groton, Massachusetts. He describes the fierce fighting on Bunker Hill.

Diary of Amos Farnsworth[1]

. . . About sun-set we was drawn up and herd prayers; and about dusk marched for Bunker's Hill under command of our own Col. Prescott . . . About sixty men was taken out of our battalion to go into Charlestown, I being one of them . . . Our men marched to Bunker-Hill and begun thair intrenchment and careerd it on with the utmost viger all night. Early in the morning I joined them.

Saturday June 17. The enemy appeared to be much alarmed on Saturday morning when they discovered our operations and immediately began a heavy cannonading . . . from the ships in the harbour . . . We discovered a large body of the enemy crossing Charles-River from Boston. Thay [they] landed on a point of land about a mile eastward of our intrenchment and immediately disposed their army for an attack, previous to which they set fire to the town of Charlestown. It is supposed that the enemy intended to attack us under the cover of the smoke from the burning houses . . . As the enemy approached, our men was not only exposed to the attack of a very numerous musketry, but to the heavy fire of the battery.[2] . . . Notwithstanding we within the intrenchment . . . sustained the enemy's attacks with great bravery and resolution, killed and wounded great numbers, and repulsed them several times; and after bearing, for about 2 hours, as sever [severe]

[2]The battery was a tactical artillery unit with cannon.

106

and heavy a fire as perhaps ever was known, and many having fired away all their ammunition, and having no reinforcement . . . we ware over-powered by numbers and obliged to leave the intrenchment . . . The town of Charlestown supposed to contain about 300 dwelling-houses, a great number of which ware large and elegant, besides 150 or 200 other buildings, are almost laid in ashes by the barbarity and wanton cruelty of that infernal villain Thomas Gage.[3]

Oh, the goodness of God in preserving my life althoe thay fell on my right hand and on my left![4] O, may this act of deliverance of thine, Oh God, lead me never to distrust the(e); but may I ever trust in the(e) and put confidence in no arm of flesh![5]

Source: *Proceedings of the Massachusetts Historical Society*, 2nd Series, Volume XII. (Boston: Published by the Society, 1835), 83–84.

Colonel William Prescott to John Adams, Camp at Cambridge, August 25, 1775[6]

. . . On the 16th of June, in the evening, I received orders to march to Breed's Hill in Charlestown, with a party of about one thousand men . . . we arrived at the spot, the lines were drawn by the engineer, and we began the intrenchment about twelve o'clock . . . Just before sunrising, when the enemy began a very heavy cannonading and bombardment . . . About this time, the field officers, being indisposed, could render but little service, and the most of the men under their command deserted the party. The enemy continuing an incessant fire with their artillery, about two o'clock in the afternoon on the 17th, the enemy began to land a north-easterly point from the fort . . . Another party of the enemy landed and fired the town . . . About an hour after the enemy landed, they began to march to the attack . . . I was now left with perhaps one hundred and fifty men in the fort, and meeting with a warm reception, there was a very smart firing on both sides. After a considerable time, finding our ammunition was almost spent, I commanded a cessation till the enemy advanced within thirty yards, which we gave them such a hot fire that they were obliged to retire nearly one hundred and fifty yards before they could rally and come up again to the attack.

Our ammunition being nearly exhausted, could keep up only a scattering fire. The enemy, being numerous, surrounded our little fort, began to mount our lines and enter the fort with their bayonets.[7]

[3]Thomas Gage was commander of the British forces in the colonies.

[4]The fighting was so fierce that men were being killed all around him.

[5]I will trust not that which is human flesh.

[6] During the night of August 16, 1775, 1,600 Americans under the command of Colonel William Prescott dug in on a little hill known as Breed's Hill.

[7]This was a blade adapted to fit the muzzle end of a rifle, and it was used as a weapon in close combat.

hot a fire as it was possible for them to make. We, having very few bayonets, could make no resistance. We kept the fort about one hour and twenty minutes after the attack with small arms . . .

[8]They retreated to Bunker Hill, higher up the rise overlooking Boston, where Prescott took command of the battle. Years later, contemporaries asserted that the battle should be called "Prescott's Battle."

Source: Richard Frothingham, Jr., *History of the Siege of Boston.* (Boston: C.C. Little and James Brown, 1851), 395–396.

An Eyewitness Narrative Prepared about Two Weeks after the Battle of Bunker's Hill by Peter Thacher[9]

[9]The Reverend Peter Thacher was asked to report on the battle by the Massachusetts Committee of Public Safety. He had witnessed the fighting from the shore of the Mystic River, not far from the hill.

In consequence of undoubted information received from Boston by the commanders of the continental Army at Cambridge that Genl Gage with a part of his troops purposed the next day to take possession of Bunker's Hill . . . they determined with the advice of the Committee of Safety of the Massachusetts Province to send a party who might erect some fortifications upon the hill and prevent this design. Accordingly on the 16th of June, orders were issued that a party of about one thousand men should that evening march to Charlestown and entrench upon the hill. . . . By the dawn of the day they had nearly completed a small redoubt about eight rods square.[10] At this time an heavy fire began . . . . . . These kept up an incessant shower of shot and bombs . . . A number of boats and barges filled with soldiers were observed approaching towards Charlestown. . . . They began a very slow march towards our lines. At this instant flames and smoke were seen to arise in large clouds from the town of Charlestown (which) had been set on fire from some of the enemy batterys[11] with a design to favor their attack upon our lines by the smoke which they imagined would have been blown directly that way and thence covered them in their attack, but the wind changing at this instant it was carried another way.

[10]A redoubt was a fortification built to defend a hill. The rod is a unit of length and surveyors tool. For example, 160 square rods equal an acre. Young George Washington surveyed and used rods that were semi-flexible and could be folded and transported through brush. The rod unit of length is equal to 5½ yards or 16½ feet.

[11]Batteries were tactical artillery units with cannon.

The provincials in the redoubts and the lines reserved their fire till the enemy had come within about 10 or 12 yards and then discharged at once upon them. The fire threw their body into very great confusion, and all of them after having kept a fire for some time retreated in very great disorder . . . At this time their officers were observed . . . to . . . use the most passionate gestures and even to push forward the men with their swords. At length by their exertions the troops were again rallied and marched up to the entrenchments. The Americans reserved their fire and a second time put the regulars to flights who once more retreated in precipitation to their boats.

The fire from the ships and batteries as well as from the cannon in front of their army was redoubled. Innumerable bombs were sent into the fort. The officers behind the army of the regulars were observed to goad forward their men with renewed exertion . . . The ammunition of the provincials expended, the enemy advanced on three sides of the fort at once and scaled the walls. Can it be wondered at then that the word was given to retreat? But even this was not done till the redoubt was half filled with regulars, and the provincials had for some time kept up an engagement with the butt ends of their muskets which unfortunately were not fixed with bayonets . . . With very great signs of exultation the British troops again took possession of the hill . . . Of 3 thousand who marched out on the expedition, no less than 1500 . . . were killed and wounded, a more severe blow than the British troops had ever before met with in proportion to the number who were engaged, and the time the engagement lasted from the first fire of the musketry to the last was exactly an hour and an half.

Source: *The Historical Magazine*, 2nd Series, Volume III, 382–384, 1868.

Francis, Lord Rawdon, to His Uncle, Francis, Tenth Earl of Huntington, Camp on the Heights of Charlestown, June 20, 1775[12]

. . . On Saturday last, the 17th of this month, a large party of them were observed at work on the hills above Charlestown, throwing up a battery which would, if perfected, have probably destroyed the greatest part of Boston . . . About noon the Grenadiers . . . in all about 2,400 men, were ordered to embark under the command of General Howe . . . We landed without opposition within half a mile of Charlestown, which the fire from the vessels had forced the rebels to abandon . . . Our men . . . grew impatient, and all crying out, "Push on! push on!" advanced with infinite spirit to attack the work[13] with their small arms. As soon as the rebels perceived this, they rose up and poured in so heavy a fire upon us that the oldest officers say they never saw a sharper action. They kept up this fire till we were within ten yards of them . . . Nothing . . . could long resist the courage of our men. The rebels were obliged to abandon the post, but continued a running fight from one fence, or wall, to another, till we entirely drove them off . . .[14]

Source: *Report on the Manuscripts of the Late Reginald Rawdon Hastings*, Great Britain Historical Manuscript Commission, Hastings Manuscripts, Volume III. (London: Her Majesty's Stationery Office, 1934), 154–155.

[12]Francis, Lord Rawdon's account, is that of a participant. He was in the thick of the fighting and later went on to a distinguished career in the Napoleonic Wars.

[13]He says his men wanted to attack the defenses of the rebel forces.

[14]Like his peers from the British nobility, he seems to be writing for the consumption of Parliament and the British upper class. He is astonished at the abilities of the provincials to resist superior British forces.

Sir William Howe was personally brave but weak as a tactician. He was used to fighting in the formal European style and was stymied by the rebels' nonorthodox tactics. Howe's mismanagement of the affair contributed to the huge British losses. He is quoted in the *New York Gazette* as saying, "You may talk of other battles, but I never saw nor heard of such carnage in so short a time." Bunker Hill was the bloodiest battle of the revolution.

16The British captured the small fort.

17An aide-de-camp is a military officer acting as a confidential assistant to a senior officer. Sherwin was killed from wounds inflicted during the battle.

18Colonel James Abercrombie was a British Army officer.

19"Just between us I have heard the rumor."

Sir William Howe to His Majesty George III, Camp upon the Heights of Charlestown (June 22 and 24)[15]

. . . The troops were no sooner ashore than it was instantly perceived the enemy were very strongly posted, the redoubt upon their right being large and full of men with cannon. To the right of the redoubt they had troops in the houses of Charles Town . . . Close upon the Mystic River, they had a breast work made with strong railing taken from the fences and stuffed with hay, which effectively secured those behind it . . . We began the attack (the troops in two lines) . . . by a sharp cannonade the line moving slowly and frequently halting to give time for the artillery to fire . . . The Grenadiers being directed to attack . . . their orders were executed . . . with a laudable perseverance, but not with the greatest share of discipline, for as soon as the order with which they set forward to the attack with bayonets was checked by a difficulty they met with in getting over some very high fences of strong railing, under a heavy fire, well kept up by the Rebels, they began firing, and by crowding fell into disorder . . . At the 2d onset they carried the redoubt[16] in the handsomest manner, tho' it was most obstinately defended to the last. Thirty of the Rebels not having time to get away were killed with bayonets in it . . . But I now come to the fatal consequences of this action—92 officers killed and wounded—a most dreadful account. I have lost my aid de camp Sherwin,[17] who was shot thro' the body and died the next day. Our friend Abercrombie[18] is also gone—he had only a flesh wound, but is said to have been in a very bad habit of body. The General's returns will give you the particulars of what I call this unhappy day. I freely confess to you, when I look to the consequences of it, in the loss of so many brave officers, I do it with horror. The success is too dearly bought. Our killed, sergeants and rank and file, about 160; 300 wounded and in hospital, with as many more incapable of present duty. The Rebels left near 100 killed and 30 wounded, but I have this morning learnt from a deserter from them that they had 300 killed and a great number wounded . . .

Entire nous, I have heard a bird sing[19] that we can do no more this campaign than endeavor to preserve the town of Boston, which it is supposed the Rebels mean to destroy by fire or sword or both—and it is my opinion . . . that we must not risk . . . the loss of Boston. The intentions of these wretches are to fortify every post in our way; wait to be attacked at every one, having their rear secure, destroying as many of us as they can before they set out to their next strong situation, and, in this defensive mode . . . they must in the end get the better of our small numbers. We can not . . . muster more now than 3400 rank and file for duty . . .

Source: J.W. Fortescue, ed., *Correspondence of King George the Third*, Volume III. (London: J. Murray, 1928), 220–224.

Report of General John Burgoyne to His Nephew, Lord Stanley, Boston, June 25, 1775[20]

. . . On the 17th, at dawn of day, we found the enemy had pushed intrenchments with great diligence during the night, on the heights of Charlestown, and we evidently saw that every hour gave them fresh strength . . . Howe, as second in command, was detached with about two thousand men, and landed . . . without opposition . . . He was to advance . . . up the hill which was over Charlestown, where the strength of the enemy lay . . . Clinton and myself took our stand . . . in a large battery directly opposite to Charlestown . . . thereby facilitating Howe's attack.

Howe's disposition . . . it was perfect.[21] As his first arm advanced up the hill they met with a thousand impediments from strong fences . . . They were also exceedingly hurt by musketry . . . Howe sent us word by a boat and desired us to set fire to the town, which was immediately done; we threw a parcel of shells, and the whole was instantly in flames . . . And now ensued one of the greatest scenes of war that can be conceived . . .

Straight before us a large and noble town in one great blaze; the church-steeples and heights of our own camp covered with spectators; the enemy all in anxious suspense; the roar of the cannon, mortars and musketry; the crash of churches, ships upon the stocks, and whole streets falling together, to fill the ear; the storm of the redoubts, with the objects above described, to fill the eye; and the reflection that, perhaps, a defeat was a final loss to the British Empire in America, to fill the mind . . . beyond any thing that ever came to my lot to be witness to[22] . . . The day ended with glory, and the success was most important, considering the ascendancy it gave the Regular troops; but the loss was uncommon in officers for the numbers engaged . . .

Source: Peter Force, *Containing a Documentary History of the English Colonies in N. America.* American Archives: 4th Series, Volume 2. (Washington: M. St. Clair Clarke and P. Force, 1837), 1094–1095.

[20]This report of General John Burgoyne to his nephew in London reflects the seriousness with which he regarded the engagement. His colleagues Generals Howe and Clinton still maintained the official attitude that the colonials were inferior and disorganized.

[21]Burgoyne means that the position of Howe's army was perfect.

[22]Although Bunker Hill was technically a British victory, Burgoyne saw the handwriting on the wall.

[23]In 1774, General Thomas Gage was appointed governor of Massachusetts and concentrated his troops within the city of Boston, effectively ceding the surrounding areas to the colonials. After Lexington and Concord, his army was effectively walled in the city. Bunker Hill was an attempt to break up the military isolation of Boston.

[24]The French and Indian or Seven Years' War, 1754–1761, ended with the British taking French possessions in the New World. Because the colonists did not fight the French with enthusiasm, the British thought they were poor fighters. Gage is saying that to judge the rebels as poor fighters because of the last war has led the British forces to greatly underestimate them.

[25]Reinforcements are not arriving in time.

[26]The rebels set up defensive works so as to protect against attack.

[27]He refers here to Boston.

[28]He means conquer and reduce the rebels into servitude.

[29]He wants to employ German troops from the state of Hesse (known as Hessians).

[30]This is the equivalent of modern armies trying to win a war with air power thus avoiding "boots on the ground."

[31]He was correct. New York was full of Loyalists.

General Gage to Lord Barrington, Secretary of State for War, Boston, June 26, 1775[23]

My Lord: You will receive an account of some success against the Rebels, but attended with a long list of killed and wounded on our side; so many of the latter that the hospital has hardly hands sufficient to take care of them. These people shew a spirit and conduct against us they never shrewd against the French, and every body has judged of them from their former appearance and behavior when joyned with the King's forces in the last war, which has led many into great mistakes.[24]

They are now spirited up by a rage and enthusiasm as great as ever people were possessed of, and you must proceed in earnest or give the business up. A small body acting in one spot will not avail. You must have large armys, making diversions on different sides, to divide their force.

The loss we have sustained is greater than we can bear. Small armys can't afford such losses, especially when the advantage gained tends to little more than the gaining of a post . . . The troops are sent out too late,[25] the Rebels were at least two months before-hand with us, and your Lordship would be astonished to see the tract of country they have entrenched and fortifyed,[26] their number is great, so many hands have been employed.

We are here, to use a common expression, taking the bull by the horns, attacking the enemy in their strong parts. I wish this cursed place[27] was burned. The only use is its harbour, which may be said to be material; but in all other respects it is the worst place either to act offensively from, or defencively. I have before wrote your Lordship my opinion that a large army must at length be employed to reduce these people,[28] and mentioned the hiring of foreign troops.[29] I fear it must come to that, or else to avoid a land war and make use only of your fleet.[30] I don't find one province in appearance better disposed than another, tho' I think if this army was in New York, that we should find many friends, and be able to raise forces in that province on the side of Government . . .[31]

Source: Clarence Edwin Carter, *Correspondence of Gage*, Volume II. (New Haven: Yale University Press, 1933), 686–687.

Letter of a British Officer, July 5, 1775[32]

We have lost 1000 men killed and wounded. We burned Charlestown during the engagement . . . Too great a confidence in ourselves . . . is always dangerous, occasioned this dreadful loss . . . We went to battle without even reconnoitering the position of the enemy. Had we only wanted to drive them from their ground, without the loss of a man, the Cemetery transport, which drew little water[33] and mounted 18 nine-pounders,[34] could have been towed up Mystic Channel, and brought to within musket-shot of their left flank, which was quite naked[35] . . . One charge on their uncovered flank would have dislodged them in a moment. Had we intended to have taken the whole rebel army prisoners, we needed only have landed in their heart and occupied the high ground above Bunker's Hill . . . But from an absurd and destructive confidence, carelessness or ignorance, we have lost a thousand of our best men and officers and have given the rebels great matter of triumph by showing them what mischief they can do us. They were not followed, though Clinton proposed it . . . [Even if we] had seen and rejected all the advantages I have mentioned above, even our manner of attacking in front was ruinous. In advancing, not a shot should have been fired, as it retarded the troops, whose movement should have been as rapid as possible. They should not have been brought up in line, but in columns[36] with light infantry in the intervals, to keep up a smart fire against the top of the breastwork. If this had been done, their works would have been carried in three minutes, with not a tenth part of our present loss. We should have been forced to retire, if Gen. Clinton had not come up with a reinforcement of 5 or 600 men. This re-established the left under Pigot and saved our honor.

The wretched blunder of the over-sized balls sprung from the dotage of an officer of rank in that corps, who spends his whole time in dallying with the schoolmaster's daughters.[37] God knows he is old enough; he is no Samson, yet he must have his Dalilah.[38]

Another circumstance equally true and astonishing is that Gen. Gage had undoubted intelligence early in May that the rebels intended to possess Bunker's Hill; yet no step was taken to secure that important post, though it commanded all the north part of the town. He likewise had an exact return of the corps that composed the rebel army then investing the town; of every piece of cannon they possessed; of their intended lines of blockade; and of the numbers expected and on their march from the other provinces.

[32]This report by an unidentified British officer is an exacting critique of the British action. Although it may be seen as an example of "Monday morning quarterbacking," in fact it supplies enough evidence to prove that the British losses were the result of entrenched incompetence.

[33]The *Cemetery* was a light ship capable of sailing in shallow water.
[34]Pounders were a small ship's cannon.
[35]Their flank was exposed to attack.

[36]Moving in columns presented less of a target to enemy fire.

[37]A feeble-minded idiotic officer was spending time fooling around with the schoolmaster's daughters. Thus, they were shooting cannon balls too heavy to reach their target.
[38]Samson was the biblical Hebrew warrior who lost his power by fooling around with a Philistine princess, Delilah.

[39] An archaic reference meaning "To begin with."

We are all wrong at the head.[39] My mind cannot help dwelling upon our cursed mistakes. Such ill conduct at the first outset argues a gross ignorance of the most common rules of the profession, and gives us, for the future, anxious forebodings. I have lost some of those I most valued. This madness of ignorance nothing can excuse. The brave men's lives were wantonly thrown away. Our Commander has as much murdered them as if he had cut their throats himself on Boston Common. Had he fallen, ought we to have regretted him?[40]

[40] A harsh criticism of their commander, General Gage. The author blames Gage for the needless loss of British troops and asks, "Would we have mourned Gage if he had been killed?"

Source: *Detail and Conduct of the American War, under Generals Gage, Howe, Burgoyne, and Vice Admiral Lord Howe*, 3rd edition. (London: Royal Exchange, 1780), 14–15.

Ann Hutton's Account, Boston, June 20, 1775[41]

[41] Ann Hutton was an upper-class Bostonian who had no sympathy for the revolutionary cause. Her account of the battle is important because it reflects the passion that characterized the opponents of the rebellion. This woman of privilege was determined to preserve the status quo.

. . . Last Saturday I was a spectator of a most awful scene my eyes ever beheld . . . The rebels had thrown up a breastwork, and were preparing to open a battery upon the heights above Charlestown . . . Soon after eleven o'clock the grenadiers . . . marched out of their encampments . . . and were landed on a point of land to the eastward of Charlestown . . . It seems very strong lines were thrown up and were occupied by many thousands of the rebels. The troops advanced with great ardor towards the intrenchment, but were much galled in the assault, both from the artillery and the small arms, and many brave officers and men were killed and wounded. As soon as they got to the intrenchments, the rebels fled, and many of them were killed in the trenches and in their flight. The marines, in marching through part of Charlestown, were fired at from the houses . . . Upon the firing from the houses, the town was immediately set in flames, and at four o'clock we saw the fire and the sword, all the horrors of war raging. The town was burning all night . . . We were exulting in seeing the flight of our enemies, but in an hour or two we had occasion to mourn and lament. Dear was the purchase of our safety! In the evening the streets were filled with the wounded and the dying . . . It grieves one that gentlemen, brave British soldiers, should fall by the hands of such despicable wretches as compose the banditti[42] of the country; amongst whom there is not one that has the least pretension to be called a gentleman.[43] They are a most rude, depraved, degenerate race, and it is a mortification to us that they speak English and can trace themselves from that stock . . .

[42] An archaic Italian word for bandits.
[43] Even in the account of a battle, British snobbery is seen. To this Loyalist woman it seems the rebellion was more wicked because it was led by lower-class men!

Source: Ann Hutton, *Letters of a Loyalist Lady*. Edited by E. Rhys Jones, 97–100. (Cambridge: Harvard University Press, 1927).

Application of Johnathan Brigham for a Pension[44]

In the year 1774 . . . Excitement was high and the moment of actual hostilities constantly anticipated by the inhabitants. Under these circumstances, I, with others of my townsmen, voluntarily formed ourselves into a military company . . . That I and the company to which I belonged equipped ourselves and met punctually through the year two days each week for the purpose of military exercise and improvement and, as a minuteman, continued to serve . . . in the early part of April 1775 . . . Declarant[45] was ever ready on all occasions to defend my country and her rights. On the nineteenth of April, 1775, declarant . . . marched to Concord for the protection of the military stores on the first notice of the hostile approach of the British forces. Great efforts were made to keep secret the march . . . but the battle at Lexington roused the country. Declarant heard of the affair at Lexington about nine or ten o'clock in the forenoon and arrived at Concord . . . at about two or three o'clock in the afternoon. When declarant arrived, the British had effected their object and were retreating, when declarant and his company immediately pursued . . . when in pursuit, they saw numbers of dead bodies, as the enemy's retreat was harassed by the yeomanry[46] firing upon them from behind walls, hedges, and buildings. The British . . . continued their retreat to Bunker's Hill and the next morning crossed to Boston . . . On the seventeenth June, 1775, declarant was engaged in the battle at Bunker's Hill. The firing on the part of the British commenced at an early hour in the morning from their ships and batteries.[47] But the engagement did not become general until a little after noon, when their forces crossed Charles River and attempted to dislodge the Americans from the redoubt which they had erected the preceding night. The battle was severe and the British repulsed at every charge until, for want of ammunition, the Americans were compelled to retire. The awful solemnities of that day are still deeply impressed upon declarant's mind, and the scenes of carnage and death and the inconceivable grandeur of the immense volume of flames illuminating the battlefield from the burning of Charlestown appear as vivid as if the events of yesterday . . .

Source: Revolutionary War Pension and Bounty Land Warrant Application File S. 22,665. Jonathan Brigham, Continental Mass. Identifier 540550789, National Archives.

[44]After the conclusion of the war, Congress agreed to pay pensions for veterans of the fighting. In order to qualify, a "declarant" had to present a sworn account of his or her actions. Brigham's soldier's eye accounts of Lexington, Concord, and Bunker Hill corroborates the reports of American and British officers.

[45]Brigham, in his application for a pension, refers to himself in the third person. "Declarant" is a person making a formal legal statement.

[46]Yeomanry were farmers who owned their own land; they were fighting to protect their property.

[47]Two or more cannon used for combined action formed a small artillery unit called a battery.

[48]This report on the Battle of Bunker Hill was published in London on November 27, 1775, along with a map of the battle. It was an attempt to energize British support for the conflict. It was propaganda. Not a word here about British miscalculations or weaknesses.

Letter Written by General Burgoyne to His Nephew Lord Stanley, Boston, June 25, 1775[48]

Boston is a peninsula . . . to the North is Charles-Town (or rather was, for it is now rubbish), and over it a large hill . . . to the South of the town is a still larger scope of ground . . . called Dorchester Neck: the heights as above described . . . command the town, that is, give an opportunity of erecting batteries that you can make against them . . . It was absolutely necessary we should make ourselves masters of these heights . . . my two colleagues and myself . . . had, in concert with Gen. Gage, formed the plan: Howe was to land the transports on one point, Clinton in the center, and I was to cannonade from the Causeway . . . this was to have been executed on the Eighteenth. On the 17th, at dawn of day, we found the enemy had pushed intrenchments with great diligence, during the night, on the heights of Charles-Town . . . every hour gave them fresh strength . . . it therefore became necessary . . . to attack . . . Howe . . . was detached with about 2000 men, and landed on the outward side of the peninsula . . . he was to advance from thence up the hill which was over Charles-Town . . .

[49]Howe's infantry advanced up the hill.

[50]This is the technique of bringing small arms fire on specific targets.

Howe's disposition was exceedingly soldier-like . . . As his first arm advanced up the hill,[49] they met with a thousand impediments from strong fences, and were much exposed. They were also exceedingly hurt by musketry[50] from Charles-Town . . . We threw a parcel of shells, and the whole was instantly in flames . . . And now ensued one of the greatest scenes of war that can be conceived . . . Howe's corps ascending the hill was much engaged . . . to the left the enemy pouring in fresh troops by thousands . . . our ships and floating batteries cannonading them: strait before us a large and a noble town in one great blaze; the church steeples, being of timber, were great pyramids of fire above the rest . . . the hills round the country covered with spectators . . . Howe's left were staggered;[51] two battalions had been sent to reinforce them, but we perceived them on the beach seeming in embarrassment what way to march . . . the day ended with glory, and the success was most important, considering the ascendancy it gave the regular troops; but the loss was uncommon in officers for the numbers engaged . . .[52]

[51]Howe's left wing was crippled by the fire of Americans from Charlestown.

[52]The British dead and wounded included 100 commissioned officers, which was a significant portion of the British officer corps in North America.

Source: Peter Force, ed., *American Archives*: 4th Series, Volume 2. (Washington: M. St Clair Clarke and Peter Force, 1839), 1094–1095.

A Letter from Joseph Palmer to John Adams, Cambridge, June 19, 1775[53]

Saturday last, the 17th, the Regulars attacked us upon one of the Charlestown Hills, where we had begun to entrench, and obliged us to retreat . . . the Enemy have not much to boast; for tho' they kept the Field . . . yet they lost, by the best acctts we can yet obtain: about 500 kill'd and wounded, and among the former are, as we have reason to believe, Several Officers of distinction: our loss in numbers is not great . . . about 60 or 70 kill'd and missing . . . the Regulars landed, then Set Fire to the Town of Charlestown . . . and they have . . . encamped upon Bunker's Hill and . . . our people, by Small Parties have picked off some of their out Guards . . . Do send us Powder, and then we Shall, by the blessing of Heaven, soon destroy this Hornets Nest. This put me in mind of Saltpeter . . . I must beg you to Send the best process of making it . . . [54]

Source: Letter from Joseph Palmer to John Adams, June 19, 1775. Adams family papers. https://www.masshist.org/database/797. Massachusetts Historical Society. Used by permission.

[53]While John Adams was a resident in Philadelphia (1774–1776), he carried on an extensive correspondence with distinguished friends in Massachusetts. This letter gives us an insight into a little-recognized aspect of Adams—the practical revolutionary.

[54]Saltpeter is a key ingredient for gunpowder. The knowledge on how to manufacture it was freely distributed during the revolution, and both states and individuals did their part in making it for the American cause. Adams responded by providing his recipe (not included here).

Letter from Abigail Adams to John Adams, June 18–20, 1775[55]

. . . Charlstown is laid in ashes. The Battle began upon our intrenchments upon Bunker's Hill, a Saturday morning about 3 o'clock and has not ceased yet and tis now 3 o'clock Sabbeth afternoon . . . the constant roar of the cannon is so [distre]ssing that we can not Eat, Drink or Sleep. . . .

I am not able to give you any authentick account of last Saturday[56] . . . The Spirits of the people are very good. The loss of Charlstown affects them no more than a Drop in the Bucket.

Source: Letter from Abigail Adams to John Adams, June 18–20, 1775. Adams family papers. https://www.masshist.org/database/3301. Massachusetts Historical Society. Used by permission.

[55]The correspondence between Adams and his wife is one of the great monuments of the revolution.

[56]Abigail was a faithful reporter of events back home but, more than that, she was an advocate for a new role for women in the republic her husband was creating. "Remember the ladies!" she famously wrote to him.

Nathaniel Ober, Diary Entry, June 17, 1775[57]

Our people and The Kings Trops Began a warm ingaigment about three a Clock this after none this was a melancly Day not only a grait number of our Braive friends fel But a grait Deal of

[57]Nathanial Ober was a private in the Continental Army. He fought in the Battles of Lexington and Concord.

Substance was Consumed by fire for our unatrel Enemies. Sat fier to the Town of Charlestown wich Consumed almost Every house in that town.[58]

Source: June 17, 1775, entry. Nathaniel Ober diary, 1775–1781. https://www.masshist.org/database/1900. Massachusetts Historical Society. Used by permission.

[59]Peter Brown gives an account from the American side. He was a native of Westward, Massachusetts, and served under Colonel Prescott.

Letters Home from Peter Brown to His Mother from Bunker's Hill, June 25, 1775[59]

. . . We marched down on to Charlestown Hill . . . where we entrenched, & made a Fort . . . about half after 5 in the Morn, we not having above half the Fort done, they began to fire. .pretty briskly for a few minutes, then stopt, and then again to the Number of about 20 or more. . . . about 11 o'clock and then they began pretty brisk again; and that caused some of our young Country ppl to desert . . . We began to be almost beat out, being tired by our Labour and having no sleep the night before, but little vituals, no Drink but Rum . . . They fired very warm from Boston & from on board till about 2 o'clock . . . Our Officers sent time after Time after the Cannon from Cambridge in the Morning & could get but four . . . it being about 3 o'clock there was a little Cessation of the Cannon Roaring. Come to look there was a matter of 40 Barges full of Regulars coming over to us: it is supposed there were about 3000 of them and about 700 of us left not deserted, besides 500 Reinforcement that could not get so nigh to us to do any good hardly till they saw that we must all be cut off, or some of them, and then they advanced . . . When our Officers saw that the Regulars would land they ordered the Artillery to go out of the fort & prevent their Landing if possible, from which the Artillery Captain took his pieces and went right off home to Cambridge fast as he could, for which he is now confined & we expect will be shot for it. But the enemy landed & fronted before us & formed themselves in an Oblong Square so as to surround us which they did in part & After they were well formed they advanced towards us in Order to swallow us up . . . 'tho we could do nothing with our small Arms as yet for Distance, & had *but two Cannon, & nary* A. *Gunner.* And they from Boston & from the ships firing and throwing Bombs, keeping us down, till they got almost round us. But God in Mercy to us fought our Battle for us, & altho' we were but few & so were suffered to be defeated by them, we were preserved in a most wonderful Manner far beyond Expectation . . . for out of our Regiment there were *about 37 killed, 4 or 5 taken* captive, and about 47 wounded . . . I was preserved while others were suffer'd to fall a prey to our Cruel enemies. O may That God whose Mercy was so far extended in my preservation, grant me his grace to devote my future Life to his divine service . . . if we should be called into Action again I hope to have Courage & strength to act my part valiantly in Defence of our Liberties & our Country, trusting in him who hath yet kept me & hath covered my head in the day of Battle[60] . . . I was not suffered to be touched altho' I was in the fort till the Regulars came in & I jumped over the Walls, & ran for about half a Mile where Balls flew like Hailstones, & Cannon roared like Thunder. But tho' I escaped then it may be my Turn next. So I must conclude with my prayers for your Welfare & wishing you the best of Blessings I still remain Your dutiful Son.

Source: F.B. Dexter, ed., *The Literary Diary of Ezra Stiles*, D.D. NY. Volume 1. (New York: Charles Scribner's Sons, 1901), 595–596.

[60]His is the fullest account of the feelings and observations of a participant in the ranks.

Lieutenant John Waller to a Friend, Boston, June 21, 1775[61]

[61]John Waller gives an account of the battle from the British point of view.

. . . On the 17th, Inst. we were ordered to March to the North Battery in Boston, and there to wait till order'd to Embark for Charles Town side . . . the Light Infantry had then (tho' at a great distance) began the Attack. We Landed accordingly where we were attack'd before I could get those in the first Boat for'd, however, we soon form'd into tolerable order with the loss of one Man only, and then March'd into a Field where we form'd in Line with the 43rd, and 47th. Regt. and were then order'd to shelter ourselves by laying on the Grass. We were soon order'd to advance and attack the natural defense of the Redoubt and to storm that also at all Events. We gained Ground on the Enemy but slowly, as the Rails Hedges and stone walls, broke at every time we got over them and several Men were shot, in the Act of climbing them . . . we received a Check . . . from the very heavy and severe Fire from Enemy in the Redoubt, and in this Spot we lost a number of Men . . . I requested Colnel Nesbit to form upon our Left in order that we might advance to the Enemy with our Bayonets without firing . . . I cannot pretend to describe the Horror of the Scene within the Redoubt when we enter'd it, it 'was streaming with Blood and strew'd with dead and dying Men the Soldiers stabbing some and dashing out the Brains of others was a sight too dreadful

[62]A breastwork is a temporary fortification, often an earthwork thrown up to breast height to provide protection to defenders firing over it from a standing position.

for me to dwell any longer on; therefore I must now tell you that the Enemy retreated to a very strong brest work[62] where they had 3 pieces of Artillery . . .

Source: Letter from J. Waller to unidentified recipient, June 21, 1775. Massachusetts Historical Society. https://www.masshist.org/bh/waller.html.

[63]Colonel William Prescott was commander of the American troops at Bunker Hill.

Letter from William Prescott to John Adams, Camp at Cambridge, August 25, 1775[63]

. . . On the 16 June in the Evening I received orders to march to Breed's Hill in Charlestown, with a party of about one thousand men . . . We arrived at the spot, the lines were drawn by the engineer . . . the enemy began a very heavy cannonading and bombardment . . . About this time, the above field officers, being indisposed, could render me but little service, and the most of the men under their command deserted the Party. The enemy continuing an incessant fire with their artillery, about two o'clock in the afternoon, on the seventeenth, the enemy began to land a north-easterly point from the fort, and I ordered the train, with two field-pieces, to go and oppose them, and the Connecticut forces to support them; but the train marched a different course, and I believe those sent to their support followed, I suppose to Bunker's Hill. Another party of the enemy landed and fired the town . . . after the enemy landed, they began to march to the attack in three columns . . . I was now left with perhaps one hundred and fifty men in the fort.[64] The enemy advanced and fired very hotly on the fort, and meeting with a warm reception, there was a very smart firing on both sides. After a considerable time, finding our ammunition was almost spent, I commanded a cessation till the enemy advanced within thirty yards,[65] when we gave them such a hot fire that they were obliged to retire nearly one hundred and fifty yards before they could rally and come again to the attack. Our ammunition being nearly exhausted, could keep up only a scattering fire. The enemy being numerous, surrounded our little fort, began to mount our lines and enter the fort with their bayonets. We was obliged to retreat through them, while they kept up as hot a fire as it was possible for them to make. We having very few bayonets, could make no resistance. We kept the fort about one hour and twenty minutes after the attack with small arms. This is nearly the state of facts, though imperfect and too general,

[64]This report to John Adams reflects the bloody violence of the battle.

[65]This is colloquially reported as "Don't fire until you see the whites of their eyes!" but there is little evidence that phrase was actually spoken.

which, if any ways satisfactory to you, will afford pleasure to your most obedient humble servant,

William Prescott

Source: R. Frothingham, *A History of the Siege of Boston, and the Battles of Lexington, Concord, and Bunker Hill*, 2nd edition. (Boston: Charles C. Little and James Brown, 1851), 395–396.

Broadside, June 18, 1775[66]

On Friday night, the 17th Instant, fifteen hundred of the Provincials went to Bunker's-Hill . . . Saturday ten o'clock, when 2000 Regulars marched out of Boston, landed in Charlestown . . . set fire to it in ten different places at once; then dividing their army, part of it marched up in the front of the Provincial entrenchment, and began to attack the Provincials . . . The Provincial entries discovered the Regulars . . . Captain Nolton . . . with 400 of paid forces, immediately repaired to, and pulled up a post and railfence, and carried the posts and rails to another fence, put them together for a breast work. Captain Nolton gave orders to the men not to fire until the enemy were got within fifteen rods,[67] and then not till the word was given. At the words being given, the enemy fell surprisingly; it was thought by spectators who stood at a distance, that our men did great execution.

The action continued about two hours, when the Regulars on the right wing were out in confusion and gave way . . . They retreated with precipitation across the causeway to Winter's Hill, in which they were exposed to the fire of the enemy, from their shipping and floating batteries. We sustained our principal losses passing the causeway. The enemy pursued our troops to Winter's Hill, where the Provincials being reinforced by General Putnam, renewed the battle with great spirit, repulsed the enemy with great slaughter, and pursued them until they got under cover of their cannon from the shipping . . . they on Monday began to fire upon the Regulars on Bunker's-Hill . . . The number of Provincials killed is between 40 and 70; 140 are wounded . . . The number of Regulars . . . was not less than two thousand, the number of the Provincials was only fifteen hundred . . . This account was taken from Elijah Hide, of Lebanon, who was a spectator on Winter's Hill, during the whole action . . .

Source: *Broadside Printed at Lancaster*, Pennsylvania, by Francis Bailey, June 26, 1775. In *An Authentic History of Lancaster County, in the State of Pennsylvania.* Edited by J.I. Mombert, 232–234. (Lancaster, PA: J.E. Barr & Co., 1869).

[66] A broadside is a large sheet of paper printed on one side only. Historically, broadsides were posters, announcing events or proclamations, or simply advertisements. They were one of the most common forms of printed material between the 16th and 19th centuries, particularly in Britain, Ireland, and North America. These broadsides were the agency through which the average citizen got news of the war. They were widely distributed in Philadelphia, Baltimore, and Charlestown.

[67] The rod unit of length is equal to 5½ yards, or 16½ feet.

Official Account of General Gage, Whitehall, July 25, 1775[68]

My Lord, I am to acquaint your Lordship of an action that happened on the 17th instant between His majesty's troops and a large body of the rebel forces . . . advice was soon afterwards received, that the rebels had broke ground, and were raising a battery on the heights of the peninsula of Charlestown, against the town of Boston . . . in a few hours, a battery of six guns played upon their works. Preparations were instantly made for landing a body of men to drive them off . . . landed on the peninsula without opposition . . . The rebels upon the heights were perceived to be in great force, and strongly posted. A redoubt, thrown up on the 17th, at night, with other works, full of men, defended in Charlestown . . . This appearance of the rebel's strength, and the large columns seen pouring in to their assistance, occasioned an application for the troops to be reinforced . . . the whole, when in conjunction, making a body of something above 2000 men. These troops advanced, formed in two lines, and the attack began by a sharp cannonade from our field-pieces and howitzers, the lines advancing slowly, and frequently halting to give time for the artillery to fire. The light-infantry was directed to force the left point of the breastwork . . . and the grenadiers to attack in front . . . These orders were executed . . . under a heavy fire from the vast numbers of the rebels . . . Brigadier-general Pigot, who engaged also with the rebels of Charlestown, which, at a critical moment, was set on fire, the brigadier pursued his point, and carried the redoubt. The rebels were then forced from other strongholds, and pursued till they were drove clear off the peninsula, leaving five pieces of cannon behind them . . . This action has shown the superiority of the King's troops, who, under every disadvantage, attacked and defeated above three times their own number, strongly posted, and covered by breastworks . . . in justice to Brigadier-general Pigot, I am to add, that the success of the day must, in great measure, be attributed to his firmness and gallantry[69] . . . the valor of the British officers and soldiers . . . was at no time more conspicuous than in this action.

I have the honor to be, andc.,
THO. GAGE

Source: R. Frothingham, *A History of the Siege of Boston, and the Battles of Lexington, Concord, and Bunker Hill*, 2nd edition. (Boston: Charles C. Little and James Brown, 1851), 386–387.

The Invasion of Montreal and Quebec
(1775)

INTRODUCTION

It is a cliché of battle that it is invariably a mistake to underestimate your enemy. The Continentals not only made this mistake; they based their campaign against Canada on a delusion—a fatal misreading of the mind-set of the Canadians. The Americans assumed that their neighbors to the north resented the British tyranny as much as they did. In fact, the Second Continental Congress assumed that Canada could be persuaded to enter the union as a 14th colony.

This was the official position; but it was supported by one of the most—perhaps the most—problematic figures of the revolution: Benedict Arnold. Arnold, whose name has become a synonym for traitor because of his later activities undermining the American cause, was at the outset, a fierce patriot, longing for the glory that the battlefield might bring him. He, along with Ethan Allen, had conquered at Ticonderoga, and he was anxious to conquer Canada as well.

Arnold convinced Washington to allow him to move north through the wilderness and attack Quebec City. Richard Montgomery was assigned the attack on Montreal. Montgomery took Montreal and set out to meet up with Arnold's army, conquer Quebec, and win the Canadian conflict.

But this neat plan of battle made the fatal mistake of underestimating the defense of the city under the leadership of General Guy Carleton. Montgomery was killed, Arnold was wounded, and the Continental Troops, wasted and wanting from the murderous trek north through the Maine wilderness, met total defeat. Arnold lived to fight another day and cover himself with anything but glory. The following documents present eyewitness accounts of these unfortunate events.

A Letter from Colonel Benedict Arnold, Probably to General Schuyler, Pointe Aux Trembles, November 27, 1775[1]

. . . Thus in about 8 weeks we completed a march of near six hundred miles, not to be paraleled in history; the men having with the greatest fortitude and perseverance hauled their batteaux[2] up rapid

[1] After choosing Washington as commander in chief, Congress appointed Phillip Schuyler major general. Schulyer was a New Yorker who had distinguished himself in the French and Indian War. He was an aristocrat with zealous support for the revolutionary cause. Colonel Benedict Arnold

²A bateau, batteau, or batteaux is a shallow-draft, flat-bottomed boat that was used extensively across North America, especially in the colonial period and in the fur trade.
³A ration is the allowance of food for the subsistence of one person for one day; his meaning here is that the men did not have a full ration of food each day for a week.

streams, being obliged to wade almost the whole way, near 180 miles, carried them on their shoulders near forty miles, over hills, swamps and bogs almost impenetrable, and to their knees in mire; being often obliged to cross three or four times with their baggage. Short of provisions, part of the detachment disheartened had gone back; famine staring us in the face; an enemy's country and uncertainty ahead. Not withstanding all these obstacles, the officers and men, inspired and fired with the love of liberty and their country, pushed on with a fortitude superior to every obstacle, and most of them had not one day's provision for a week.³

I have thus given you a short but imperfect sketch of our march . . . the enemy being appraised of our coming, we found it impracticable to attack them without too great a risk . . . On a strict scrutiny into our ammunition, found many of our cartridges (which to appearance were good) and not ten rounds each for the men, who were almost naked, bare footed and much fatigued; and as the garrison was daily increasing and nearly double our numbers, we thought it prudent to retire to this place and wait the arrival of Gen. Montgomery, with artillery, clothing, etc., who to our great joy has this morning joined us with about 300 men. We propose immediately investing the town and make no doubt in a few days to bring Gov. Carlton to terms. You will excuse the incorrectness of my letter and believe me with the greatest esteem.

Source: *Collections of the Maine Historical Society*, Volume 1. (Portland: Day, Fraser & Co., 1831), 384–385.

⁴General Richard Montgomery (1737–1775) was born in Ireland. He settled in America and married into the distinguished Livingston family. He, along with Benedict Arnold, was sent to lead the invasion of Canada and after repeated acts of bravery was cut down on December 31, 1775. He was buried at Quebec but in 1818 a special act of the New York legislature brought his body to New York City where it was interred with full military honors in St. Paul's Cemetery (Trinity Parish). Abner Stocking was a private in Arnold's army.

Journal of Abner Stocking on the Death of Montgomery⁴

Between four and five in the morning [of Jan 1 1776] the signal was given and the several divisions moved to the assault, under a violent storm of snow . . . Montgomery, at the head of the New York troops, advanced along the St. Lawrence . . . The guard placed at the block-house, being chiefly Canadians, having given a random and harmless fire, threw away their arms and fled in confusion to the barrier.

Unfortunately, the difficulties of the route rendered it impossible for Montgomery instantly to avail himself of this first impression. Along the scanty path leading under the projecting rocks of the precipice, the Americans pressed forward in a narrow file, until they reached the block house and picket.[5] Montgomery, who was himself in front, assisted with his own hands to cut down or pull up the pickets, and open a passage for his troops . . .

Having reassembled about two hundred men, whom he encouraged alike by his voice and his example, he advanced boldly and rapidly at their head to force the barrier. One or two persons had now ventured to return to the battery, and seizing a slow-match,[6] standing by one of the guns, discharged the piece . . . This single accidental fire was a fatal one. The general . . . together with his orderly sergeant and a private, were killed on the spot. The loss of their general, in whom their confidence had been so justly placed, discouraged the troops; and Colonel Campbell, on whom the command devolved but who did not partake of that spirit of heroism which had animated their departed chief, made no attempt to prosecute the enterprise. This whole division retired precipitately from the action and left the garrison at leisure, after recovering from the consternation into which they had been thrown, to direct their undivided force against Arnold.

Source: *An Interesting Journal of Abner Stocking of Chatham, Connecticut.* (Catskill, NY: Eagle Office, 1810), 28–30.

Benedict Arnold to His Wife Hannah, January 6, 1776[7]

Before this reaches you I make no doubt you will have heard of our misfortune of the 31st ultimo and will be anxious for my safety . . . The command of the army, by the death of my truly great and good friend, General Montgomery, devolved on me; a task, I find, too heavy under my present circumstances. I received a wound by a ball through my left leg . . . which, by the loss of blood, rendered me very weak . . . I returned to the hospital, near a mile, on foot, being obliged to draw one left after me, and a great part of the way under the continual fire of the enemy . . . I providentially escaped . . . I soon learned the death of our general; who attacked the town at the side opposite to me; he behaved heroically . . . This occasioned the disaster that afterwards happened to my detachment, which, after the general's defeat, had the whole garrison to encounter . . . To return was impossible, as the route was within fifty yards and exposed to the fire of the whole garrison . . . In this situation, they maintained their ground near three hours, but being overpowered with numbers, were obliged to lay down their arms; about three hundred . . . were taken prisoners and, as near as I can judge, about sixty killed and wounded . . . The prisoners are treated politely and supplied with

[5] A blockhouse is a small, isolated fort in the form of a single building. It serves as a defensive strong point against any enemy that does not possess siege equipment or, in modern times, artillery. A picket is an advance guard whose job it is to warn of the enemy approach. Pickets are also barriers such as fences.

[6] This is a slow-burning piece of wood used to produce fire.

[7] This excerpt from a letter reflects the bravery and stubborn character of the man, attributes that led both to his success on the battlefield and to his eventual downfall.

every thing the garrison affords. Governor Carleton sent to let me know that the soldiers' baggage, if I pleased, might be sent to them, which I shall immediately send.

Though the enemy are now double our number, they have made no attempt to come out. We are as well prepared to receive them as we can possibly be in our present situation . . . I expect General Wooster from Montreal in a few days with a reinforcement. I hope we shall be properly supported with troops by the Congress. I have no thoughts of leaving this proud town until I first enter it in triumph[8] . . . I know you will be anxious for me. That Providence which has carried me through so many dangers is still my protection. I am in the way of my duty and know no fear.

Source: Peter Force, *American Archives, Fourth Series*, Volume 4. (Washington, DC: M. St. Clair Clarke and Peter Force, 1843), 589–590.

[8]Arnold boasts that he will not leave until the job is done.

Journal of Thomas Ainslie[9]

The drums beat to arms:[10] the different corps assembled on the Parade. It was there proposed that the volunteers of the British and Canadian militia should join the troops and sailors to engage the Rebels on the plains; to their credit be it said that almost to a man both corps were anxious to be led to action . . .

A few shots were exchanged by our advanced party and the rear guard of the enemy; their balls whistled over us without hurting a man. They fled most precipitately as soon as ourfield pieces began to play on their guard houses and advanced posts. They left cannon, mortars, field pieces, muskets and even their cloths behind them. As we pursued them we found the road strewed with arms, cartridges, cloaths, bread, pork, etc.

Their confusion was so great, their panic so violent, that they left orderly books and papers, which for their own credit should not have been left. Look whatsoever way one would, he saw men flying and loaden carts driving full speed . . .

The frigates fired on bateaus full of runaways; the turning of the tide unfortunately forced them to come to an anchor, and the boats rowed close to shore and got off.

[9]Thomas Ainslie was collector of Customs of the Port of Quebec. He had literary ambitions, and his journal is distinguished by its style from many contemporary accounts. His description of the American desertion of comrades is unique among the accounts of this action.

[10]Drums were sounded to alert soldiers to assemble, armed and ready.

To lighten their boats they inhumanely threw out many of their sick men upon the beach. Some of them expired before our parties could get to their relief; those objects of compassion whom we found alive were sent to the general Hospital. Thus was the country round Quebec freed from a swarm of misguided people, led by designing men, enemies to the liberties of their country, under the specious title of the Assertors of American Rights.

Source: Fred C. Wurtele, *Blockade of Quebec in 1775–1776 by the American Revolutionist*s. (Quebec: Literary and Historical Society of Quebec, 1905), 83–84.

Pension Application of Richard Vining

When Congress voted to award pensions to veterans, it opened a Pandora's box and established a precedent that was followed after each of America's wars.

. . . About the first of September (1775), General Arnold had orders to march to Quebec, when deponent[11] volunteered his services . . . I . . . was in the woods alone three days without a mouthful of provisions . . . When the sun shone again I then struck for the river and came up with the rear company of the army, and there I got half allowance which was allowed to the army on account of the scarcity of provisions . . . General Arnold took five or six men, pushed on to the French inhabitants as fast as possible to provide provisions for us. The general . . . procured a cow and sent back to relieve the army . . . Previous to this, our company was obliged to kill a dog and eat it for our breakfast, and in the course of that day I killed an owl, and two of my messmates and myself fared in the repast.[12] However we came up with the cow and cooked a portion of it and drinked the broth of the beef and owl cooked together, and the next day ate the meat. The second day after we got the beef, it rained heavily and turned into a snowstorm, and the snow fell needle deep. The day following, we waded a river thirty rods wide. We soon came to a house where we drew a pound of beef and three potatoes each . . . Went on five miles and came to another house where we got one pound of beef, three potatoes, and a pint of oatmeal each. We then went on, when I became so feeble that myself and two more hired a Frenchman to carry us on at our own expense for thirteen miles. There we found common rations. We then went on, all very much enfeebled by reason of sickness and hardship, for four or five days until reached Quebec.

[11]A deponent is someone who gives evidence or acts as a witness.

[12]There were swindles based on absurd claims, but nevertheless, many of the details contained in the applications provide colorful insight into aspects of the conflict not available in official military accounts.

At Quebec we lay on the opposite side of the river from the town for about one week. General Arnold ordered all who were fit for duty to cross the river, who crossed and presented themselves in front of the fort when the British fired upon them. No injury down except that one man had a leg shot off by a cannonball. The general then ordered a retreat. We retreated up the river towards Montreal . . . We lay there about four weeks until General Montgomery had secured Montreal, when he came and joined us, and we returned to Quebec.

Source: Revolutionary War Pension and Bounty-Land Warrant Application Files, Pension No. S. 11638, Record Group 15, National Archives.

The Siege of Boston

(1775)

The Battles of Lexington, Concord, and Bunker Hill were all fought in Massachusetts by what was essentially a ragtag assembly of enthusiastic but inexperienced volunteers. After these events, Parliament declared the colonies to be in rebellion and determined to put down the rebellion with the full force of the British Empire. The Continental Congress meeting at Philadelphia knew that it was absolutely imperative to create an organized army, an army made up of volunteers from many colonies and led by officers from the South as well as from the North; an army that was fully representative of united American colonies. Thus, there existed a united army before there was a United States. On June 14, 1775, a day that was later memorialized in the American patriotic calendar as "Flag Day," the Congress resolved to raise companies from Pennsylvania, Maryland, and Virginia. These companies were ordered to join the Massachusetts militia. But who was to become commander in chief of this united force? The Congress wisely elevated a Virginian to the command, a Virginian whose only military experience had been during the war with the French and Indians. Tasked with the mission of defending American liberty, General George Washington accepted, reluctantly, as the Congress expressed its "special trust and confidence" in his patriotism, valor, conduct, and fidelity. The date was June 17, 1775. That trust was not misplaced.

In January 1776, cannon and other materiel captured at Fort Ticonderoga were transported to the heights south of Boston. Moving heavy equipment by oxcart became impossible because of the heavy ice and snow in the Berkshire Mountains. Sleighs were used to pull the load, but several cannon fell through the ice while being moved across frozen rivers. Despite the logistical difficulties, the precious armaments reached Cambridge, and on March 4 Washington took command of Dorchester Heights and laid siege to the city and harbor. Placed in a position where they could not defend the city, the British took ship for Halifax and the victorious Continentals marched into Boston.

Extract of a Letter from John Andrews to William Barrell, June 1, 1775[1]

[1] John Andrews was a prosperous Boston merchant who remained in the city to guard his property.

. . . Its hard to stay coop'd up here and feed upon salt provissions, more especially without one's wife, Bill, but at the same time

[2] This letter to William Barrell, a Philadelphia businessman and friend, gives us a picture of what it was like to try to survive under British occupation.

would not wish to have her here under the present disagreable circumstances . . . We have now and then a carcase offer'd for sale in the market, which formerly we would not have pick'd up in the street; but bad as it is, it readily sells for eight pence Lawful money per lb., and a quarter of lamb when it makes its appearance, which is rarely once a week, sells for a dollar . . . wood not scarcely to be got at twenty two shillings a cord. Was it not for triffle of salt provissions that we have, 'twould be impossible for us to live. Pork and beans one day, and beans and pork another, and fish when we can catch it . . .[2]

Source: Winthrop Sargent, *Letters of John Andrews, esq, of Boston 1772–1776.* (Cambridge: Press of John Wilson and Sons, 1866), 95.

[3] The correspondence between John Adams, leading patriotic spirit of the revolution and second president of the United States, and his wife Abigail is one of the great resources of information about home front conditions. Adams was in Philadelphia with the Continental Congress; Abigail remained in Massachusetts to oversee the family property and raise their family.

[4] This regulation was promulgated to keep the residents of Boston from watching the fighting on Bunker Hill.

[5] These were permits to leave Boston.

[6] The 18th-century monetary system was very confusing by today's standards. There were three general types of money in the pre-revolutionary colonies; commodity money (such as tobacco, beaver skins, and wampum), specie (coins), and paper money. Commodity money was used when cash such as coins and paper money were scarce. To make matters worse, before the revolution each colony had a distinct currency. Most people in the 1700s were self-employed, and there is simply not enough information about annual incomes. There was also no income tax, so no tax records on income exist. However, $10, $20, $30, and $40 would have been a small fortune.

Letter from Abigail Adams to John Adams, Braintree, July 5, 1775[3]

I should have been more particular, but I thought you knew every thing that passed here. The present state of the inhabitants of Boston is that of the most abject slaves under the most cruel and despotic of tyrants . . . Upon the 17th of June, printed handbills were posted up at the corners of the streets and upon houses, forbidding any inhabitants to go upon their houses, or upon any eminence, on pain of death . . .[4]

Our prisoners were brought over to the Long Wharf, and lay there all night, without any care of their wounds or any resting-place but the pavements, until the next day, when they exchanged it for the jail, since which we hear they are civilly treated . . . as they can have no fresh provisions . . . and their own wounded men die very fast, so that they have a report that the bullets were poisoned . . . The money that has been paid for passes[5] is incredible. Some have been given ten, twenty, thirty and forty dollars, to get out with a small proportion of their things.[6] It is reported and believed that they have taken up a number of persons and committed them to jail, we know not for what in particular . . . God alone knows to what length these wretches will go, and I hope restrain their malice . . .

Source: Charles Francis Adams, ed., *Letters of Mrs. Adams*, Volume 1, 2nd edition. (Boston: Charles C. Little and James Brown, 1840), 48–49.

From an Officer of Distinction at Boston to a Person in London, March 3, 1776[7]

For the last six weeks, or near two months, we have been better amused than could possibly be expected in our situation. We had a theatre, we had balls, and there is actually a subscription on foot for a masquerade. England seems to have forgot us, and we endeavored to forget ourselves.[8] But we were roused to a sense of our situation last night, in a manner unpleasant enough. The rebels have been for some time past erecting a bomb battery, and last night began to play upon us. Two shells fell not far from me. One fell upon Col. Moncton's house, and broke all the windows but luckily did not burst till it had crossed the street . . . The rebel army is not brave I believe, but it is agreed on all hands, that their artillery officers are at least equal to our own . . . March 5th. This is, I believe, likely to prove as important a day to the British Empire as any in our annals. We underwent last night a very severe cannonade, which damaged a number of houses, and killed some men. This morning at daybreak we discovered two redoubts on the hills on Dorchester Point . . . From these hills they commanded the whole town, so that we must drive them from their post, or desert the place. The former is determined upon, and five regiments are already embarked . . . 6th March. A wind more violent than any thing I ever heard prevented our last night's purposed expedition, and so saved the lives of thousands. Today they have made themselves too strong to make a dislodgment possible. We are under their fire whenever they chuse to begin; so that we are now evacuating the town with the utmost expedition, and leaving behind us half our worldly goods.[9] Adieu! I hope to embark in a few hours . . .

Source: *Celebration of the Centennial Anniversary of the Evacuation of Boston by the British Army.* (Boston: By Order of the City Council, 1876), 175–176.

Letter Sent to England by an Officer at Boston, August 18, 1775[10]

Boston, the metropolis of North America (where we now are, and have been so long cooped up) may very justly be termed the grave of England and the slaughter house of America. Nothing is to be heard in it but execrations and clamour. Nothing is to be seen but

[7] This letter reflects the transformation of life in Boston for the British forces.

[8] At first life went on as usual, with parties and fund-raising events.

[9] As soon as the bombardment began from Washington's cannon, reality set in and, soon enough the British prepared to evacuate the town.

[10] This is a picture of the demoralized state of the British Army, isolated and trapped in the city.

distractions and melancholy, disease and death. The soldiery, and inhabitants likewise, I am sure have done sufficient penance here for their whole lives. The latter are all ruined; many that were worth 16 or 20 thousand pounds have not a sixpence left; and if any one of them in the anguish of his heart, or the bitterness of his soul, dares mutter like resentment for the loss of his fortune, a distressed family or a murdered friend, he is immediately thrown into a loathsome prison . . .

[11]Desertion was not an option; they had nowhere to go.

"Tis well for our generals that we have nowhere to run to; for could the men desert, I am full of opinion that they would soon be left by themselves, but situated as we are, we must unavoidably live and die together" . . .[11]

Source: Margaret Willard, ed., *Letters on the American Revolution; 1774–1775.* (Boston: Houghton Mifflin Co, 1925), 190.

[12]Samuel Larrabee was a private soldier in Washington's army at Dorchester Heights. In his application for a veteran's pension, he describes the British evacuation of Boston.

Pension Application of Samuel Larrabee[12]

. . . in the month of February, 1776, at North Yarmouth . . . we marched to Dorchester, near Boston . . . and served on Dorchester Heights, the road to which was across a low piece of land where we were exposed to the fire of Lord Howe's guns, to protect ourselves from which we placed bundles of hay. The last fortnight before Howe evacuated Boston, we kept up a smart cannonading every pleasant night from twelve o'clock till sunrise . . . About sunrise and on a day in the middle of March, the seventeenth I believe, Howe's fleet began to move. The drums beat to arms[13] from Dorchester Heights all round to Cambridge, and we instantly left our fort and hastened to our regiment . . . We immediately formed, took up our line of march and . . . were met by two men who had just thrown open the gates and let down the bridge to receive us into the town. At twelve o'clock we were in the State House . . . At half past twelve all the English were embarked, and while the fleet were sailing out of the harbor, I heard the explosion of Castle William and the lighthouse as they were blown up by the English.[14] Lord Howe left ten or twelve transports and other armed vessels to blockade the harbor . . . In July we were paraded on the east side of the State House and heard the Declaration of Independence read . . .

[13]The signal for the troops to form up for the march.

[14]As a final event, the departing British destroyed Castle William at the entrance to the harbor. The fortification had served as a customs house, refuge, and prison at various times. It had become a symbol of British occupation.

Source: Revolutionary War Pension and Bounty-Land Warrant Application Files, Record Group 15, Pension No. W. 26773, National Archives.

A Letter from Colonel Charles Stuart to Lord Bute, Halifax, April 18, 1776[15]

... About the middle of Feb. we were informed that the Rebels had a quantity of fascines and entrenching tools[16] on Dorchester Neck for the purpose of throwing up works. Deserters informed the General that the enemy intended to bombard the town, and preparations were made to hinder their work . . . The Rebels at the same time made a battery within point-blank cannon shot of our lines, and with such caution that we could not discover that it was intended for a battery . . . On the 3rd March at 9 o'clock at even they began a pretty hot cannonade and bombardment. Their shells were thrown in an excellent direction, they took effect near the centre of the town, and tore several houses to pieces; the cannon was usually well fired, one shot killed 8 men of the 22nd Regt. and houses were pierced through and through with balls they fired from Phipps's Farm. Our lines were raked from the new battery they had made and tho' we returned shot and shell, I am very, very sorry to say with not quite so much judgement. The bombardment continued for five nights . . . The inhabitants were in a horrid situation, particularly the women who were several times drove from their houses by shot, and crying for protection. On the 8th or 9th of March, I forgot which, they ceased firing, and at daybreak next morning we perceived two posts[17] upon the highest hills of Dorchester peninsula, that appeared more like majick than the work of human beings. They were each of them near 200 ft. long on the side next the town, and seemed to be strong cases of packed hay about 10 ft. high with an abattis[18] of vast thickness round both. We discovered near 6000 people, most of them at work; they opened embrasures[19] before 9 o'clock and out 2 clock had made a ditch and connected the two hills by a breastwork.

We fired a few shots, but the position was too strong to be affected; the General therefore determined to attack it. A quantity of artillery and three regiments immediately embarked . . . amounting in all to 2500 men . . . the whole was to have gone in boats and landed . . . so high a wind arose that it was impossible for the boats to take to sea. The next day the General assembled the field officers and acquainted us that the intended attack had failed through the inclemency of the weather, that he had consulted the engineers, who declared that the works had been so strengthened as to render their works upon that peninsula from such a commanding height we should inevitably be drove from the town.

[15]Colonel Charles Stuart was later promoted to lieutenant general and here reports, after the evacuation, to Lord Bute. Bute, a Scots Tory, was a favorite of George III and leader of the Tory factions in Parliament. From the safety of Halifax, Nova Scotia, Stuart reports on the evacuation to Bute, one of the most vigorous opponents of the American cause.

[16]The fascine knife was used by colonial military as a personal weapon and to cut fascines. Fascines were rough bundles of sticks or other material used for strengthening an earthen structure, or making a path across uneven or wet terrain. An entrenching tool is a collapsible spade used by the military.

[17]They saw two military defense lines with sentries.

[18]An abattis is an opening in a wall through which guns are fired.

[19]An embrasure is an obstacle made of felled trees with sharpened branches pointed at the enemy.

He also told us that there was no more than 6 week's provisions in the garrison, which obliged him to go to Halifax instead of New York. The principal citizens, on hearing that the town was to be evacuated, came to General Howe, and requested that the town might not be burnt; the General made answer that if the enemy molested him in his retreat he would certainly burn it; if not, he would leave the town standing. This was made known by a flag of truce to the Rebels; in consequence of which we made our retreat unmolested.

Source: William Bell Clark, *Naval Documents of the American Revolution*, Volume 4. (Washington, DC: Government Printing Office, 1969), 1292–1293.

Journal of Timothy Newell, a Selectman of Boston[20]

[20]Deacon Timothy Newell was pastor of the Brattle Street Church. His journal provides a day-to-day record of the last year of British occupation.
[21]"Chevaux de freze" is French for a portable barrier covered with barbed wire; "crow feet" is a reference to debris.

March 17th, Lord's Day. This morning at 3 o'clock, the troops began to move-guards, chevaux de freze, crow feet[21] strewed in the streets to prevent being pursued. They all embarked at about 9 o'clock and the whole fleet came to sail. Every vessel which they did not carry off, they rendered unfit for use. Not even a boat left to cross the river.

Thus was this unhappy distressed town . . . relieved from a set of men whose unparalleled wickedness, profanity, debauchery and cruelty is inexpressible,[22] enduring a siege from the 19th April 1775 to the 17th March 1776. Immediately upon the fleet's sailing the Select Men set off through the lines to Roxbury to acquaint General Washington of the evacuation of the town . . . The General immediately ordered a detachment of 2000 troops to take possession of the town under the command of General Putnam[23] who the next day began their works in fortifying Foothill, etc., for the better security of the town.

[22]Here, like many others, Newell records the British "scorched earth" policy leaving behind ruins and destruction.

[23]General Israel Putnam was one of the leaders of the defense at Bunker Hill.

Source: Timothy Newal, "A Journal Kept during the Time That Boston Was Shut Up in 1775–6." *In Collections of the Massachusetts Historical Society*, 4th Series, Volume I. (Boston: Published by the Society, 1852), 275–276.

The Evacuation of Boston, March 17, 1776[24]

[24]In the latter end of the year 1821 and early in 1822, a series of papers were published in the *Boston Centinel* under the head of "Recollections of a Bostonian."

The British army evacuated Boston on the forenoon of Sunday, the 17th March, 1776 . . . On crossing the common we found it very much disfigured with ditches and cellars, which had been dug by the British troops for their accommodation when in camp. To our great regret, we saw several large trees lying in the mall, which had been cut down that morning. We were informed that the tories were so exasperated at being obliged to leave the town, that they were determined to do all the mischief possible, and had commenced destroying that beautiful promenade . . . On passing into the town, it presented an indescribable scene of desolation and gloominess, for notwithstanding the joyous occasion of having driven our enemies from our land, our minds were impressed with an awful sadness at the sight of the ruins of many houses which had been taken down for fuel—the dirtiness of the streets—the wretched appearance of the very few inhabitants who remained during the siege . . . We entered the Old South church . . . it had been turned into a riding school for the use of General Burgoyne's regiment of cavalry . . . The pulpit and all the pews were taken away and burnt for fuel, and many hundred loads of dirt and gravel were carted in, and spread upon the floor. The south door was closed, and a bar was fixed, over which the cavalry, were taught to leap their horses at full speed. A grog shop was erected in the gallery, where liquor was sold to the soldiery, and consequently produced scenes of riot and debauchery in that holy temple . . . [25] Amidst the sadness of the scene, there was a pleasing satisfaction in the hope that men capable of such atrocities, could not have the blessing of Heaven in the nefarious plan of subjugating our beloved country . . .

[25]The public was presented with many curious facts in relation to the condition of and proceedings in Boston many years ago.

Source: H. Niles, *Principles and Acts of the Revolution in America.* (Baltimore: Printed by W.O. Niles, 1822), 479–480.

PROCLAMATION of General Washington on Taking Possession of the Town of Boston, March 21, 1776[26]

By his excellency, George Washington, Esq., general and commander in chief of the thirteen united colonies. "Whereas the ministerial army[27] has abandoned the town of Boston, and the forces of the untied colonies, under my command, are in possession of the same: I have therefore thought it necessary for the preservation of peace, good order and the discipline, to publish the following orders, that no persons offending therein, may plead ignorance as an excuse for their misconduct." "All officers and soldiers are hereby ordered to live in the strictest amity with the inhabitants; and no inhabitant, or other person, employed in his lawful business in the town, is to be molested in his person or property, on any pretense whatever."[28]

[26]George Washington's proclamation is designed to promote an orderly transition from occupation to colonial government.

[27]He refers to the British Army.

[28]In light of the disorder and destruction that characterized the British withdrawal, Washington forbids his troops from taking vengeance on citizens who may have supported the Tory cause.

"If any officer or soldier shall presume to strike, imprison, or otherwise ill-treat any of the inhabitants, they may depend on being punished with the utmost severity; and if any officer or soldier shall receive any insult from any of the inhabitants, he is to seek redress in a legal way, and no other." "Any non-commissioned officer or soldier or others under my command, who shall be guilty of robbing or plundering in the town, are to be immediately confined, and will be most rigidly punished. All officers are therefore ordered to be very vigilant in the discovery of such offenders, and to report their names and crime to the commanding officer in the town as soon as may be."

"The inhabitants and others, are called upon to make known to the quarter-master-general, or any of his deputies, all stores belonging to the ministerial army, that may be remaining or secreted in the town: any person or persons whatever, that shall be known to have concealed any of the said stores, or to appropriate them to his or their own use, will be considered as an enemy to America, and treated accordingly."[29] "The select men and the magistrates of the town, are desired to return to the commander-in-chief, the names of all or any person or persons, they may suspect of being employed as spies upon the continental army, that they may be dealt with accordingly.

"All officers of the continental army, are enjoined to assist the civil magistrates in the execution of their duty, and to promote peace and good order. They are to prevent, as much as possible, the soldiers from frequenting tippling-houses,[30] and strolling from their posts. Particular notice will be taken of such officers as are inattentive and remiss in their duty; and on the contrary, such only as are active and vigilant will be entitled to future favor and promotion.

'Given under my hand, at head-quarters, in Cambridge, the 21st day of March, one thousand seven hundred and seventy-six.'

George Washington."
Boston, March 29.

Source: H. Niles, *Principles and Acts of the Revolution in America.* (Baltimore: Printed by W.O. Niles, 1822), 143.

[29]He forbids citizens taking advantage of "spoils of war" left behind by the redcoats and does all he can to promote domestic order and peace.

[30]A tippling-house was a place that sold liquor, often illegally.

The Battle for Long Island, Northern Manhattan, and White Plains

(1776)

INTRODUCTION

Fresh from the humiliation of the defeat at Boston, the British badly needed a triumph to balance the scales. It wasn't long in coming. August 1776 brought with it the opportunity for Howe's forces to reclaim their reputation with the might of the British Navy's guns supporting the activity of the redcoats and their mercenary German allies. Howe's troops made short work of Washington's Continentals encamped in Brooklyn. Not only were the Americans outnumbered two to one, but they were led into battle by a score of incompetent generals: Greene, who fell ill early in his command; Sullivan, whose vanity had led to several disasters; and Putnam, an officer distinguished by equal parts of courage and inexperience. The battles for Long Island, northern Manhattan, and White Plains ended in a series of defeats for Washington, who felt that the fate of the new nation hung in the balance. And so it seemed until Christmas night 1776, when Washington's successful attack at Trenton prepared the way for the eventual triumph at Saratoga and Yorktown that wrote finis to the history of the British Empire in America.

Colonel Miles Describes the Battle of Long Island[1]

On the landing of the British army on Long Island, I was ordered over with my rifle regiment to watch their motions . . . I will here state my position and conduct. I lay directly in front of the village of Flat Bush . . . where the Hessians were encamped. We were so near each other that the shells they sometimes fired went many rods beyond my camp. The main body of the enemy . . . lay about 2 miles to my left . . . There were several small bodies of Americans dispersed to my right, but not a man to my left, although the main body of the enemy lay to my left . . . This was our situation on the 26th of August.

About one o'clock at night Gen. Grant, on the right, and Gen. Howe, on my left, began their march, and by daylight Grant had got within a mile of our entrenchments . . . The Hessians[2] kept their

[1] Colonel Samuel Miles of the Pennsylvania militia was on the staff of General John Sullivan. His journal account of the Battle of Long Island is the most complete account of that action. It is distinguished by the detail of military technique and its lack of special pleading.

[2] "Hessians" is the term given to 18th-century German auxiliaries contracted for military service by the British government, who found it easier to borrow money to pay for their service than to recruit its own soldiers. They took their name from the German state of Hesse.

3The American Army was made up of three parts: (a) the Continentals established by the Second Continental Congress; (b) state militia "Commissions" who were considered inferior in command to the Continentals; (c) individual volunteers like the "minutemen" whose interest was local.

4In military terminology, baggage is any equipment that can be carried or hauled along.

5A grenadier was a specialized soldier responsible for the throwing of grenades and sometimes assault operations. Grenadiers were chosen from the strongest and largest soldiers and would often lead assaults in the field of battle.
6He interrogated him.

position until 7 in the morning. As soon as they moved the firing began . . . I immediately marched towards where firing was, but had not proceeded more than 1 or 200 yards until I was stopped by Colonel Wyllys, who told me that I could not pass on; that we were to defend a road that lead from Flatbush road to the Jamaica road. Col. Wyllys being a Continental, and I a State commission, he was considered a senior officer and I was obliged to submit;3 but I told him I was convinced the main body of the enemy would take the Jamaica road, that there was no probability of their coming along the road he was then guarding, and if he would not let me proceed to where the firing was, I would return and endeavor to get into the Jamaica road before Gen. Howe. To this he consented, and I immediately made a retrograde march, and after marching nearly two miles, the whole distance through woods, I arrived within sight of the Jamaica road, and to my great mortification I saw the main body of the enemy in full march between me and our lines, and the baggage guard4 just coming into the road.

A thought struck me of attacking the baggage guard, and if possible, to cut my way through them and proceed to Hell Gate to cross the Sound . . . I saw a grenadier5 stepping into the woods. I got a tree between him and me until he came near, and I took him prisoner and examined him.6 I found that there was a whole brigade with the baggage, commanded by a general officer. I immediately returned to the battalion and called a council of the officers and laid three propositions before them: 1st, to attack the baggage guard and . . . 2nd, to lay where we were until the whole had passed us . . . or, 3rd, to endeavor to force our way through the enemy's flank guards into our line at Brooklyn . . . The 3rd proposition was therefore adopted, and we immediately began our march, but had not proceeded more than half a mile until we fell in with a body of 7 or 800 light infantry, which we attacked without any hesitation, but their superiority of numbers encouraged them to march up with their bayonets, which we could not withstand, having none ourselves . . . We had proceeded but a short distance before we were again engaged with a superior body of the enemy, and here we lost a number of men, but took their commanding officer prisoner . . . Finding that the enemy had possession of the ground between us and our lines, and that it was impossible to cut our way through as a body, I directed the men to make the best of their way as well as they could; some few got in safe, but there were 159 taken prisoners. I was myself entirely cut off from our lines and therefore endeavored to conceal myself with a few men who would not leave me. I hoped to remain until night, when I intended to try to get to Hell Gate and cross the Sound, but about 3 o'clock in the afternoon was discovered by a party of Hessians and obliged to surrender. Thus ended the career of that day.

Source: Benson J. Lossing, *The American Historical Record*, Volume 2. (Philadelphia: Samuel P. Town, 1873), 115–117.

Extract of a Letter from an Officer in General Frazier's Battalion,[7] September 3, 1776

[7]General Frazier was a member of General Putnam's staff.

Rejoice, my friend, that we had given the Rebels a d—d [damn] crush. We landed on Long Island the 22 ult.,[8] without opposition. On the 27th we had a very warm action, in which the Scots regiments behaved with the greatest bravery and carried the day after an obstinate resistance on the Rebel side . . . The Hessians and our brave Highlanders gave no quarter; and it was a fine sight to see with what alacrity they dispatched the Rebels with their bayonets after we had surrounded them so that they could not resist. Multitudes were drowned and suffocated in morasses—a proper punishment for all Rebels . . . It was a glorious achievement my friend, and will immortalize us and crush Rebel colonies. Our loss was nothing.[9] We took care to tell the Hessians that the Rebels had resolved to give no quarter to them in particular, which made them fight desperately and put all to death that fell into their hands. You know all strategies are lawful in war, especially against such vile enemies to their King and country. The island is all ours, and we shall soon take New York, for the Rebels dare not look us in the face. I expect the affair will be over this campaign, and we shall all return covered with American laurels and have the cream of American lands allotted us for our services.

[8]Calendar reference meaning "of last month."

[9]This triumphant cry was ill-timed. On the night of August 26–27, the British successfully attacked the American position giving rise to jubilation. But when they decided to lay siege to Washington's army instead of pressing their advantage, this gave Washington the opportunity to withdraw to Manhattan and the chance to destroy the American force was missed.

Source: Peter Force, ed., *American Archives*, 5th Series, Volume 1. (Washington, DC: M. St. Clair Clarke and Peter Force, 1848), 1259–1260.

General Washington's Proclamation,[10] August 17, 1776

[10]When it became clear to Washington that the battle for Long Island and Manhattan was lost, he issued this order arranging for the evacuation of women, children, and the infirm, aided by his troops, to find safety in the Jerseys.

Whereas a bombardment and attack upon the city of New York by our cruel and inveterate enemy may be hourly expected; and as there are great numbers of women, children, and infirm persons yet remaining in the city,[11] whose continuance will rather be prejudicial than advantageous to the army, and their persons exposed to

[11]Even in defeat Washington never lost his concern for the innocent.

great danger and hazard: I do therefore recommend it to all persons, as they value their own safety and preservation, to remove with all expedition out of the said town at this critical period—trusting that with the blessing of heaven upon the American arms they may soon return to it in perfect security. And I do enjoin and require all the officers and soldiers in the army under my command, to forward and assist all such persons in their compliance with this recommendation,

Given under my hand, at head-quarters, New York, August 17, 1776.

George Washington.

Response of Convention.

In convention of the Representation of the State of New York, held at Harlem, Aug. 17, 1776.

Resolved, That the women and children, and infirm persons in the city of New York, be immediately removed from the said city, agreeable to General Washington's request of this house in his letter of this date.

Robert Benson, Secretary

Source: H. Niles, *Principles and Acts of the Revolution in America.* (Baltimore: Printed by W.O. Niles, 1822), 177.

The Battle of Trenton

(1776)

In the 18th century, it was standard military practice to move to winter quarters and wait to fight until spring. Washington, aware that the Hessian troops at Trenton would follow this routine, seized the opportunity to take the offensive and launch a surprise attack on the garrison on Christmas night 1776. Washington was in a desperate situation. Fresh from defeat at the battles in and around New York City, he had withdrawn his army to the relative safety of Pennsylvania. It was more than the weather and string of defeats that threatened him. Most of the troops under his command had enlisted for a period of service that expired on New Year's Day 1777. And the condition of that army was inferior to say the least. Colonel Rall, commander of the Hessians, described it as "naked, dying of cold, without blankets, and very poorly supplied with provisions." Rall's description was accurate—but he neglected to reckon with Washington's inspiring leadership. For, beaten down as they were, the Americans took courage from their Commander's example. Washington was famous for his personal contact with the troops. He was always in the thick of the fighting and was as much a father figure to the young men in his charge as he was a mentor and inspiration.

Washington divided his force into three groups. One crossed the Delaware River north of Trenton; the other two were to cross opposite and south of the city to prevent the Hessians' retreat. The winter weather was a barrier to the plan. It proved impossible for the southern force to move their arms across the ice-blanketed river. But the northern crossing was successful, and the Continentals attacked the Hessians. It was a total surprise. Rall was killed and the Hessians—1,000 strong—surrendered. The Americans lost five troops.

It was a victory that Washington badly needed. The Continental Army was now filled with a new spirit. The taste of victory, so long in coming, was now on every tongue. Cheers rang through the American camps and every three-cornered hat was in the air.

Intelligence by Samuel Brown,[1] December 22, 1776

Gen. Washingtons whole army does not consist of more than 8000 men, about 5000 of them Troops formerly enlisted . . . the rest are new raised Militia. That the time of enlistment of Ewing's brigade

[1] This intelligence report, which describes the poor conditions of Washington's army, buoyed the spirits of the British who, in spite of their recent victories in New York, were tiring of a conflict that dragged on and on.

of 600 men[2] all expire the first of Jan. next and that the officers and men and Gen. Ewing himself have declared they will serve no longer . . . than the Term of their Enlistment, which expires also the first of Jan'y next; that these troops compose the main Part of Washington's Army. Mr. Hovenden further says that there are four regiments or rather the remains of them, whose time expires the 1st of Jan'y and that he was informed by their principal officers that they would serve no longer out of their own Province.

Source: William Stryker, *The Battles of Trenton and Princeton.* (Boston: Houghton, Mifflin and Co., 1898), 337–338.

[3]Joseph Reed was an attorney who attained the rank of colonel in Washington's army. Reed was an intimate of the commander and one of the few people to whom Washington unburdened himself.

[4]This letter follows an extensive correspondence dating from November 1775 in which the general expresses his despair and discouragement with the conditions of raising and maintaining an army.

Colonel Joseph Reed to George Washington,[3]
December 22, 1776

We are all of opinion, my dear General, that something must be attempted to revive our expiring credit, give our cause some degree of reputation, and prevent a total depreciation of the Continental money, which is coming on very fast; that even a failure cannot be more fatal than to remain in our present situation;[4] in short, some enterprise must be undertaken in our present circumstances or we must give up the cause. In a little time the Continental Army will be dissolved. The militia must be taken before their spirits and patience are exhausted; and the scattered, divided state of the enemy affords us a fair opportunity to trying what our men will do when called to an offensive attack. Will it not be possible, my dear general, for your troops, or such part of them as can act with advantage, to make a diversion, or something more, at or about Trenton? . . .

[5]Later promoted to adjutant general, Reed did not hesitate to urge Washington to take strong action. Some sort of victory was needed to rescue the Continental cause.

[6]To "take benefit" means to retire.

Allow me to hope that you will consult your own good judgment and spirit . . . something must be attempted before the sixty days expire[5] . . . I am confident that unless some more favorable appearance attends out arms and cause before that time, a very large number of the militia officers here will follow the example of those of Jersey and take benefit from it.[6] I will not disguise my own sentiments, that our cause is desperate and hopeless if we do not take the opportunity of the collection of troops at present to strike some stroke. Our affairs are hastening fast to ruin if we do not retrieve them by some happy event. Delay with us is now equal to a total defeat . . . Pardon the freedom I have used. The love of my country, a wife and four children in the enemy's hands, the respect and attachment I have to you, the ruin and poverty that must attend me and thousands of others will plead my excuse for so much freedom.

Your obedient and affectionate humble servant
Joseph Reed

> **Source:** Jared Sparks, *The Writings of George Washington*, Volume 4. (Boston: Ferdinand Andrews, 1839), 543–544.

George Washington to Joseph Reed,[7] December 23, 1776

[7]This is Washington's response to Reed's letter.

The bearer is sent down . . . to inform you, that Christmas-day at night, one hour before day is the time fixed upon for our attempt on Trenton. For Heaven's sake keep this to yourself, as the discovery of it may prove fatal to us[8] . . . Attack as many of their posts as you possibly can with a prospect of success; the more we can attack at the same instant, the more confusion we shall spread and greater good will result from it . . . I have ordered our men to be provided with three days' provisions ready cooked, with which, and their blankets, they are to march: for if we are successful, which Heaven grant, and the circumstances favor, we may push on . . .

[8]It seems that Washington had already determined to attack even before he received Reed's communication.

> **Source:** Benson Lossing, *Life of Washington: A Biography*, Volume 2. (New York: Virtue and Company, 1860), 369.

Memoirs of Elisha Bostwick of the Seventh Connecticut Regiment[9]

[9]Elisha Bostnick was a private soldier in the Seventh Connecticut Regiment. He crossed the Delaware with Washington and left an extensive description of the action.

. . . [O]ur whole army was then set on motion and toward evening began to recross the Delaware but by obstruction of ice in the river did not all get across till quite late in the evening, and all the time a constant fall of snow with some rain, and finally our march began with the torches of our field pieces stuck in the exhalters.[10] [They] sparkled and blazed in the storm all night and about day light a halt was made, at which time his Excellency as he was coming on speaking to and encouraging the soldiers. The words he spoke as he passed by where I stood and in my hearing were these:

[10]These are braces used to stabilize something.

"Soldiers, keep by your officers. For God's sake, keep by your officers!" Spoke in a deep and solemn voice . . . We marched on and it was not long before we heard the out centries of the enemy both on the road we were in and the eastern road, and their out yards retreated firing, and our army, then with a quick step pushing on upon both roads, at the same time entered the town. Their artillery taken, they resigned with little opposition, about nine hundred all Hessians, with 4 brass field pieces . . . the next day recrossed the Delaware again and returned back to Trenton, and there on the first of January 1777 our years' service expired, and then by the pressing solicitation of his Excellency a part of those whose time was out consented on a ten dollar bounty to stay six weeks longer[11] . . .

Source: Nathan Hale Collection. General Collection, Beinecke Rare Book and Manuscript Library, Yale University.

[11]The success was twofold: a defeat of the Hessian troops and the agreement of the regiment to extend its term of service.

[12]Major General Henry Knox was an important ally of Washington from the earliest days of the war. It was he who supervised the transport of cannon from Ticonderoga to Dorchester, making Washington's siege of Boston possible. By trade a bookseller, his correspondence reflects a literary élan not typical of many contemporary accounts.

[13] An amazing feat, considering that many of the troops did not have boots, so they were forced to wear rags around their feet. Some of the men's feet bled, turning the snow to a dark red.

[14]Washington knew his men could not hold Trenton against British reinforcements, so he withdrew his troops back across the

Letter from Henry Knox to His Wife,[12] December 28, 1776

. . . Trenton is an open town . . . accessible all sides. Our army was scattered along the river for twenty-five miles. Our intelligence agreed that the force of the enemy in Trenton was from two to three thousand . . . that they were Hessians—no British troops . . . A part of the army . . . passed the river on Christmas night, with almost infinite difficulty, with eighteen field pieces. The floating ice in the river made the labor almost impossible. However, perseverance accomplished what at first seemed impossible . . . The night was cold and stormy; it hailed with great violence; the troops marched with the most profound silence and good order . . .[13] About half a mile from the town was an advanced guard on each road, consisting of a Captain's guard. These we forced and entered the town . . . and here succeeded a scene of war of which I had often conceived, but never saw before.

The hurry, fright and confusion of the enemy was [not] unlike that which will be when the last trump shall sound . . . During the contest in the streets measures were taken for putting an entire stop to their retreat by posting troops and cannon in such passes and roads as it was possible for them get away by. The poor fellows . . . saw themselves completely surrounded . . . The Hessians . . . were obliged to surrender upon the spot, with all their artillery, six brass pieces, army colors, etc. . . . The number of prisoners was above 1,200, including officers—all Hessians . . . After having marched off the prisoners and secured the cannon, stores, etc., we returned to the place, nine miles distant, where we had embarked.[14] Providence seemed to have smiled upon every part of this enterprise . . .

Source: F.S. Drake, *Life and Correspondence of Henry Knox.* (Boston: S.G. Drake, 1873), 36–37.

An Eyewitness Account of Trenton by an Officer on George Washington's Staff,[15] December 26, 1776

It was broad daylight when we came to a house where a man was chopping wood. . . "Can you tell me where the Hessian picket is?" Washington asked. The man hesitated, but I said, "You need not be frightened, it is General Washington who asked the question." His face brightened and he pointed toward the house of Mr. Howell. It was just 8 o'clock. Looking down the road I saw a Hessian running out from the house. He yelled in Dutch [German] and swung his arms. Three or four others came out with their guns. Two of them fired at us but the bullets whistled over our heads . . . twenty men . . . came running out of the house. The Captain flourished his sword and tried to form his men. Some of them fired at us, others ran towards the village. The next moment we heard drums beat and a bugle sound, and then from the west came the boom of a cannon. General Washington's face lighted up instantly, for he knew that it was one of Sullivan's guns. We could see a great commotion down toward the meeting-house, men running here and there, officers swinging their swords, artillery men harnessing their horses . . . Washington gave the order to advance . . . We saw Rall come riding up the street[16] . . . We could hear him shouting in Dutch, "My brave soldiers, advance." His men were frightened and confused, for our men were firing upon them from fences and houses and they were falling fast. Instead of advancing they ran into an apple orchard. The officers tried to rally them, but our men kept advancing and picking off the officers. It was not long before Rall tumbled from his horse and his soldiers threw down their guns[17] and gave themselves up as prisoners.

Source: Wm Stryker, *The Battles of Trenton.* (Princeton, Boston, New York: Houghton, Mifflin and Co., 1898), 362–363.

George Washington to Continental Congress, December 27, 1776[18]

Sir: I have the pleasure of Congratulating you upon the success of an enterprise which I had formed against a detachment of the

Delaware. However, on December 30, he crossed back into New Jersey with an army of 2,000.

[15]The Hessian forces had 22 killed in action, 83 wounded, and 896 captured. The Americans suffered only two deaths from bare feet causing frostbite and five wounded from battle, including a near-fatal bullet wound to future U.S. president James Monroe. Monroe recovered but carried the bullet in his shoulder for the rest of his life.

[16]Colonel Johann Rall was commander of the Hessian Garrison at Trenton. Rall was mortally wounded and died later that day at his headquarters.

[17]One of the Hessian troops provided this fitting epitaph. "Hier liegt der Oberst Rall, mit ihm ist alles all!" Here lies Colonel Rall, with him it's all over!

[18]Washington's concise report reflects his character. His text is, matter of fact, the voice of the professional soldier.

Enemy lying in Trenton, and which was executed yesterday Morning. The evening of the 25th I ordered the Troops . . . to parade back of McKinley's ferry, that they might begin to pass as soon as it grew dark . . . But the Quantity of Ice made that Night impeded the passage of the Boats so much, that it was three O'Clock before the Artillery could all get over, and near four, before the Troops took up their line of march. This made me despair of surprising the Town, as I well knew we could not reach it before the day was fairly broke . . . I determined to push on at all Events. I form'd my detachments into two divisions one to March by the lower . . . the other by the upper . . . road . . . I ordered each of them . . . to push directly into the town, that they might charge the Enemy before they had time to form. The upper Division arrived . . . exactly Eight O'Clock, and in three Minutes after, I found, from the fire on the lower Road that, that Division had also got up. The out Guards made but small Opposition . . . We presently saw their main Body formed, but from their Motions, they seemed undetermined how to act. Being hard pressed by our . . . Troops . . . they attempted to file off by a road on their right leading to Princetown, but perceiving their Intention, I threw a body of Troops in their Way which immediately checked them. Finding from our disposition that they were surrounded . . . they agreed to lay down their Arms . . . the Detachment of the Enemy consisted of the three Hessian Regiments . . . We found no Stores of any Consequence in the Town. In justice to the Officers and Men, I must add, that their Behavior upon this Occasion, reflects the highest honor upon them. The difficulty of passing the River in a very severe Night, and their march thro' a violent Storm of Snow and hail, did not in the least abate their Ardor. But when they came to the Charge, each seemed to vie with the other in pressing forward . . . [19]

[19]Only in his closing remarks does Washington allow himself emotion, and that in his praise for his troops.

Source: John C. Fitzpatrick, ed., *The Writings of George Washington from the Original Sources*, 1745–1799, Volume VI. (Washington, DC: U.S. Government Printing Office, 1932), 441–444.

The Skirmish of Sag Harbor

(1777)

INTRODUCTION

Since its first settlements in the 17th century, the eastern reaches of Long Island had known great prosperity. Large tracts of fertile land were diverted to agriculture and ranching, and the sea provided rich bounty to the fleets of whaling ships, which moored at the top of Long Island at Sag Harbor. As late as the end of the 19th century, Teddy Roosevelt maintained a farm at Oyster Bay, and when the war with Spain broke out in 1898, Teddy mustered his "Rough Riders" and set forth for Cuba from bays just west of Montauk Point. The area was of such strategic importance that George Washington himself directed that a huge lighthouse be erected at the point—an installation that is still active today.

Nathan Jennings, who was born and raised on the East End, went to school in a building that the British later commandeered as a guard house. In his application for a veteran pension under the congressional resolution of 1818, Jennings submitted this account of the daring maneuver, an exploit now unfairly forgotten and overshadowed by the great triumphs at Saratoga and Yorktown.

I . . . was born in . . . Southhampton . . . I was drafted in the militia . . . for the term of six months; then was ordered to march to Montauk Point on the very end of Long Island to prevent the British from taking off cattle and sheep,[1] as part of their fleet then lay in Gardiner's Bay, within three-quarters of a mile of Long Island shore . . .

[1] During the revolution, the livestock and produce of the island were a rich bounty for whichever army could take charge of them.

A very short time after, I was recommended to . . . take command of three whaleboats with ten men each to pilot them to Sag Harbor, and in Southold Sound to take vessels and boats that was found guilty of supplying the British with wood and any kind of stores.[2] We soon captured three vessels loaded with flour and wood . . .

[2] The whaling fleet and its catch were a source of wealth to those who could control it.

I . . . volunteered myself to Colonel Meigs, stating the situation of Sag Harbor and the strength of the British guard and how easy they might be taken, and that I would pilot him and a detachment of troops across the sound to Long Island and carry our boats across

[3]A fervent patriot, Jennings conceived a plan to deny the British the rich stores of the area and to destroy the whaling fleet. He lay his plan before Washington, who delighted in the opportunity to achieve the victory in New York so long denied him.

[4]The revolution was fought and won not just on the grand battlefields of the war, but in the small skirmishes. Sag Harbor is an example of a skirmish that provided the underpinning for the great triumphs that history remembers. The May 23, 1777, raid netted 6 killed, 12 ships burned, and 90 taken prisoner, without the loss of a man on the American side.

Oysterpond Branch . . . into Southold Bay. Then we could land and come on the back of the guard. The colonel was highly pleased with my plan. Then Colonel Meigs showed it to His Excellency George Washington. Then the general sent for me to come to headquarters with Colonel Meigs. Then, after asking me many questions, he was highly pleased with my conversation and plan.[3]

The next day . . . The orders was . . . that about 110 men of good oarsmen to volunteer themselves to go on a private expedition, and when the word march was given there was upwards of 300 men stepped four paces in front in less than three minutes, and, after Colonel Meigs had picked out 110 men, the rest fell back in the ranks. At the same time, there was a number of whaleboat[s] lying at the Long Wharf at New Haven. Then we crossed over the sound to Long Island, carried our boats across the beach into Southold Bay, crossed the bay, landed just before daylight on Joseph's Island, and carried our boats into a thicket of red cedars. There lay all day. The next night, I conducted the boats within about two miles and a half of Sag Harbor, on the back of the guardhouse. The guard was kept in a schoolhouse where I had gone to school. After landed, we left a few men to keep our boats afloat. Then I conducted our detachment a back way across fields and through thick brush until we came in sight of the guardhouse. We kept under the side of a thick swamp within about fifty yards of the two sentries. We immediately surrounded the guard and sentries and took all except one sentry that made his escape through a piece of marsh. Then we left a guard with our prisoners and marched down about two hundred yards . . .

Then we marched about one [hundred] yards to their barracks. We made prisoners of all that was there. Then we went on the Long Wharf. There we took more prisoners and burnt twelve brigs and schooners, a quantity of hay and corn. Then the British was playing on us with grapeshot. Then we returned back to our boats with ninety prisoners the same way to the Oyster Point beach, carried our boats across the beach, then put our prisoners on board of two small vessels and guarded them across the sound to Black Rock, and from there we marched our prisoners to New Haven without the loss of a man.[4]

There was not a man in the attachment that ever had been on Long Island except myself and one man who said that about twenty years ago he was ashore about two hours. And, in a few days after, we guarded our prisoners from New Haven to Hartford prison up Connecticut River, then returned back to New Haven. There I fell in with two young men that was looking for me. We had been schoolboys together. They had made their escape from Sag Harbor in a boat. They told me not to venture over there no more, for the Tories and the British swore that if they could . . . get ahold of me, they swore they would put me to death without judge or jury . . .

Source: Nathan B. Jennings, *Pension Application.* Revolutionary War Pension and Bounty-Land Warrant Application Files, Record Group 15, Pension No. R. 5577, National Archives.

The Battles of Brandywine, Valley Forge, and the Paoli Massacre

(1777–1778)

INTRODUCTION

Though Washington's army had tasted victory at Trenton and known occasional bright events such as Sag Harbor, the fall and winter of 1777 were to prove a time of testing and bitter, bloody defeat.

Yet at the same time, to the north at Saratoga the Continentals achieved a signal victory—one which resulted in the decision of the French to come to the aid of the Americans and thus tip the scales in their favor. The year 1777 was one in which the fickle fortunes of war seemed to be playing with the American efforts: defeat in the central colonies, victory in the North. It was a mixed bag of events; despair and hope mingled in the minds of both armies and no one at this point could be certain that the Gods of War were on their side. Sudden, unpredictable change seemed to be the only realistic assessment of the situation.

The British badly needed a victory, and General Howe determined to occupy Philadelphia. He sailed from New York to Chesapeake Bay and prepared to march on the city. Washington placed his forces between Howe and the city, and the two armies met at Brandywine Creek. The British outmaneuvered the Americans and quickly occupied the city. Then Washington attacked the redcoats at Germantown, north of Philadelphia, but bad weather and fog resulted in confusion in the Continental ranks. The Americans fired on one another and were forced to retreat to Valley Forge, barefoot, bloodied, and beaten. This double defeat horribly concluded with a massacre of Anthony Wayne's troops at Paoli. It was only news of victory at Saratoga that rescued the patriot cause from psychological disaster.

The winters of 1777 and 1778 were extremely severe, and the men short of provisions. Soldiers deserted in great numbers as hardships at camp overcame their motivation and dedication to fight. Some 2,000 soldiers died by the end of the winter of disease, malnutrition, and exposure to freezing temperatures. Log huts had been built as shelters, but they were damp and crowded. Washington repeatedly appealed to Congress to provide more relief. Finally, on January 24, 1778, five Congressmen came to Valley Forge to examine the conditions of the Continental Army. Washington was quite frank that things needed to change; something needed to be done. Washington also informed them that he wanted Congress to take control of the army supply system, pay for the supplies, and replenish them when necessities were scarce. By the end of February, there were adequate supplies flowing throughout camp after Congress gave full support to monetarily funding the supply lines of the army, along with reorganizing the commissioner department (which controlled the gathering of the supplies for the army).

Journal of Colonel Timothy Pickering of Massachusetts,[1] September 11, 1777

This morning a cannonade took place, the enemy having advanced to the heights opposite to those occupied by us, on the other side of the ford.[2] A hot skirmish took place between our light troops under Maxwell, and a party of Hessians, in which the latter were chiefly killed and wounded, not thirty running away . . . three hundred of them were killed and wounded. The enemy made no attempt to cross at this place. The cannonade was mutual, theirs did us no harm, save killing one man.

The enemy remaining paraded on the distant heights . . . indicated me to think they did not intend to cross at Chad's Ford, but only to amuse us while their main army crossed at some other place. The event proved the conjecture right. The enemy's main body crossed the Brandywine six or eight miles above on our right. The General had intelligence of this by some messengers but it was contradicted by other;[3] and, the information remaining a long time surprisingly uncertain, it was late before a disposition was made to receive the enemy on that quarter. The consequence was that the divisions first engaged, being too far distant to be supported by others, were repulsed; and this laid the foundation for a final defeat . . . The whole army this night retired to Chester. It was fortunate for us that the night came on, for under its cover the fatigued stragglers and some wounded made their escape.

Source: O. Pickering, *The Life of Timothy Pickering.* (Boston: Little, Brown and Co., 1867), 154–155.

George Washington to the President of Congress,[4] Midnight, September 11, 1777

Sir: I am sorry to inform you that in today's engagement we have been obliged to leave the enemy masters of the field. Unfortunately the intelligence received of the enemy's advancing up the

[1]Pickering, a brave soldier in the Continental cause, was Washington's adjutant general during the Battle of Brandywine.

[2]A ford is a shallow place with good footing where a river or stream may be crossed by wading.

[3]Pickering thought that staff problems, like this failure to gather correct information, was the reason for the loss at Brandywine.

[4] Washington's report on the defeat at Brandywine is important because it contains the earliest account of the activities of the Marquis De Lafayette.

[5] A disposition is a decision to deploy troops.

[6] The Marquis de Lafayette was a French aristocrat who, at 19 years of age, set sail for America and fought for the United States in the revolution. He and George Washington remained close friends for the rest of their lives. He was also friends with Alexander Hamilton and Thomas Jefferson. Lafayette was a key figure in the French Revolution of 1789 and the July Revolution of 1830. For his accomplishments in the service of both France and the United States, he is sometimes known as "the Hero of the Two Worlds."

Brandywine, and crossing at a ford about six mile above us, was uncertain and contradictory, notwithstanding all my plans to get the best. This prevented my making a disposition,[5] adequate to the force with which the Enemy attacked us on the right; in consequence of which the troops first engaged, were obliged to return before they could be reinforced . . . But though we fought under many disadvantages, and were from the causes above mentioned obliged to retire, yet our loss of men is not, I am persuaded, very considerable: I believe much less than the enemy's. We have also lost about seven or eight pieces of cannon . . .

Notwithstanding the misfortune of the day, I am happy to find the troops in good spirits; and I hope another time we shall compensate for the losses now sustained. The Marquis La Fayette was wounded in the leg[6] . . . other Officers were wounded and some slain . . .

Source: J.C. Fitzpatrick, *The Writings of George Washington*, Volume IX. (Washington, DC: U.S. Govt. Printing Office, 1939), 207–208.

[7] The history of General John Sullivan's career is one of a combination of poor talent and worse luck. This letter from Thomas Burke, member of the Congress from North Carolina, is almost the last straw.

Thomas Burke to General Sullivan,[7] October 12, 1777

I was present at the action of Brandywine and saw and heard enough to convince me that the fortune of the day was injured by miscarriages where you commanded . . . I heard officers in the field lamenting in the bitterest terms that they were cursed with such a commander and I overheard numbers during the retreat complain of you as an officer whose evil conduct was forever productive of misfortunes to the army. From these facts I concluded that your duty as a general was not well performed[8] . . . I also concluded that the troops under your command had no confidence in your conduct, and from the many accounts I had officially received of your miscarriages, I conceived, and am still possessed of an opinion, that you have not sufficient talents for your rank and office, tho' I believe you have strong disposition to discharge your duty well.

[8] Although Sullivan was no inspiring leader, his weakness at Brandywine led to a call for his replacement. But Washington was also active there, and his operation was far from distinguished. At this point it seems that Sullivan is being made a scapegoat for the general debacle.

I consider it as one essential part of my duty to attend to the appointments of the army, and where I perceive that any person so unqualified as I deem you to be has got into a command where incompetence may be productive of disasters and disgrace, it is my duty to endeavor at removing him. In discharge of this I gave to Congress all of the information I was able, carefully distinguishing what I saw, what I heard, and from whom . . . I urged your recall with all the force I could, and thought it, and still do think it, necessary for the public good because, in all your enterprises and in every part of your conduct . . . you seem to be void of judgment and foresight in concerting, of deliberate vigor in executing, and of presence of mind under accidents and emergencies; and from these defects seem to me to arise your repeated ill success . . .

I should have had great pleasure in justly forming a better opinion of you, but no reason can induce me to overlook the defects of officers on whom so much depends. Nor will any thing deter me from pursuing the measures suggested by my own judgment . . . My objection to you is want of sufficient talents, and I consider it as your misfortune, not fault.[9] It is my duty, as far as I can, to prevent its being the misfortunes of my country.

Source: O.G. Hammond, *Letters and Papers of Major-General John Sullivan*, Volume 1. (New Hampshire: New Hampshire Historical Society, 1930), 534–536.

[9]Sullivan was not relieved of command and was active in the battles of Rhode Island. In command of 4,000 troops, he was particularly successful in campaigns against the Indian Nations in New York State.

General John Armstrong to General Gates,[10] October 9, 1777

[10]General John Armstrong was commander of the militia of Brandywine, and an aide to General Horatio Gates, commander of Continental forces under Washington.

. . . On the fourth instant General Washington attacked the enemy, marching his troops by various routes about fifteen miles the preceding night. The British troops were encamped chiefly at Germantown . . . the surprise was not total but partial.

At the head of Germantown the continental troops attacked with vigour, and drove the British who frequently rallied and were drove again and again about the space of two miles, when some unhappy spirit of infatuation seized our troops . . . whereby they began to retreat and fled in wild disorder unknown to the General,[11] that is, without his orders and beyond his power to prevent. So that a victory, a glorious victory fought for and eight-tenths won, was shamefully but mysteriously lost, for no one to this moment can or at least will give any good reason for the flight. The conjectures are these, the morning was foggy and so far unfavorable. It is said ours took the manoeuvres of part of our own people, for large reinforcements of the enemy, and thereby took fright at themselves or at one another. Some unhappy officer is said to have called out *we are surrounded, we are surrounded*. . . . every intelligence from town assures us that the continental troops in the morning gave the enemy a severe drubbing . . . the triumphant torys again struck to the centre, and the

[11]The confusion of battle was typical of the war at this period and mutiny of the troops, who were poorly clothed and fed and had not been paid for months, was understandable.

drooping spirits of the whigs again relieved.[12] Thus God supports our otherwise sinking spirits, which were also animated by your northern success.

Source: James Wilkinson, *Memoirs of My Own Times*, Volume 1. (Philadelphia: Abraham Small, 1816), 353–355.

[12]During the American Revolution, Whigs were supporters of the war against England while a Tory, or Loyalist, described an American who favored the British side.

Lieutenant William Barton to His Father from Valley Forge,[13] November 22, 1777

[13]The encampment at Valley Forge has become a symbol of the determination and courage that eventually led to victory for the American forces. Washington's inspiring leadership pulled the army together and by March events had turned a corner. These letters allow us to hear the voice of a line soldier—a personal picture of courage and suffering.

[14] Half-naked and facing starvation and bitter cold, the troops refused to mutiny.

. . . "Camp Valley Forge, Feb Eighteenth 1778 . . . I should wrote oftener but have been in expectation of Coming home but this day find my expectations blasted and have no manner of hope to get home Until April . . . I have Received my Coat and boots[14] by Capt. Weycoff and am Inform'd you have procured me some shirts which I am Extremely Glad of as I Shall be in great need of them in a short time . . . I have not Receiv'd a Letter from you since at home, should be very Glad to be favored with a few lines if Convenient and Likewise a few pounds of Sugar and A little Chocolate . . . there is a Scarcity of those articles in this Place . . . Camp does not very well agree with me . . ."

[15] This letter was written by Barton's friend, Lieutenant John Blair, as Barton was in dire straits.

Valley Forge 24th Febry. 1778 . . .[15] By request of your Son Wm. Barton I embrace the opportunity of Informing that he is very unwell these ten Days and no appearance of getting any better, and is very Desirous that you would send a Wagon or Chease for him as he is too weak to Ride a horseback, he likewise beggs that you would appeal to Colo. Brearely to Write to Major Cumming to give him leave to go home as Genl. Orders is very strict against any Officer leaving Camp . . .

Source: *Letters Home from a Valley Forge Soldier.* Available online at http://www.americanrevolution .org/vlyfrgeltrs.php.

A Letter to Doctor Samuel Mather from Ezra Selden,[16] Valley Forge, May 15, 1778

[16]This letter from Captain Seldon gives us an eyewitness account of Baron von Steuben's training.

[17]Baron Frederick von Steuben, a Prussian veteran of the army of Frederick the Great, tipped the scales in favor of the Americans at Valley Forge. An unrelenting master of tactics, he whipped the Continentals into shape and set the stage for victories to come.

. . . Our Army is at present very busy and intent upon a New mode of Exercise Pointed by Major General Baron Stuben from Prussia.[17] His knowledge in discipline is very great, his method of maneuvering is very Difficult; but mostly satisfactory, he never infers what is to be Done in future; but gives Lessons and we Practice until he gives us new Directions; he allows no music while we are maneuvering . . . at the word march to step right off and always with the left foot. Our manual Exercise as yet continues the same—excepting in the Charging the Bayonet . . . Our encampment is strongly fortified and Picqueted, I have no suspicions that we shall be attacked in Quarters.

This is a very Different spirit in the Army to what there was when I left it,[18] the Troops considerably well clothed . . . I am content should they remove almost any General Except his Excellency . . . even Congress are not aware of the Confidence the Army Places in him or motions would never have been made for Gates to take the Command . . .

[18]Seldon had been captured by the British at the Battle of Kip's Bay, had made his escape, and rejoined Washington's army. He was later promoted to colonel.

Source: *Letters Home from a Valley Forge Soldier.* Available online at http://www.americanrevolution .org/vlyfrgeltrs.php.

William Hutchinson Describes the Paoli Massacre,[19] September 21, 1777

. . . The second morning after the Paoli Massacre . . . a circumstance took place which the declarant asks permission to relate . . . A Quaker, a stranger, came to our quarters and brought with him a man which he said he had found lying in the woods whose clothes, coat, vest, and trousers were stiff with gore. And declarant believes they would have stood alone when taken off him. He was a Virginian and had shared in the consequences of the massacre; had been singled out at the close thereof as a special subject for the exercise of the savage cruelty of the British soldiers. He told us that more than a dozen soldiers had with fixed bayonets[20] formed a cordon round him, and that every one of them in sport had indulged their brutal ferocity by stabbing him in different parts of his body and limbs, and that by a last desperate effort, he got without their circle and fled. And as he rushed out, one of the soldiers struck at him to knock him down as the finis to the catastrophe, in which only the front of the bayonet reached his head and laid it on with a gash as if it had been cut with a knife. He made, however, his escape, and when brought to our captain, he had laid in the woods twenty-four hours. He had neither hat, shoes, nor stockings, and his legs and feet were covered with mud and sand which had been fastened to his skin by mixing with his own blood as it ran down his limbs.

[19]Wayne's Troops were surprised by General Grey's forces. At General Grey's direction, the flints, hard pieces of stone used to ignite the firing of flintlock weapon, had been removed from his men's muskets to ensure that no shots gave warning to the Americans. The attack was to be at the point of the bayonet. General Grey thereby acquired the nickname of "No flints" Grey.

[20]Soldiers were bayoneted without mercy. Several hundred were wounded.

Our captain immediately dispatched his lieutenant for a physician, who, when he returned, was so fortunate as to bring two with him. We then procured the means of washing and cleansing the wounded man, and upon examining him there was found, as our captain afterwards announced to the men, forty-six distinct bayonet wounds in different parts of his body, wither of which were deep and sufficiently large to have been fatal if they had been in vital parts. But they were mostly flesh wounds, and every one of them had bled profusely, and many of them commenced bleeding again upon being washed. His wounds were dressed, his bloody garments were burned, and by orders of our captain, he was waited upon with strict attention until he was able to walk, and then was by Lieutenant Corry (our lieutenant) taken somewhere not distant to an hospital . . .

I had occasion to enter . . . the hospital in which the wounded were dressing and where the necessary surgical operations were performing and there beheld a most horrid sight. The floor was covered with human blood; amputated arms and legs lay in different places in appalling array, the mournful memorials of an unfortunate and fatal battle, which indeed it truly was.[21] From Germantown we were marched by White Marsh to Chestnut Hill and in eight or ten days afterwards were discharged after having served two months and one week . . .

[21]Major General Grey was a fierce competitor, known for his "Take no prisoners" attitude. Major General Anthony Wayne, also known as "Mad Anthony," earned the nickname from his military exploits and fiery personality.

Source: William Hutchinson, *Pension Application.* Revolutionary War Pension and Bounty-Land Warrant Application Files, Record Group 15, Pension No. W. 10133, National Archives.

The Battle of Monmouth

(1778)

Under Washington's watchful eye, Baron von Steuben had succeeded in transforming the Continentals from a disorganized collection of enthusiastic but inexperienced patriots into a disciplined fighting machine. In June 1778, word came to headquarters at Valley Forge that the British were planning to abandon Philadelphia and march to reinforce their garrison at New York. This maneuver would entail a march across New Jersey. The American commanders were divided on what action to take. General Lee opposed an attack on the retreating British. Alexander Hamilton (Washington's aide de camp) and General Green favored an aggressive movement. The Marquis de Lafayette also favored action and was given the command responsibility, but shortly Lee once again asserted his authority. Washington thought he had settled the matter and ordered a military strike at Monmouth Court House. But when the commander in chief moved to the scene of action, he was outraged to find that Lee had ordered a retreat. Lee was court martialed, relieved of command, and removed from the American Army. Washington took command and on June 28, 1778, 26,000 soldiers fought the battle. The day was excruciatingly hot. As one soldier reported "The sun shone full upon the field . . . the mouth of a heated oven seemed to me but a trifle hotter than this ploughed field; it was almost impossible to breathe."

The result of the battle was a draw. The British successfully reached New York, ending the last significant battle of the revolution in the North. The British now adopted a southern strategy, hoping to find more loyalist sympathy in Virginia and the Carolinas, and thus to defeat the rebellion by splitting the rebels while maintaining control of New York. The first move was to capture a major southern port, Savannah. This was accomplished by the new year. The British then successfully moved against Charleston. By May, the British controlled Georgia and South Carolina. Although the Americans raised a second army in 1780, it was defeated at the Battle of Camden, a disaster for the patriot cause. The new year brought new hope. General Green led new offensives at King's Mountain, Cowpens, and Guilford Courthouse. These engagements brought a new courage and hope to the patriot cause, and although neither side proved victorious, these battles proved that the Americans were still a force to be reckoned with in the South.

Memoirs of the Marquis de Lafayette[1]

[1] The Marquis de Lafayette helped the American cause. A favorite of Washington, he became a major general and persuaded France to send military aid to the Continental Army. He was wounded at Brandywine and fought at Monmouth, Rhode Island, and Yorktown. He also helped negotiate the Treaty of Paris that ended the American Revolution.

On the 17th of June, [1778], Philadelphia was evacuated . . . the army marched, in two columns, each consisting of seven thousand men . . . towards New York. The army of the United States, which was of nearly equal force, directed itself from Valley Forge to Coryell's Ferry . . . it was thus left at the option of the Americans, either to follow on their track or to repair to White Plains. In a council held on the subject, Lee very eloquently endeavored to prove that . . . every thing ought not to be placed at hazard; that the English army had never been so excellent and so well disciplined; he declared himself to be for White Plains . . . M. de Lafayette, placed on the other side, spoke late, and asserted that it would be disgraceful for the chiefs, and humiliating for the troops, to allow the enemy to traverse the Jerseys tranquilly; that, without running any improper risk, the rear guard might be attacked; that it was necessary to follow the English . . . and . . . seize the most favourable opportunities and situations. This advice was approved by many of the council . . . The majority were, however, in favor of Lee; but M. de Lafayette spoke again to the general on this subject in the evening, and was seconded by Hamilton, and by Greene . . .

Several of the general officers changed their opinion; and the troops having already begun their march, were halted in order to form a detachment. When united, there were 3,000 continentalists and 1,200 militia; the command fell to the share of Lee, but, by the express desire of the general, M.de Lafayette succeeded in obtaining it. Everything was going on extremely well, when Lee changed his mind and chose to command the troops himself; having again yielded this point, he rechanged once more . . . The enemy, unfortunately, continued their march . . . The two columns of the English army had united together at Monmouth Courthouse, from whence they departed on the morning of the 28th.

Source: *Memoirs, Correspondence, and Manuscripts of General Lafayette, Published by His Family,* Volume I. (New York: Saunders and Otley, 1837), 50–52.

Testimony at the Court Martial of General Lee[2]

[2] This is the testimony of Lieutenant Colonel Richard Harrison of the Continental Army.

[3] General Washington's.

On the 28th of June, as one of His Excellency's[3] suite, I marched with him till we passed the Meetinghouse near Monmouth . . . When we came to where the roads forked, His Excellency made a halt for a few minutes, in order to direct a disposition of the army. The wing under General Greene was then ordered to go to the right to prevent the enemy's turning our right flank. After order was given in this matter, and His Excellency was proceeding down the road, we met a fifer, who appeared to be a good deal frighted. The General asked him whether he was a soldier belonging to the army, and the cause of his returning that way; he answered that he was a soldier, and that the Continental troops that had been advanced were retreating. On this answer the General seemed to be exceedingly surprised, and rather more exasperated, appearing to discredit the account, and threatened the man, if he mentioned a thing of the sort, he would have him whipped . . . We then moved a few paces forward . . . where we met two or three persons more on that road; one was, I think, in the habit of a soldier. General asked them from whence they came, and whether they belonged to the army; one of them replied that he did, and that all the troops that had been advanced, the whole of them, were retreating . . . I offered my services to the General to go forward and to bring him a true account of the situation . . . The next officer was Lieutenant-Colonel William Smith. I addressed myself to Colonel Smith and asked him what was the cause of the troops retreating, as I had come to gain information, who replied that he could not tell, that they had lost but one man[4] . . . I . . . galloped down the line to meet General Washington, to report to him the state of our troops and the progress of the enemy . . . adding that the enemy was pressing hard and would soon be upon him in a march of fifteen minutes . . . We remained there a few minutes until the extreme rear of our troops got up.

[4]Despite the war council's decision to attack the British withdrawal to New York, Lee, on his own authority, countermanded the decision. He was court-martialed, suspended from command for one year, and then dropped from the army.

Source: *Proceedings of a General Court-Martial . . . for the Trial of Major-General Lee.* (New York: Privately Reprinted, 1864), 82–86.

Narrative Attributed to James Sullivan Martin[5]

After all things were put in order, we marched, but halted a few minutes in the village, where we were joined by a few other troops and then proceeded on . . . we received orders to retreat, as all the left wing of the army[6] were retreating. Grating as this order was to our feelings, we were obliged to comply. We had not retreated far before we came to a . . . muddy sloughy brook; while the artillery were passing this place, we sat down by the road side; in a few minutes the Commander-in-chief and suit crossed the road just where we were sitting. I heard him ask our officers, "by whose order the troops

[5]Martin was a private soldier from Connecticut in the Continental Army. Later promoted to Sergeant, his "narratives" give us a vibrant picture of life in the Continental Army.

[6]Under the command of General Lee.

were retreating," and being answered, "by General Lee's," he said something, but as he was moving forward all the time this was passing, he was too far off for me to hear it distinctly; those that were nearer to him said that his words were "Damn him"; whether he did thus express himself or not I do not know; it was certainly very unlike him, but he seemed at the instant to be in a great passion; his looks if not his words seemed to indicate as much . . .

Source: Joseph Plumb Martin, *A Narrative of Some of the Adventures, Dangers, and Sufferings of a Revolutionary Soldier.* (Hallowell, ME: Glazier, Masters & Co., 1830), 92–93.

A Letter to John Jay from Alexander Hamilton on the Emancipation of Black Troops, Middlebrook, New Jersey, March 14, 1779[7]

[7]Alexander Hamilton's contributions to the revolution and the establishment of the American republic cannot be overestimated. He served as Washington's aide-de-camp at the Battle of Monmouth, as a member of the Continental Congress, as an author of the *Federalist Papers* that promoted support for the Constitution, and as first secretary of the Treasury in Washington's cabinet. No one did more for the cause than perhaps Washington himself. Here, in a letter to John Jay, first chief justice of the Supreme Court, Hamilton advocates emancipation and equal treatment of blacks, 84 years before Lincoln.

Dear Sir,

Col. Laurens, who will have the honor of delivering you this letter, is on his way to South Carolina, on a project, which I think, in the present situation of affairs there, is a very good one and deserves every kind of support and encouragement. This is to raise two, three or four battalions of negroes; with the assistance of the government of that state . . . He wishes to have recommended by Congress to the state, and, as an inducement, that they would engage to take those battalions into Continental pay. It appears to me, that an expedient of this kind, in the present state of southern affairs, is the most rational, that can be adopted, and promises very important advantages. Indeed, I hardly see how a sufficient force can be collected in that quarter without it . . . I have not the least doubt, that the negroes will make very excellent soldiers, with proper management . . . It is a maxim with some great military judges, that with sensible officers soldiers can hardly be too stupid . . . I mention this, because I frequently hear it objected to the scheme of embodying negroes that they are too stupid to make soldiers. This is so far from appearing to me a valid objection that I think their want of cultivation (for their natural faculties are probably as good as ours) joined to that habit of subordination which they acquire from a life of servitude, will make them sooner became soldiers than our White inhabitants. Let officers be men of sense and sentiment and the nearer the soldiers approach to machines perhaps the better.

I foresee that this project will have to combat much opposition from prejudice and self-interest. The contempt we have been taught to entertain for the blacks, makes us fancy many things that are founded neither in reason nor experience; and . . . it should be considered, that if we do not make use of them in this way, the enemy probably will; and that the best way to counteract the temptations they will hold out will be to offer them ourselves. An essential part of the plan is to give them their freedom with their muskets. This will secure their fidelity, animate their courage, and I believe will have a good influence upon those who remain, by opening a door to their emancipation. This circumstance, I confess, has no small weight in inducing me to wish the success of the project; for the dictates of humanity and true policy equally interest me in favor of this unfortunate class of men . . . With the truest respect and esteem I am Sir Your most Obed servant

Alex Hamilton
Want of time to copy it, will apologize for sending this letter in its present state.
Head Quarters March 14th. 79

Book: John C. Hamilton, *The Life of Alexander Hamilton*, Volume 1. (London: O. Rich, 1834), 231–234.

The Battle of Saratoga

(1777)

The victory of the Americans at Saratoga marks the turning point of the revolution for two reasons: it demonstrated decisively the weakness of the British strategy that planned to defeat the Continentals in the North and forced the British to adopt a southern strategy that eventually failed at Yorktown; and it persuaded the French that the Americans might win and therefore that supporting the rebel cause was in their best interests. When the French entered the conflict, the British were forced to realign their land and sea power in defense of an empire that stretched from the Caribbean to the Far East. The result was that the forces available to face the Americans were seriously reduced.

General John Burgoyne had recaptured Fort Ticonderoga for the British and now moved his army south to Saratoga. The Continental Congress had recently appointed the popular General Horatio Gates to the northern command, and hundreds of patriots now flocked to join his force. Gates set up fortifications at Freeman's Farm near Saratoga on September 19, 1777. The British attacked but were stymied by the patriot defense. Only nightfall spared the British a serious loss. Although greatly outnumbered, Burgoyne returned to the attack on October 7, but the Americans won the second battle of Freeman's Farm.

Burgoyne held a council of war and planned a retreat, but this proved impossible. The Americans had surrounded his troops and Burgoyne surrendered. The Americans had lost only 450 men; the British had 1,200 killed and 6,000 wounded.

For pure eloquence and delicious sarcasm, nothing in the documents of the American Revolution approached the exchange of proclamations that preceded the fighting at Saratoga. Burgoyne issued his evaluation of the situation and made an offer of peace to any who would desert the rebellion and swear fealty to king and country. The Continentals' response is a biting rebuttal to the mighty general. It flings his own words back in his face. The two statements mirror the frame of mind of the adversaries on the eve of battle: unbridled arrogance versus courageous confidence.

[1]"Gentleman Johnny" Burgoyne is one of the most fascinating characters to play on the revolutionary stage, so much so that G. B. Shaw made him a leading figure of his comedy *The Devil's Disciple*. Burgoyne first

Proclamation by John Burgoyne[1]

Proclamation by John Burgoyne Esq., Lieutenant General of His Majesty's Armies in America, Colonel of the Queen's Regiment of Light Dragoons, Governor of Fort William in North Britain, One of the Representatives of the Commons of Great Britain, and Commanding an Army and Fleet Employed on an Expedition from Canada, Etc., Etc.,

The forces entrusted to my command, are designed to act in concert, and upon a common principle, with the numerous armies and fleets which already display in every quarter of America, the power, the justice, and, when properly sought, the mercy of the King. The cause in which the British arms is thus exerted, applies to the most affecting interests of the human heart; and the military servants of the crown, at first called forth for sole purpose of restoring the rights of the constitution,[2] now combine with love of their country, and duty to their sovereign . . . To the eyes and ears of the temperate part of the public, and the breasts of suffering thousands in the provinces, be the melancholy appeal, whether the present unnatural rebellion has not been made a foundation for the completest system of tyranny that ever God, in his displeasure, suffered for a time to be exercised over a froward[3] and stubborn generation. Arbitrary imprisonment, confiscation of property, persecution, and torture, unprecedented in the inquisition of the Romish church, are among the palpable enormities[4] that verify the affirmative. These are inflicted, by assemblies and committees, who dare to profess themselves friends to liberty, upon the most quiet subjects, without distinction of age or sex, for the sole crime, often for the sole suspicion, of having adhered in principle to the government under which they were born, and to which, by every tie, divine and human, they owe allegiance. To consummate these shocking proceedings, the profanation of religion is added to the most profligate prostitution of common reason,[5] the consciences of men are set at nought; and multitudes are compelled not only to bear arms, but also to swear subjection to an usurpation[6] they abhor.

Animated by these considerations, at the head of troops in the full powers of health, discipline, and valor, determined to strike where necessary, and anxious to spare where possible, I, by these presents, invite and exhort all persons, in all places where the progress of this army may point, and by the blessings of God I will extend it far, to maintain such a conduct as may justify me in protecting their lands, habitations, and families. The intention of this address is to hold forth security, not depredation to the country. To those, whom spirit and principle may induce to partake the glorious task

appears at the Battle of Bunker Hill; from then on his ambition and ego drove him to leading roles at Champlain, Ticonderoga, Bennington, and finally at Saratoga where his reputation, if not his arrogance, finally collapsed.

[2] The English Constitution, that is, the power of king and Parliament.

[3] "Froward" is an archaic term for disobedient.

[4] He refers here to "obvious offenses."

[5] After Burgoyne's war career, he dabbled in politics and wrote two plays, *Maid of the Oaks* and *The Heiress*. He was very eloquent in his use of words. Here, he refers to an extravagant use of reason for an unholy purpose.

[6] The term "usurpation" refers to a wrongful seizure of Royal Authority.

of redeeming their countrymen from dungeons, and re-establishing the blessings of legal government, I offer encouragement and employment; and upon the first intelligence of their association, I will find means to assist their undertakings. The domestic, the industrious, the infirm, and even the timid inhabitants, I am desirous to protect, provided they remain quietly at their houses; that they do not suffer their cattle to be removed, nor their corn or forage to be secreted or destroyed; that they do not break up their bridges or roads; nor by any other act, directly or indirectly, endeavor to obstruct the operations of the king's troops, or supply or assist those of the enemy . . .[7]

In consciousness of Christianity, my royal master's clemency, and the honor of soldiership, I have dwelt upon this invitation . . . And let not people to be led to disregard it, by considering their distance from the immediate situation of my camp. I have but to give stretch to the Indian forces under my direction, and they amount to thousands, to overtake the hardened enemies of Great Britain and America. I consider them the same, wherever they may lurk.

If, notwithstanding these endeavors, and sincere inclination to effect them, the frenzy of hostility should remain, I trust I shall stand acquitted in the eyes of God and man in denouncing and executing the vengeance of the estate against the willful outcasts. The messengers of justice and of wrath await them in the field; and devastation, famine, and every concomitant horror, that a reluctant, but indispensable prosecution of military duty must occasion, will bar the way to their return.

John Burgoyne.
Camp, at Ticonderoga, July 2, 1777.
By order of his excellency the lieut. general.
Robert Kingston, Secretary.

Source: H. Niles, *Principles and Acts of the Revolution in America.* (Baltimore: Printed by W.O. Niles, 1822), 262–263.

[7] Patriots had destroyed bridges and cut down trees to block Burgoyne's movements from Ticonderoga to Saratoga, while raiders harassed the redcoats, firing at them from the cover of field and forest.

[8] Burgoyne's arrogant offer to the Americans to accept their surrender receives an appropriate reply, couched in the same orotund language style in which the general expresses himself.

A Reply to Burgoyne's Proclamation[8]

To John Burgoyne, Esq. lieutenant general of his majesty's armies in America, colonel of the queen's regiment of light dragoons, governor of Fort William in North Britain, one of the representatives of Great Britain, and commanding an army and fleet employed on an expedition from Canada, etc, etc.

Most high, most mighty, most puissant[9] and sublime general!

When the forces under your command arrived at Quebec in order to act in concert and upon a common principle with the numerous fleets and armies which already display in every quarter of America, the justice and mercy of your king, we, the reptiles of America, were struck with unusual trepidation and astonishment. But what words can express the plentitude of our horror, when the colonel of the queen's regiment of light dragoons advanced toward Ticonderoga. The mountains shook before thee, and the trees of the forest bowed their lofty heads; the vast lakes of the north were chilled at thy presence, and the mighty cataracts stopped their tremendous career, and were suspended in awe at thy approach.[10] Judge, then, Oh! Ineffable governor of Fort William in North Britain, what must have been the terror, dismay, and despair that overspread this paltry continent of America, and us, its wretched inhabitants. Dark and dreary indeed, was the prospect before us, till, like the sun in the horizon, your most gracious, sublime, and irresistible proclamation, opened the doors of mercy, and snatched us, as it were, from the jaws of annihilation.

We foolishly thought, blind as we were, that your gracious master's fleets and armies were come to destroy us and our liberties; but we are happy in hearing from you (and who can doubt what you assert?) that they were called forth for the sole purpose of restoring the rights of the constitution, to a froward and stubborn generation. And it is for this, Oh! sublime lieutenant general, that you have given yourself the trouble to cross the wide Atlantic, and with incredible fatigues traverse uncultivated wilds? And we ungratefully refuse the proffered blessing? To restore the rights of the constitution you have called together an amiable host of savages, and turned them loose to scalp our women and children, and lay our country waste; this they have performed with their usual skill and clemency and yet we remain insensible of the benefit, and unthankful for so much goodness.

Our Congress have declared independence, and our assemblies, as your highness justly observes, have most wickedly imprisoned

[9]Puissant means powerful.

[10]This paragraph is written in the style of the King James Bible, implying that Burgoyne obviously thinks he is God. Cataracts refer to mighty waterfalls.

the avowed friends of that power with which they are at war, and most profanely compelled those, whose consciences will not permit them to fight, to pay some small part toward the expenses their country is at, in supporting what is called a necessary defensive war. If we go on thus in our obstinacy and ingratitude, what can we expect, but that you should, in your anger, give a stretch to the Indian forces under your direction amounting to thousands, to overtake and destroy us! or, which is ten times worse, that you should leave us to our own misery, without completing the benevolent task you have begun, of restoring to us the rights of the constitution.

We submit—we submit—most puissant colonel of the queen's regiment of light dragoons, and governor of Fort William in North Britain! We offer our heads to the scalping knife, and our bellies to the bayonet. Who can resist the force of your eloquence? Who can withstand the terror of your arms? The invitation you have made, in the consciousness of Christianity, your royal master's clemency, and the honor of soldiership, we thankfully accept. The blood of the slain, the cries of injured virgins and innocent children, and the never ceasing sighs and groans of starving wretches, now languishing in the jails and prison ships of New York, call on us in vain; while your sublime proclamation is sounded in our ears. Forgive us, O our country! Forgive us, dear posterity! Forgive us, all ye foreign powers, who are anxiously watching our conduct in this important struggle, if we yield implicitly to the persuasive tongue of the most elegant colonel of her majesty's regiment of light dragoons.

Forbear, then, thou magnanimous lieutenant general! Forbear to denounce the vengeance against us; Forbear to give a stretch to those restorers of constitutional rights, the Indian forces under your direction. Let not the messengers of justice and wrath await us in the field, and devastation, and every concomitant horror, bar our return to the allegiance of a prince, who, by his royal will, would deprive us of life, with all possible clemency. We are domestic, we are industrious, we are infirm and timid: we shall remain quietly at home, and not remove our cattle, our corn, our forage, in hopes that you will come, at the head of troops, in the full powers of health, discipline, and valor, and take charge of them for yourselves. Behold our wives and daughters, our flocks and herds, our goods and chattels, are they not at the mercy of our lord the king, and of his lieutenant general, member of the house of commons, and governor of Fort William in North Britain?

A.B.
C.D.
E.F. etc, etc.
Saratoga, 10th July, 1777

Source: H. Niles, *Principles and Acts of the Revolution in America.* (Baltimore: Printed by W.O. Niles, 1822), 263–264.

A Letter from General Burgoyne to Lord George Germain[11]

I am afraid the expectations of Sir J. Johnson greatly fail in the rising[12] of the country. On this side I find daily reason to doubt the sincerity of the resolution of the professing Loyalists. I have about 400 (but not half of them armed) who may be depended upon; they are trimmers,[13] merely actuated by interest. The great bulk of the country is undoubtedly with the Congress, in principle and in zeal; and their measures are executed with a secrecy and dispatch that are not to be equaled. Wherever the King's forces point, militia, to the amount of three to four thousand, assemble in twenty-four hours; they bring with them their subsistence, etc., and, the alarm over, they return to their farms. The Hampshire Grants, in particular, a country unpeopled and almost unknown in the last war,[14] now abounds in the most active and most rebellious race of the continent, and hangs like a gathering storm upon my left . . .

Another most embarrassing circumstance is the want of communication with Sir William Howe; of the messengers I have sent, I know of two being hanged, and am ignorant whether any of the rest arrived . . . Washington has detached Sullivan, with 2500 men, to Albany . . . after my arrival at Albany the movements of the enemy must guide mine . . . Had I a latitude in my orders, I should think it my duty to wait in this position, or perhaps as far back as Fort Edward, where my communication with Lake George would be perfectly secure, till some event happened to assist my movement forward; but my orders being positive to "force a junction with Sir William Howe," I apprehend I am not at liberty to remain inactive longer than shall be necessary to collect twenty-five days provisions, and to receive the reinforcement of the additional companies, the German drafts and recruits now (and unfortunately only now) on

[11]Lord George Germain was one of the fiercest opponents of the Continental cause. A highly ambitious member of Parliament, he had been guilty of misconduct during the Seven Years' War. Nevertheless, George III had appointed him secretary of state for the colonies. As such he made a great contribution to Britain's loss of its colonies, but was quick to blame others for his failure, up to and including the Battle of Yorktown, the final campaign of the revolution.

[12] The "rising" refers to the rebellion.

[13]A trimmer is a person who holds no strong political belief but changes his position to please both sides in a dispute.

[14]The last war was the French and Indian War, also known as the Seven Years' War, fought between Great Britain and France between 1756 and 1763.

Lake Champlain. The waiting the arrival of this reinforcement is of indispensable necessity, because from the hour I pass the Hudson's River and proceed towards Albany, all safety of communication ceases. I must expect a large body of the enemy from my left will take post behind me . . .

When I wrote more confidently, I little foresaw that I was to be left to pursue my way through such a tract of country and hosts of foes, without any co-operation from New York; I yet do not despond. Should I succeed in forcing my way to Albany, and find that country in a state to subsist my army, I shall think no more of a retreat, but at the worst fortify there and await Sir W. Howe's operations. Whatever may be my fate, my Lord, I submit my actions to the breast of the King, and to the candid judgment of my profession, when all the motives become public; and I rest in the confidence that, whatever decision may be passed upon my conduct, my good intent will not be questioned.

I cannot close so serious a letter without expressing my fullest satisfaction in the behavior and countenance of the troops, and my compleat confidence that in all trials they will do whatever can be expected from men devoted to their King and country.

Source: Gen. John Burgoyne, *A State of the Expedition from Canada.* (London: J. Almon, 1780), 46–48.

[15]George Germain was a British soldier and politician who was secretary of state for the colonies during the revolution; William Knox was undersecretary of state for the colonies.

Letters from George Germain to William Knox,[15] September 29, 1777

I am sorry the Canada army will be disappointed in the junction they expect with Sir William Howe, but the more honor for Burgoyne if he does the business without any assistance from New York.

October 31, 1777

I am sorry to find that Burgoyne's campaign is so totally ruined; the best wish I can form is that he may have returned to Ticonderoga without much loss. His private letter to me, being dated the 20th of August, contains nothing material about the affair near Bennington but military reasoning about the propriety of that attack; but what alarms me most is that he thinks his orders to go to Albany to force a junction with Sir William Howe are so positive that he must attempt at all events the obeying of them, tho' at the same time he acquaints me that Sir William Howe has sent him word that he has gone to Philadelphia, and indeed nothing that Sir William says could give him reason to hope that any effort would be made in his favor.

Source: *Reports from Commissioners, Inspectors, and Others*, Volume 60. Historical Manuscripts Commission. Seventeenth Report of the Royal Commission on Historical Manuscripts. (London: His Majesty's Stationery Office, 1908), 139–140.

Journal of Lieutenant William Digby,[16]
September 19, 1777

[16]William Digby was a member of the Shropshire Regiment, a British light infantry unit attached to Burgoyne's force.

At day break intelligence was received that Colonel Morgan, with the advance party of the enemy consisting of a corps of rifle men, were strong about 3 miles from us . . . A little after 12 our advanced picquets came up with Colonel Morgan and engaged, but from the great superiority of fire received from him . . . they were obliged to fall back . . . the line came up to their support and obliged Morgan in his turn to retreat with loss . . . Between 2 and 3 the action became general on their side . . . Such an explosion of fire I never had any idea of before, and the heavy artillery joining in concert like great peals of thunder, assisted by the echoes of the woods, almost deafened us with the noise . . . The crash of cannon and musketry never ceased till darkness parted us, when they retired to their camp, leaving us masters of the field; but it was a dear bought victory if I can give it that name, as we have lost many brave men . . . General Burgoyne was every where and did every thing that could be expected from a brave officer . . . During the night we remained in our ranks, and tho we heard the groans of our wounded and dying at a small distance, yet could not assist them till morning, not knowing the position of the enemy, and expecting the action would be renewed at day break. Sleep was a stranger to us, but we were all in good spirits and ready to obey with cheerfulness any orders the general might issue before morning dawned . . .

Source: James P. Baxter, *The British Invasion from the North.* (Albany, NY: J. Munsell's Sons, 1887), 270–274.

Recollections of Captain E. Wakefield of the American Army[17]

[17]Captain Wakefield is writing about Colonel (later General) Daniel Morgan. Morgan was a cousin to Daniel Boone. He was considered one of the great tacticians of the Continental Army. Morgan's troops were riflemen, not grenadiers, and their fire was particularly

A persistent effort has been made from the day of the battle to rob Arnold of the glory . . . I shall never forget the opening scene of the

accurate and deadly. Morgan had fought alongside Washington in the French and Indian War and along with Benedict Arnold was responsible for the triumph of American arms at Saratoga.

first day's conflict. The riflemen and light infantry were ordered to clear the woods of the Indians. Arnold rode up, and with his sword pointing to the enemy emerging from the woods into an opening partially cleared, covered with stumps and fallen timber, addressing Morgan, he said, "Colonel Morgan, you and I have seen too many redskins to be deceived by that garb of paint and feathers; they are asses in Lions' skins, Canadians and Tories; let your riflemen cure them of their borrowed plumes."... And so they did, for in less than fifteen minutes the "Wagon Boy"[18] with his Virginia riflemen, sent the painted devils with a howl back to the British lines. Morgan was in his glory, catching the inspiration of Arnold, as he thrilled his men; when he hurled them against the enemy, he astonished the English and Germans with the deadly fire of his rifles.

[18]This was a nickname for Morgan.

Nothing could exceed the bravery of Arnold on this day; he seemed the very genius of war. Infuriated by the conflict and maddened by Gates' refusal to send reinforcements, which he repeatedly called for, and knowing he was meeting the brunt of the battle, he seemed inspired with the fury of a demon.

Source: R.A. Guild,. *Chaplain Smith and the Baptists.* (Philadelphia: American Baptist Publications Society, 1885), 213.

[19]This letter is the first evidence we have of Benedict Arnold's dissatisfaction with his treatment by Gates. Here we find the roots of his traitorous conduct. Gates was adjutant to Washington and had been an effective commander. But he was not one to press his advantage. Arnold, on the other hand, was fearless and aggressive and the dissention between the two commanders led to Arnold's relief from command. He was even barred from headquarters!

Correspondence between Benedict Arnold and Horatio Gates,[19] Camp at Stillwater, September 22, 1777

When I joined the army at Vanschaick's Island, the first instant you were pleased to order me to Loudon's ferry to take the command of Generals Poor's and Learned's brigades and Colonel Morgan's battalion of riflemen and light infantry. Your commands were immediately obeyed, I have repeatedly since received your orders respecting those corps, as belonging to my division, which has often been mentioned in general orders, and the gentlemen commanding those corps have understood themselves as my division. On the 9th instant you desired me to annex the New York and Connecticut Militia to such brigades as I thought proper in my division, which I accordingly did . . . The next day I was surprised to observe in general orders, the New York militia annexed to General Glover's brigade, which placed me in the ridiculous light of presuming to give orders I had no right to do, and having them publicly contradicted . . . You then observed that the mistake was your own, and that it should be mentioned as such in the ensuing orders, which has never been done.

On the 19th inst. when advice was received that the enemy were approaching, I took the liberty to give it as my opinion that we ought to march out and attack them. You desired me to send Colonel Morgan and the light infantry, and support them; I obeyed your orders; and before the action was over, I found it necessary to send out the whole of my division to support the attack . . . I have been informed that in the returns transmitted to Congress of the killed and wounded in the action, the troops were mentioned as a detachment from the army, and in the orders of this day I observe it is mentioned that Colonel Morgan's corps, not being in any brigade or division of this army, are to make returns and reports only to head-quarters from whence they are alone to receive orders; although it is notorious to the whole army, they have been in and done duty with my division for some time past.

When I mentioned these matters to you this day, you were pleased to say in contradiction to your repeated orders, you did not know I was a Major-general or had any command in the army. I have ever supposed a Major-general's command of four thousand men, a proper division, and no detachment when composed of brigades, forming one wing of the army, and that the general and troops, if guilty of misconduct or cowardly behaviour in time of action were justly chargeable as a division. And that if on the other hand they behaved with spirit and firmness in action, they were justly entitled to the applause due to a proper division, not a detachment of the army . . .

From what reason I know not (as I am conscious of no offence or neglect of duty,) but I have lately observed little or no attention paid to any proposals I have thought it my duty to make for the public service, and when a measure I have proposed has been agreed to, it has been immediately contradicted. I have been received with the greatest coolness at head quarters, and often huffed in such a manner as must mortify a person with less pride than I have and in my station in the army. You observed you expected General Lincoln in a day or two, when I should have no command of a division, that you thought me of little consequence to the army, and that you would with all your heart give me a pass to leave it, whenever I thought proper. As I find your observation very just, that I am not or that you wish me of little consequence in the army, and as I have the interest and safety of my country at heart, I wish to be where I can be of the most service to her. I therefore, as General Lincoln is arrived, have to request your pass to Philadelphia with my two aid-de-camps and their servants, where I propose to join General Washington, and may possibly have it in my power to serve my country, although I am thought of no consequence in this department.

Reply from Gates to Arnold, Headquarters, September 23, 1777

You wrote me nothing last night but what had been sufficiently altercated between us in the evening. I then gave such answers to all your objections as I think were satisfactory. I know not what you mean by insult or indignity. I made you such replies only as I conceived proper. As to the open letter I sent you to Mr. Hancock, it was the civilest method I could devise of acquainting Congress with your leaving the army. And is to all intents and purposes as full a pass as can be desired. I sent it unsealed, as being the more complaisant to you, and is what is commonly done upon such occasions. That not being so agreeable to you as a common pass, I send you one inclosed.

Source: James Wilkinson, *Memoirs of My Own Times*, Volume 1. (Philadelphia, Abraham Small, 1816), 254–256, 258.

[20]Colonel Livingston had been an active commander since the Canadian Campaign. Philip Schuyler was one of four generals appointed by the Continental Congress to assist Washington (May 1775). Livingston had distinguished himself in the French and Indian War, came from a wealthy New York family, and was a zealous champion of the cause of liberty. Here he writes to Schuyler to set the record straight concerning the conflict between Arnold and Gates. It is very clear that Gates's professional jealousy of Arnold's competence and leadership ability was behind his effort to denigrate Arnold's contribution to the victory at Saratoga.
[21] General Gates.

Colonel Henry Brockholst Livingston to General Schuyler,[20] September 23, 1777

I am much distressed at Gen. Arnold's determination to retire from the army at this important crisis. His presence was never more necessary. He is the life and soul of the troops. Believe me, Sir, to him and him alone is due the honor of our late victory. Whatever share his superiors may claim they are entitled to none. He enjoys the confidence and affection of officers and soldiers. They would, to a man, follow him to conquest or death. His absence will dishearten them to such a degree as to render them of but little service.

The difference between him and Mr G[21] has arisen to too great a height to admit of a compromise. I have, for some time past, observed the great coolness and, in many instances, even disrespect with which Gen. Arnold has been treated at Head Quarters. His proposals have been rejected with marks of indignity, his own orders have frequently been countermanded, and himself set in a ridiculous light by those of the Commander in Chief. His remonstrances on those occasions, have been termed presumptuous. In short he has pocketed many insults for the sake of his country, which a man of less pride would have resented. The repeated indignities he received at length roused his spirit and determination again to remonstrate. He waited on Mr. Gates in person last evening. Matters were altercated in a very high strain. Both were warm—the latter rather passionate and very assuming. Towards the end of the debate Mr Gates told Arnold, "He did not know of his being a Major-General. He had sent in his resignation to Congress. He had never given him the command of any division of the army. General Lincoln would be here in a day or two, and that then he should have no occasion for him, and would give him a pass to go to Philadelphia, whenever he chose it."

Arnold's spirit could not brooke this usage.[22] He returned to his quarters, represented what had passed in a letter to Mr. Gates and requested his permission to go to Philadelphia. This morning, in compliance to his letter, he received a permit, by way of a letter directed to Mr. Hancock. He sent this back and requested one in proper form, which was complied with. Tomorrow he will set out for Albany. The reason of the present disagreement between two old cronies is simply this: Arnold is your friend. I shall attend the general down,[23] chagrining as it may be for me to leave the army at a time when an opportunity for every young fellow to distinguish himself. I can no longer submit to the command of a man whom I abhor from my very soul. His conduct is disgusting to every one except his flatterers and dependents, among whom are some whom profess to be your friends. A cloud is gathering and may ere long burst on his head.

[22]He could not put up with this treatment.

[23]Livingston intends to accompany General Arnold to Philadelphia.

Source: Isaac Arnold, *The Life of Benedict Arnold.* (Chicago: Jansen, McClurg & Company, 1880), 180–181.

Memoirs of James Wilkenson[24]

On the afternoon of the 7th October, the advanced guard of the centre beat to arms; the alarm was repeated throughout the line, and the troops repaired to their alarm posts. I was at head quarters when this happened, and with the approbation of the General mounted my horse to inquire the cause; but on reaching the guard where the beat commenced, I could obtain no other satisfaction but that some person had reported the enemy to be advancing against our left. . . .

[24]Morgan's Raiders were famed throughout the corps for their bravery and the excellence of their tactics. Although accounts of their successes had become the stuff of legend, there is no doubt that they were justly celebrated. This account is one of many that we have that underscores their reputation.

I perceived, about half a mile from the line of our encampment, several columns of the enemy . . . entering a wheat field which had not been cut . . . I could distinctly mark their every movement . . . Having satisfied myself . . . that no attack was meditated, I returned and reported to the General, who asked me what appeared to be the intention of the enemy . . . "They are foraging, and endeavoring to recanter your left, and I think, Sir, they offer you battle." . . . "Well, then, order on Morgan to begin the game." . . .[25] I waited on the Colonel, whose corps was formed in front of our centre, and delivered the order; he knew the ground and inquired the position of the enemy . . . Colonel Morgan, with his usual sagacity, proposed to make a circuit with his corps by our left, and under cover of the wood to gain the height on the right of the enemy, and from thence commence his attack, so soon as our fire should be opened against their left; the plan was the best which could be devised and no doubt contributed essentially to the prompt and decisive victory we gained . . .

Morgan at this critical moment poured down like a torrent from the hill, and attacked the right of the enemy in front and flank. Dearborn, at the moment when the enemy's light infantry were attempting to change front,[26] pressed forward with ardour and delivered a close fire; then leapt the fence, shouted, charged and gallantly forced them to retire in disorder . . . they were immediately rallied and reformed behind a fence in rear of their first position; but being now attacked with great audacity in front and flanks by superior numbers, resistance became vain, and the whole line, commanded by Burgoyne in person, gave way and made a precipitate and disorderly retreat to his camp, leaving two twelve and six six-pounders on the field with the loss of more than 400 officers and men killed, wounded and captured . . . The ground which had been occupied by the British grenadiers presented a scene of complicated horror and exultation. In the square space of twelve or fifteen yards lay eighteen grenadiers in the agonies of death, and three officers propped up against stumps of trees, two of them mortally wounded, bleeding and almost speechless; what a spectacle for one whose bosom glowed with philanthropy,[27] and how vehement the impulse which can excite men of sensibility to seek such scenes of barbarism!

I found the courageous Colonel Cilley astraddle on a brass twelve-pounder and exulting in the capture; whilst a surgeon, a man of great worth who was dressing one of the officers, raising his

[25]Morgan's game was to create turmoil in the enemy by having his corps first shoot the Indian guides who led the British forces and then target the officers. The British Army considered these guerrilla-style tactics to be dishonorable; but they were effective.

[26]The infantry were attempting to change position.

[27]The love of one's fellow man.

blood-besmeared hands in frenzy of patriotism, exclaimed, "Wilkenson, I have dipped my hands in British blood!" . . .

Source: James Wilkinson, *Memoirs of My Own Times*, Volume 1. (Philadelphia, Abraham Small, 1816), 267–271.

Letter from Ebenezer Mattoon to General Philip Schuyler,[28] October 7, 1835

. . . At this juncture Arnold came up with a part of Brook's regiment and gave them[29] a most deadly fire, which soon caused them to face about and retreat with a quicker step than they advanced . . . At this moment Arnold says to Col. Brooks . . . "Let us attack Balcarras's works." Brooks replied, "No, Lord Auckland's detachment has retired there, we can't carry them."[30] "Well, then, let us attack the Hessian lines." Brook replies, "With all my heart."

We all wheeled to the right and advanced. No fire was received, except from the cannon, until we got within about eight rods,[31] when we received a tremendous fire from the whole line. But a few of our men, however, fell. Still advancing, we received a second fire, in which a few men fell, and Gen. Arnold's horse fell under him, and he himself was wounded. He cried out, "Rush on, my brave boys!" After receiving the third fire, Brooks mounted their works,[32] swung his sword, and the men rushed into their works. When we entered the works, we found Col. Bremen dead, surrounded with a number of his companions, dead or wounded. We still pursued slowly, the fire, in the meantime, decreasing. Nightfall now put an end to this day's bloody contest . . . . The gloom of thee night, the groans and shreiks of the wounded and dying, and the horrors of the whole scene baffle all description.

Source: William Stone, *The Campaign of Lieut. Gen. John Burgoyne*. (Albany, NY: Joel Munsell, 1877), 374–375.

Journal of Lieutenant William Digby,[33] October 7, 1777

Brigadier General Frazer was mortally wounded . . . When General Burgoyne saw him fall, he seemed then to feel in the highest degree our disagreeable situation. Our cannon were surrounded and taken; the men and horses being all killed . . . it evidently appeared a retreat was the only thing left for us. They still advanced upon our works

[28]At the Battle at Saratoga, Benedict Arnold was still a huge factor in the Continental Army's success. This letter presents a vivid picture of Arnold in battle.

[29]The "them" were the Hessian soldiers. There were approximately 30,000 German troops hired by the British to help fight during the Revolutionary War.

[30]He means they can't defeat Auckland's troops.

[31]A rod was equivalent to approximately 5½ yards; thus approximately 16 feet.

[32] "Works" is a term for trenches dug for defense. He means here that they rushed into the trenches.

[33]As the battle turned against Burgoyne's forces, the general begins to realize that his defeat is a distinct possibility. His cause is rescued for the moment by the coming of nightfall but the general's silence speaks volumes.

under a severe fire of grape shot[34] . . . another body of the enemy stormed the German lines after meeting with a most shameful resistance, and took possession of all their camp and equipage, baggage, etc., etc., Colo. Bremen fell nobly at the head of the foreigners, and by his death blotted out part of the stain his countrymen so justly merited from that day's behavior . . . General Burgoyne appeared greatly agitated as the danger to which the lines were exposed was of the utmost serious nature at that particular period . . . He said but little, well knowing we could defend the lines or fall in the attempt. Darkness interposed (I believe fortunately for us), which put an end to the action . . .

Source: James P. Baxter, *The British Invasion from the North.* (Albany: Joel Munsell's Sons, 1887), 287–289.

[35]Samuel Woodruff, a volunteer in General Gates's force, gives us a vivid picture of the decisive second battle of Freeman's Farm in which Benedict Arnold was seriously wounded. This account is one of many from pension applications former soldiers sent to Congress in support of their requests for Federal Veterans' pensions authorized by Congress.

[36]The second battle of Freeman's Farm.

The Second Battle of Freeman's Farm[35]

. . . on or about the tenth day of August, 1777, I was enrolled as a volunteer soldier in a military company . . . and marched with them through Albany to Saratoga, where on or about the twentieth day of October, three days after the surrender of General Burgoyne with his army, our company was disbanded . . . while in this service at Saratoga I was engaged in the battle fought by the hostile armies on the seventh of October,[36] the following particulars of which, . . . I distinctly remember . . . that about eleven o'clock in the forenoon of that day, the British troops advanced ender the command of General Fraser, who led up the grenadiers,[37] drove in our pickets[38] and advanced guards, and made several unsuccessful charges with fixed bayonets upon the line of the Continental troops at the American redoubts[39] on Bemis Heights, near the headquarters of General Gates. But meeting a repulse at this point of attack, the grenadiers commenced a slow but orderly retreat, still keeping up a brisk fire. After falling back two or three hundred yards, this part of the hostile army met and joined with the main body of the royal troops commanded by Lord Balcarres and General Riedesel. Here, on a level piece of ground of considerable extent called Freeman's farms, thinly covered with yellow pines, the royal army formed an extensive line with the principal part of their artillery in front. By this time the American line was formed, consisting of Continentals, state troops, and militia. The news immediately became general through the line with renewed

[37]Grenadiers are British infantry or foot soldiers, as distinct from cavalry or horse soldiers. They are called "grenadiers" because they fought by throwing grenades.

[38]Forward lookouts.

[39]Redoubts are small fortifications meant to protect high ground.

spirit, and nearly the whole force on both sides was brought into action . . . the British grenadiers began reluctantly to give ground, and their whole line, within a few minutes, appeared broken. Still, they kept up a respectable fire, both of artillery and musketry. At about this stage in the action, General Arnold, while galloping up and down our line upon a small brown horse . . . received a musket ball which broke his leg and killed the horse under him. He was at that moment about forty yards distant from me and in fair view. Isaac Newell of said Southington, since deceased, and one or two others assisted this applicant to extricate Arnold from his fallen horse, placed him on a litter, and sent him back to the headquarters of General Gates . . . In conducting the retreat we came to a small cultivated field enclosed by a fence. Here they halted, formed, and made a stand, apparently determined to retrieve what they had lost by their repulse at the redoubts in commencement of the action. They placed in their center and at each flank a strong battery of brass fieldpieces.[40] The carnage became frightful, but the conflict was of short duration. Their gallant major received a musket ball through both legs, which placed him hors de combat.[41] Retreat immediately ensued, leaving their killed and some of their wounded with two brass fieldpieces on the ground . . .

The retreat, pursuit, and firing continued till eight o'clock. It was then dark. The royal army continued their retreat about a mile further and there bivouacked for the night. Ours returned to camp, where we arrived between nine and ten o'clock in the evening. About two hundred of our wounded men, during the afternoon, and by that time in the evening, were brought from the field of battle in wagons, and for want of tents, sheds, or any kind of buildings to receive and cover them, were placed in a circular row on the naked ground. It was a clear, but cold and frosty, night. The sufferings of the wounded were extreme, having neither beds under them nor any kind of bed clothing to cover them while extracting bullets and performing other surgical operations. This applicant, though greatly fatigued by the exercise of the day, felt no inclination to sleep, but with several others spent the whole night carrying water and administering what other comforts were in our power to the sufferers, about seventy of whom died of their wounds during the night.

The next day (October 8th), this applicant was detached from our company to assist others detached from other companies in burying

[40]Field artillery made up of short cannon that fire shells over a high short range.

[41]He means here that the major was out of the fight.

the dead remaining on the field of battle. This was a sad and laborious day's work . . .

Source: *Pension Application of Samuel Woodruff.* Revolutionary War Pension and Bounty-Land Warrant Application Files, Record Group 15, Pension No. S. 7964, National Archives.

Letter of Thomas Anburey, British Lieutenant,[42] Cambridge, Massachusetts, November 15, 1777

[42]Thomas Anburey, a lieutenant in the British force, describes the desperate situation and the circumstances under which Burgoyne's officers sued for a cease-fire and surrender.

The state and situation of our army was truly calamitous! . . . Worn down by a series of incessant toils and stubborn actions; abandoned in our utmost distress by the Indians; weakened by the desertion, and disappointed as to the efficacy of the Canadians and Provincials by their timidity; the regular troops reduced, by the late heavy losses of many of our best men and distinguished officers, to only 3500 effective men, of which number there were not quite 2000 British: in this state of weakness, no possibility of retreat, our provisions nearly exhausted, and invested by an army of four times our number that almost encircled us, who would not attack us from a knowledge of our situation, and whose works could not be assaulted in any part. In this perilous situation the men lay continually upon their arms, the enemy incessantly cannonading us, and their rifle and cannon shot reaching every part of our camp . . . After waiting the whole of the 13th day of October, in anxious expectation of what it would produce, and to which time it had been resolved to endure all extremities in maintaining our ground against the enemy; no prospect of assistance appearing, and no rational ground of hope remaining, it was thought proper, in the evening, to take an apt account of the provisions left, which amounted to no more than three days short allowance. In this state of distress, a council of war was called, to which all the Generals, Field-officers and commanding officers of corps were summoned, when it was unanimously agreed that in the present circumstances we could do no other than treat[43] with the enemy.

[43]We had no option but to discuss terms of settlement.

Source: Thomas Anburey, *Travels through the Interior Parts of America*, Volume 1. (London: William Lane, 1789), 461–464.

Journal of Lieutenant William Digby of the Shropshire Regiment,[44] October 17, 1777

[44]William Digby, a member of the Shropshire Regiment, describes the dignity of the meeting for surrender of Generals Gates and Burgoyne. The terms the Americans demanded were generous, and the demeanor of the commanding officers

Gen. Burgoyne desired a meeting of all the officers early that morning, at which he entered into a detail of his manner of acting since he had the honor of commanding the army; but he was too full[45] to speak; heaven only could tell his feelings at this time. He dwelled much on his orders to make the wished for junction with General Clinton,[46] and as to how his proceedings had turned out . . . He then read over the Articles of Convention, and informed us the terms were even easier than we could have expected from our situation, and concluded with assuring us he never would have accepted any terms, had we provisions enough, or at the least hopes of our extricating ourselves any other way.

About 10 o'clock we marched out, according to treaty, with drums beating and the honors of war, but the drums seemed to have lost their former inspiriting sounds . . . As to my own feelings, I cannot express them. Tears (though unmanly) forced their way . . . I never shall forget the appearance of their troops on our marching past them; a dead silence universally reigned through their numerous columns, and even then they seemed struck with our situation and dare scarce lift their eyes to view British troops in such situation. I must say their decent behavior during the time . . . merited the utmost approbation and praise.

The meeting between Burgoyne and Gates was well worth seeing. He paid Burgoyne almost as much respect as if he was the conquerer; indeed, his noble air, tho prisoner, seemed to command attention and respect from every person . . . Thus ended all our hopes of history, honor, glory, etc. Thus was Burgoyne's Army sacrificed to either the absurd opinions of a blundering ministerial power, the stupid inaction of a general [Howe], who, from his lethargic disposition, neglected every step he might have taken to assist their operations, or lastly, perhaps, his own misconduct in penetrating so far as to be unable to return,[47] and tho I must own my partiality to whims great, yet if he or the army under his command are guilty, let them suffer to the utmost extent, and by an unlimited punishment in part blot out and erase, if possible, the crime charged to their account.

was echoed by the silence of the victorious Continentals. In spite of the conflict, both armies remembered that they had been brothers before the war, and peace, in a sense, restored that consanguinity. Saratoga was the turning point of the revolution. It not only inspired the rest of Washington's army; it convinced the French that it would be to their advantage to give aid to the American cause.

[45]In a letter of October 20, Burgoyne described himself as "emotionally sunk in mind and body."

[46]General Clinton was supposed to bring up reinforcements to Burgoyne and attempted to divert the Americans by capturing two forts along the Hudson River. Clinton's efforts, however, were in vain; Burgoyne attacked knowing he would not receive aid in time.

[47]There was a lack of communication between Generals Howe and Burgoyne. Sir William Howe decided to attack the Rebel capital at Philadelphia rather than deploying his army to meet up with Burgoyne and cut off New England from the other colonies.

Source: James P. Baxter, *The British Invasion from the North*. (Albany: Joel Munsell's Sons, 1887), 317–323.

The Battle of Yorktown

(1781)

The victory of Yorktown, the final major battle of the revolution, was no accident. It was a triumph for both the French-American alliance and for Washington's strategic genius. Before the land battle, the French admiral De Grasse had been persuaded by Washington to attack the British fleet to prevent it from supporting Cornwallis's troops at Yorktown. This event was essential to the weakening of the British position. The other prelude to the allied victory was Washington's strategies—his trick for deceiving the enemy. Washington had maintained a force to the north of New York City and maintained the greatest secrecy as to the progress of its deployment. The question was: would they be used to attack the British stronghold at New York, or moved to support the effort in Virginia? On August 20, Washington moved his force to the Jersey shore and sent them south to Yorktown. But General Clinton had already recalled some of the troops from Virginia to reinforce the New York garrison, further weakening Cornwallis's position.

By September, the British had figured out Washington's plan and sent a naval armada south to the Chesapeake. But De Grasse arrived first and blockaded the mouth of the James River passage to Chesapeake Bay. Cornwallis, deprived of troops and his escape route blocked, was obliged to stand and fight. He dug in for defense as the Americans and French took up positions surrounding him. The fighting began on October 9; the allies carried all before them. Cornwallis considered a retreat by sea, but fate intervened in the form of a sudden storm that settled the matter. Blaming the lack of support from Clinton, a lack of ammunition, the weather, and anything else that he could think of, Cornwallis surrendered on October 19. His army of almost 9,000 men consisted of 25 percent of the entire British forces in America. The news reached Lord North, prime minister of Britain, who declared, "Oh God! It is over," and it was.

---

[1]As early as the spring of 1776, the Committee of Correspondence had sent an emissary to the Count of Vergennes to ask for French aid. Vergennes was France's foreign minister. He believed that support for American independence would weaken Britain and help restore France's prestige and power that had been lost when the

Lafayette to the Count de Vergennes,[1] New Windsor on the North River, January 20, 1781

. . . With a naval inferiority it is impossible to make war in America. It is that which prevents us from attacking any point that might be carried with two or three thousand men. It is that which reduces us to defensive operations, as dangerous as they are humiliating. The

English are conscious of this truth, and all their movements prove how much they desire to retain the empire of the sea . . . I think it is my duty to call your attention to the American soldiers, and on the part they must take in the operations of the next campaign. The Continental troops have as much courage and real discipline as those that are opposed to them. They are more inured to privation,[2] more patient than Europeans, who, on these two points, cannot be compared to them. They have several officers of great merit . . . and from their own talents have acquired knowledge intuitively; they have been formed by the daily experience of several campaigns, in which, the armies being small and the country a rugged one, all the battalions of the line were obliged to serve as advance-guards and light troops. The recruits . . . have frequently fought battles in the same regiments which they are now re-entering, and have seen more gun-shots than three-fourths of the European soldiers. As to the militia, they are only armed peasants, who have occasionally fought, and who are not deficient in ardor and discipline, but whose services would be most useful in the labors of a siege . . . The advance-guard of the Count de Rochambeau,[3] although inactive itself from want of ships, by its presence alone has rendered an essential service to America: if it had not arrived, the campaign would have been a ruinous one.

British had defeated France in the Seven Year's War. Lafayette, a soldier of fortune who had come to America, joined Washington's army, became an aide to the general, and was almost like an adopted son to him. He was instrumental in gaining French aid, especially the involvement of the French Navy. He was an important figure in the Battle of Yorktown.

[2]The Continentals were toughened by experience and used to going without provisions.

[3]Rochambeau was commander of French troops in America.

Source: Marquis de Lafayette, *Memoirs, Correspondence, and Manuscripts of General Lafayette*, Volume 1. (New York: Saunders and Otley, 1837), 374–378.

A Letter from George Washington to Lafayette,[4] Head Quarters, Philadelphia, September 2, 1781

. . . I flatter myself we shall not experience any considerable difficulties from the want of Men to carry our most favourite Projects into execution. The means for prosecuting a Siege with rapidity, energy, and success, and of supplying the Troops while they are engaged in that service . . . have been and still continue to be the great objects of my concern and attention. Heavy Cannon, Ordnance Stores and Ammunition to a pretty large Amount, are now forwarding . . . In order to introduce some kind of System and Method in our Supplies, to know with certainty what may be depended upon, and to put the business in the best possible train of execution, I shall send forward the Heads of Departments as soon as their presence can be dispensed with. I have spoken to the Surgeon General respecting Hospital Stores and Medicines, all that can be done will be done in

[4]This letter outlines Washington's battle plan for the Yorktown campaign: block Cornwallis's escape by land by Lafayette's troops and by sea by a blockade by Commander Comte de Grasse's ships. It also shows his technical concerns for materiel provisioning of his army.

[5] Count de Grasse was admiral of one of the French fleets.

that department. As to Clothing I am sorry to inform you, little is to be expected, except in the Article of Shoes, of which a full supply will be sent on . . . But my dear Marquis, I am distressed beyond expression, to know what is become of the Count de Grasse,[5] and for fear the English Fleet, by occupying the Chesapeake should frustrate all our flattering prospects in that quarter . . . Should the retreat of Lord Cornwallis by water, be cut off by the arrival of either of the French Fleets, I am persuaded you will do all in your power to prevent his escape by land. May that great felicity be reserved for you! You See, how critically important the present Moment is: for my own part I am determined still to persist, with unremitting ardor in my present Plan . . . Adieu my Dear Marquis!

Source: J.C. Fitzpatrick, ed., *The Writings of George Washington*, Volume 23. (Washington, DC: Government Printing Office, 1937), 75–77.

[6] Tucker's letters are an important soldier's eye view of the final conflict of the revolution.

Colonel St. George Tucker of the Virginia Militia to His Wife,[6] Williamsburg, September 5, 1781

[7] Louis XVI, king of France.

. . . About the middle of last week twenty-nine ships of the line and four frigates arrived in our bay, with four thousand land forces sent to our assistance by Louis the Great.[7] Besides these there are three thousand marines to be landed in case of an emergency. Of the fleet there are ten sixty-fours; eighteen seventy-fours, and one ship of an hundreds and ten guns! . . . Of the troops, three thousand five hundred landed at James Town three days ago and are now on their march to this city. Five hundred are left on board to land at York River . . . The British fleet still lies at York, and their land forces are now in the town. The Count de Grasse, by a flag, declared to the admiral or the commodore of the British fleet that he would put every man to the sword who should fall into his hands if the fleet was destroyed . . .

Our troops lie from four miles beyond this town to near James Town; so that Cornwallis is as effectively hemmed in as our troops were in Charlestown. Our force may now be reckoned to be eight thousand men; of which six thousand are regulars . . . Nor is this all, for, to my great surprise and pleasure, I was this morning informed from undoubted authority that General Washington is at the Head of Elk with five thousand troops, which are to be embarked from thence in transports sent there for that purpose, of which the Marquis last night received official accounts from General Washington in a letter dated at Chatham . . . The French fleet of ten line-of-battle ships, which lay at Rhode Island, are now actually on the way hither, and are daily expected . . .

If after such a torrent of good news I could wish to add another article, it would be that Lord Cornwallis, with his whole army, were in our possession. But this I hope, in that providence to which I prostrate myself with grateful adoration from the present happy aspect of our affairs, will be the subject of some future letter; or that I may, to the happiness of seeing you again, add that of being able to give you the first notice of so important and so happy as event.

Source: *The Magazine of American History*, Volume 8. (New York: A.S. Barnes & Company, 1881), 210.

A Letter from Colonel St. George Tucker to His Wife,[8] Williamsburg, September 15, 1781

I wrote you yesterday that General Washington had not yet arrived. About four o'clock in the afternoon his approach was announced . . . He approached without any pomp or parade, attended only by a few horsemen and his own servants . . . I met with him as I was endeavoring to get to camp from town . . . To my great surprise he recognized my features and spoke to me immediately by name . . . The Marquis rode up with precipitation, clasped the General in his arms and embraced him with an ardor not easily described . . . The General . . . rode through the French lines. The troops were paraded for the purpose and cut a most splendid figure. He then visited the Continental line. As he entered the camp the cannon from the park of artillery and from every brigade announced the happy event . . . men, women and children seemed to vie with each other in demonstrations of joy and eagerness to see their beloved countryman . . . We are all alive and so sanguine in our hopes that nothing can be conceived more different than the countenances of the same men at this time and on the first of June . . . Cornwallis may now tremble for his fate, for nothing but some extraordinary interposition of his guardian angels seems capable of saving him and his whole army from captivity . . .

Source: *William and Mary College Quarterly Historical Magazine*, Volume 16. (Richmond, VA: Whittet & Shepperson, 1908), 58–59.

[8]George Tucker continues his correspondence with an account of Washington's embrace, not only by Lafayette, but by the ordinary citizenry.

[9]Washington's battle plan was predicated on a situation in which the French fleet under de Grasse would bottle up Cornwallis's navy in the York River. But de Grasse had written to Washington to say that he could not stay at the Chesapeake after October, that he was obliged to return to his position in the West Indies. Washington sent this appeal to de Grasse by the hand of Lafayette.

A Letter from George Washington to Comte de Grasse,[9] Williamsburg, September 25, 1781

. . . Give me leave in the first place to repeat to Yr Excellency that the enterprise against York under the protection of your Ships is as certain as any military operation can be rendered by a decisive superiority of strength and means; that is in fact reducible to calculation, and that the surrender of the British Garrison will be so important in itself and its consequences, that it must necessarily go a great way towards terminating the war, and securing the invaluable objects of it to the Allies. Your Excellency's departure from the Chesapeake . . . would frustrate these brilliant prospects, and the consequence would be . . . the disbanding perhaps of the whole Army for want of provisions. The present Theatre of the War is totally deficient in means of land transportation, being intersected by large rivers, and the whole dependance for interior communication being upon small vessels . . . that our supplies can only be drawn from a distance and under cover of a fleet, Mistress of the Chesapeake. I most earnestly entreat Your Excellency farther to consider that if the present opportunity shld be missed; that if you shld withdraw your maritime force from the position agreed upon, that no future day can restore us a similar occasion for striking a decisive blow . . .

The confidence with which I feel myself inspired by the energy of character and the naval talents which so eminently distinguish Yr Excellency leaves me no doubt that upon a consideration of the consequences which must follow your departure from the Chesapeake, that Yr Excellency will determine upon the possible measure which the dearest interests of the common cause wd dictate. I had invariably flattered myself from the accounts given me by skillful mariners, that Your Excels position, moored in the Chesapeake . . . wd support the operations of a siege, secure the transportation of our supplies by

[10]"Oeconomise" is an archaic form of economize.

water and oeconomise[10] the most precious time by facilitating the debarkation of our heavy Artillery and stores conveniently to the trenches in York River . . . . Upon the whole, I shld esteem myself deficient in my duty to the common cause of France and America, if I did not persevere in entreating Yr. Excellency to resume the plans that have been so happily arranged . . .

Let me add Sir that even momentary absence of the French fleet may expose us to the loss of the British Garrison at York as in the present state of affairs Ld Cornwallis might effect the evacuation with the loss of his Artillery and baggage and such a sacrifice of men as his object would evidently justify. The Marquis de la Fayette who does me the honor to bear this to Yr Excellency will explain many peculiarities of our situation which could not well be comprised in a letter; his candor and abilities are well known to Yr. Excellency and entitle him to the fullest confidence in treating the most important interests . . .

Source: Jared Sparks, *The Writings of George Washington*, Volume 8. (New York: Harper & Brothers, 1847), 164–166.

Journal of Colonel Jonathan Trumbull, Secretary to George Washington,[11] September 28, 1781

. . . the army commences its march from Williamsburg and approaches within two miles of York Town. The enemy on our approach make some shew of opposition from their cavalry, but upon our bringing up some field pieces and making a few shot, they retire, and we take a quiet position for the night . . . By the approach of the main body, and lying of the French ships in the mouth of the river, the enemy were now completely invested, except by water above the town, where they are yet open, and their boats are troublesome up the river for some distance. To close them on this side the General has proposed it to the admiral to run some ships above the town and to take their station there.

[11]Trumbull was the son of Connecticut governor Johnathan Trumbull. He had been assigned as aide-de-camp to Washington. He presents a concise picture of the battle lines as drawn.

September 29

The American troops take their station in the front of the enemies works . . . No opposition this day except a few shots from the extream works, and small firing from their jagers[12] and our rifle men.

[12]"Jagers" was a military term for elite light infantry.

September 30

In the morning it is discovered that the enemy have evacuated all their exterior works, and retired to their interior defence near the town. We immediately take possession . . . of the enemies' redoubts, and find ourselves very unexpectedly upon very advantageous ground, commanding their line of works in near approach. Scarce a gun fired this day . . .

Source: Jonathan Trumbull, "Minutes of Occurrences Respecting the Siege and Capture of York in Virginia." *Proceedings of the Massachusetts Historical Society, 1875–1876.* (Boston: Published by the Society, 1876), 334–335.

[13]These excerpts from two diaries paint a picture of the day-to-day progress of the campaign. Colonel Butler was an associate of "mad" Anthony Wayne from the earliest days of the revolution. Duncan was a private soldier.

Journal of Colonel Richard Butler and Diary of James Duncan, Both of the Pennsylvania Line[13]

[Butler]

October 2nd: The fire of the enemy more severe this morning . . . they fired severely all day . . . the fire of the enemy continued all night. About 10 o'clock, P.M., a heavy firing of the ships in the bay . . .

October 4th: . . . the enemy very busy forming new works. Two deserters from the enemy, who report that Cornwallis' army is very sickly, to the amount of 2000 men in the hospital, and that the troops had scarce ground to live on, their shipping in a very naked state and their cavalry very scarce of forage. 2000 French marines landed on Gloster side from Count de Grasse at 9 o'clock P.M., a smart firing of small arms, which brought a very heavy cannonade all night.

October 5th: Cannonading all morning. Our part increases fast, and things go on well . . . a great deal of firing through the night . . .

October 6th: . . . The enemy kept up a severe cannonade all night . . . the allied army . . . contented themselves with going in with their work. The American part of the army on duty made great progress in forming lines and batteries without the loss of a man.

[Duncan]

[14] The Latin here, when translated to English, literally means "This hand is hostile to tyranny."

[15]This is the so-called Manual of Arms in which soldiers move their weapons through a series of maneuvers, ending with "Order Arms" by placing rifles in resting position.

October 7th . . . The trenches were this day to be enlivened with drums beating and colors flying . . . Immediately upon our arrival the colors were planted on the parapet with this motto: Manus haec inimica tyrannis.[14] Our next maneuver was rather extraordinary. We were ordered to mount the bank, front the enemy, and there by word of command go through all the ceremony of soldiery,[15] ordering and grounding our arms, and although the enemy had been firing a little before, they did not now give us a single shot. I suppose their astonishment at our conduct must have prevented them, for I can assign no other reason. Colonel Hamilton[16] gave these orders, and although I esteem him one of the first officers in the American army, must beg leave in this instance to think he wantonly exposed the lives of his men . . .

[Butler]

October 8th: The division of Steuben[17] for the trenches today . . . The enemy continued to cannonade, mounted at 12 o'clock . . . The enemy seem embarrassed, confused and indeterminate, their fire seems feeble to what might be expected; their works, too, are not formed on any regular plan, but thrown up in a hurry occasionally, and although we have not as yet fired one shot from a piece of artillery, they are as cautious as if the heaviest fire was kept up.

October 9th: . . . The Commander-in-Chief paid the allies the compliment of firing first. The shot and shells flew incessantly through the night, dismounted the guns of the enemy and destroyed many of their embrasures.[18]

Sources: "General Richard Butler's Journal of the Siege of Yorktown." *The Historical Magazine*, Volume 8. (New York: John G. Shea, 1864), 107–108; "James Duncan's Diary of the Siege of Yorktown." *The Magazine of History*, Volume 1. (New York: William Abbatt, 1905), 412.

Narrative of Sergeant James Sullivan Martin of Connecticut[19]

. . . we marched to Williamsburg, where we joined General Lafayette . . . about this time, we had orders from the Commander in Chief that, in case the enemy should come out to meet us, we should exchange but one round with them and then decide the conflict with the bayonet . . . The British did not think fit at that time to give us an opportunity to soil our bayonets in their carcasses . . . We went on and soon arrived and encamped in their neighborhood . . . we encountered our old associate, Hunger . . . No eatable stores had arrived . . . We were . . . compelled to try our hands at foraging . . . There was a plenty of shoats[20] all about this wood, fat and plump, weighing, generally, from fifty to a hundred pounds apiece . . . we made free with some of them to satisfy the calls of nature . . .

[16] Alexander Hamilton was aide-de-camp to Washington during the war, one of the authors of the *Federalist Papers* in support of the Constitution, and served in Washington's cabinet as America's first secretary of the Treasury.

[17] The Prussian general Baron von Steuben began turning the Continentals into an army at Valley Forge. He started with a group of 100 chosen men who then worked outward through other brigades. When yelling, and swearing at them in German and French didn't work, von Stuben had his aide swear at them in English. His hard work helped to turn the war around.

[18] These were openings in a wall through which guns are fired.

[19] Martin was a sergeant in the Connecticut line. His is the most vivid account we have of the action at Yorktown, including the earliest account of the treatment of runaway slaves.

[20] Shoats are young pigs.

We now began to make preparations for laying close siege to the enemy. We had holed him and nothing remained but to dig him out. Accordingly, after taking every precaution to prevent his escape, we settled our guards . . . made platforms for the batteries . . . brought on our battering pieces, ammunition, &c. On the fifth of October we began to put our plans into execution. One third part of all the troops were put in requisition to be employed in opening the trenches. A third part of our Sappers[21] and Miners were ordered out this night to assist the engineers in laying out the works. It was a very dark and rainy night . . . we . . . began by following the engineers and laying laths of pine wood end to end upon the line asked out by the officers for the trenches. We had not proceeded far in the business before the engineers ordered us to desist and remain where we were, and be sure not to straggle a foot from the spot while they were absent from us. In a few minutes after their departure, there came a man alone to us, having on a surtout,[22] . . . and inquired for the engineers. We now began to be a little jealous for our safety, being alone and without arms, and within forty rods of the British trenches. The stranger inquired what troops we were; talked familiarly with us a few minutes, when, being informed which way the officers had gone, he went off in the same direction, after strictly charging us, in case we should be taken prisoners, not to discover to the enemy what troops we were. We were obliged to him for his kind advice, but we considered ourselves as standing in no great need of it; for we knew as well as he did that sappers and miners were allowed no quarters,[23] at least are entitled to none by the laws of warfare, and of course should take care, if taken and the enemy did not find us out, not to betray our own secret. In a short time the engineers returned and the aforementioned stranger with them; they discoursed together sometime, when by the officers calling him "Your Excellency," we discovered that it was Gen. Washington. Had we dared, we might have cautioned him for exposing himself so carelessly to danger at such a time, and doubtless he would have taken it in good part if we had. But nothing ill happened to either him or ourselves.

It coming on to rain hard, we were ordered back to our tents, and nothing more was done that night. The next night, which was the sixth of October . . . We . . . completed laying out the works. The troops of the line were there ready with entrenching tools and began to entrench, after General Washington had struck a few blows with a pickaxe, a mere ceremony, that it might be said, "Gen. Washington with his own hands first broke ground at the site of Yorktown." . . .

As soon as it was day they . . . began to fire . . . They brought out a fieldpiece or two . . . and discharged several shots at the men who were at work erecting a bomb-battery; but their shot had no effect and they soon gave it over. They had a large bull-dog, and every time they fired he would follow their shots across our trenches. Our officers wished to catch him and oblige him carry a message for them into the town to his masters, but he looked too formidable for any of us to encounter. I do not remember, exactly, the number of days we were employed before we got our batteries in readiness to open upon the enemy . . . The French . . . had completed their batteries a few hours before us, but were not allowed to discharge their pieces till the American batteries were ready. Our commanding battery was on the near bank of the York river and contained ten heavy guns; the next was a bomb battery of three large mortars[24] . . . The whole number, American and French, was ninety-two cannon, mortars and howitzers.[25] Our flagstaff was in the ten-gun battery . . .

I was in the trenches the day that the batteries were to be opened.[26] All were upon the tiptoe of expectation and impatience to see the signal given to open the whole line of batteries, which was to be the hoisting of the American flag in the ten-gun battery. About noon the much wished for signal went up. I confess I felt a secret pride swell my heart when I saw the "star-spangled banner"[27] waving majestically in the very faces of our implacable adversaries; it appeared like an omen of success to our enterprise, and so it proved in reality. A simultaneous discharge of all the guns in the line followed, the French troops accompanying it with "Huzza for the Americans!" . . .

The siege was carried on warmly for several days, when most of the guns in the enemy's works were silenced . . . We arrived at the trenches a little before sunset. I saw several officers fixing bayonets on long staves. I then concluded we were about to make a general assault upon the enemy's works, but before dark I was informed of the whole plan, which was to storm the redoubts, the one by the Americans and the other by the French. The Sappers and Miners were furnished with axes and were to proceed in front and cut a passage for the troops through the abatis, which are composed of the tops of trees, the small branches cut off with a slanting stroke which renders them as sharp as spikes. The trees are then laid at a small distance from the trench or ditch, pointing outwards, and then the butts fastened to the ground in such a manner that they cannot be removed by those on the outside of them. It is almost impossible

[24]These are short, thick, and large cannon that fired an exploding shell, or "bomb," in a high trajectory. The bomb would fly over earthworks and explode while still airborne, raining shrapnel over the enemy.

[25] Howitzers are cannon that fire shells at a high angle.

[26]The batteries, or cannon, were to begin fighting.

[27]This sentence indicates the date of this text as after 1814 because of his reference to the "Star-Spangled Banner."

to get through them. Through these we were to cut a passage before we or the other assailants could enter.

At dark the detachment was formed and advanced beyond the trenches and lay down on the ground to await the signal . . . We had not lain here long before the expected signal was given, of us and the French, who were to storm the other redoubt, by the three shells with their fiery trains mounting the air in quick succession. The word "up, up" was then reiterated through the detachment. We immediately moved silently on toward the redoubt we were to attack, with unloaded muskets. Just as we arrived at the abatis, the enemy discovered us and directly opened a sharp fire upon us . . . I thought the British were killing us off at a great rate . . .

As soon as the firing began, our people began to cry, "The fort's our own!" and it was "Rush on boys." The Sappers and Miners soon cleared a passage for the infantry, who entered it rapidly. Our Miners were ordered not to enter the fort, but there was no stopping them. "We will go." said they. "Then go to the devil, if you will" said the commanding officer of our corps . . . While crossing the trench, the enemy threw hand grenades into it . . . The fort was taken and all quiet in a very short time . . . All that were in the action of storming the redoubt were exempted from further duty that night. We laid down upon the ground and rested the remainder of the night as well as a constant discharge of grape and canister shot would permit us to do . . . it. We returned to camp early in the morning, all safe and sound . . .

After we had finished our second line of trenches there was but little firing on either side. After Lord Cornwallis had failed to get off, upon the seventeenth day of October . . . he requested a cessation of hostilities for, I think, twenty four hours, when commissioners from both armies met at a house between the lines to agree upon articles of capitulation . . . Before night we were informed that the British had surrendered and that the siege was ended. The next day we were ordered to put ourselves in as good order as our circumstances would admit, to see . . . the British army march out and stack their arms . . . After breakfast, on the nineteenth, we were marched onto the ground and paraded on the right hand side of the road, and the French forces on the left. We waited two or three hours before the British made their appearance. They were . . . compelled at last, by necessity, to appear, all armed, with bayonets fixed, drums beating, and faces lengthening . . . the Americans and French beating a march as they passed out between them. It was a noble sight to us, and the more so, as it seemed to promise a speedy conclusion to the contest. The British did not make so good an appearance as the German forces . . . The English felt their honor wounded, the Germans did not greatly care who's hands they were in. The British paid the Americans, seemingly, but little attention as they passed them, but they eyed the French with considerable malice depicted in their countenances. They marched to the place appointed and stacked their arms . . . During the siege, we saw in the woods herds of Negroes which Lord Cornwallis . . . in love and pity to them, had turned adrift . . . After the siege was ended, many of the owners of these deluded creatures came to our camp and engaged some of our men to take them up, generally offering a guinea a head for them. Some of our Sappers and Miners took up several of them that belonged to a Colonel Banister; when he applied for them they refused to deliver them to him unless he would promise not to punish them. He said he had no intention of punishing them, that he did not blame them at all, the blame lay on Lord Cornwallis. I saw several of those miserable wretches delivered to their master . . . He told them that he gave them the free choice either to go with him or remain where they were, that he would not injure a hair of their heads if they returned with him to their duty. Had the poor souls received a reprieve at the gallows they could not have been more overjoyed than they appeared to be at what he promised them; their ague fit soon left them. I had a share in one of them by assisting in taking him up; the fortune I acquired was small, only one dollar . . .

Our captain at length became tired of this business and determined to go on after the other troops at all events. We accordingly left Yorktown and set our faces to the Highlands of New York . . .

Source: Joseph P. Martin, *A Narrative of Some of the Adventures, Dangers, and Sufferings of a Revolutionary Soldier.* (Hallowell, ME: Glazier, Masters, & Co., 1830), 165–175.

Journal of Dr. James Thatcher,[28] October 1781

From the 10th to the 15th, a tremendous and incessant firing from the American and French batteries is kept up, and the enemy return the fire, but with little effect . . . the engines of war have raged with redoubled fury and destruction on both sides, no cessation day or night . . . The siege is daily becoming more and more

[28]James Thatcher was a surgeon with the Continental Army. His journals recount the horrific effects of warfare. He called his diary a "military journal," and in it he says almost nothing about medical issues. But his personal observations on military actions and events are full of anecdotes that make the combat and its leading personages vivid and human.

[29]The British general Cornwallis, commander of British forces at Yorktown.

formidable and alarming, and his lordship[29] must view his situation as extremely critical, if not desperate . . . The bombshells from the besiegers and the besieged are incessantly crossing each others' path in the air. They are clearly visible in the form of a black ball in the day, but in the night they appear like a fiery meteor with a blazing tail, most beautifully brilliant, ascending majestically from the mortar to a certain altitude and gradually descending to the spot where they are destined to execute their work of destruction. It is astonishing with what accuracy an experienced gunner will make his calculations, that a shell shall fall within a few feet of a given point, and burst at the precise time, though at a great distance. When a shell falls, it whirls round, burrows, and excavates the earth to a considerable extent and, bursting, makes dreadful havoc around. I have more than once witnessed fragments of the mangled bodies and limbs of the British soldiers thrown into the air by the bursting of our shells . . .

The enemy have two redoubts . . . it was resolved to take possession of them both by assault. The one on the left . . . was assigned to our brigade of light-infantry, under the command of the Marquis de la Fayette. The advanced corps was led on by the intrepid Colonel Hamilton, who had commanded a regiment of light-infantry during the campaign . . . The assault commenced at eight o'clock in the evening, and the assailants bravely entered the fort with the point of the bayonet without firing a single gun . . . During the assault, the British kept up an incessant firing of cannon and musketry from their whole line. His Excellency General Washington, Generals Lincoln and Knox, with their aids, having dismounted, were standing in an exposed situation waiting the result.

Colonel Cobb, one of General Washington's aids, solicitous for his safety, said to His Excellency, "Sir, you are too much exposed here. Had you not better step a little back?" "Colonel Cobb," replied His Excellency, "if you are afraid, you have liberty to step back." . . .

Our artillery men, by the exactness of their aim, make every discharge take effect, so that many of the enemy's guns are entirely silenced, and their works are almost in ruins.

Source: James Thatcher, *A Military Journal during the American Revolutionary War.* (Boston: Richardson and Lord, 1823), 339–343.

Letter from Lord Cornwallis to Sir Henry Clinton,[30] Yorktown, October 20, 1781

I have the mortification to inform your Excellency that I have been forced to give up the posts of York and Gloucester, and to surrender the troops under my command by capitulation on the 19th inst. as prisoners of war to the combined forces of America and France. I never saw this post[31] in a very favorable light, but when I found I was to be attacked in it in so unprepared a state, by so powerful an army and artillery, nothing but the hopes of relief would have induced me to attempt its defence; for I would either have endeavored to escape to New York . . . or I would . . . have attacked them in the open field . . . being assured by your Excellency's letters that every possible means would be tried by the navy and army to relieve us, I could not think myself at liberty to venture upon either of those two desperate attempts; therefore, after . . . receiving on the second evening your letter of the 24th of September informing that the relief would sail about the 5th of October, I withdrew within the works on the night of the 29th of September, hoping by the labour and firmness of the soldiers to protract the defence until you could arrive . . . The enemy . . . on the night of the 30th . . . constructed . . . two redoubts . . . their batteries opened on the evening of the 9th . . . The fire continued incessant from heavy cannon and from mortars and howitzers, throwing shells from eight to sixteen inches, until all our guns on the left were silenced, our work much damaged, and our loss of men considerable . . . On the evening of the 14th, they assaulted and carried two redoubts . . .

At this time we knew that there was no part of the whole front attacked on which we could show a single gun, and our shells were nearly expended; I therefore had only to chuse between preparing to surrender next day or endeavoring to get off with the greatest part of the troops, and I determined to attempt the latter, reflecting that though it should prove unsuccessful in its immediate object, it might at least delay the enemy in the prosecution of further enterprizes. Sixteen large boats were prepared, and . . . were ordered to be in readiness to receive troops precisely at 10 o'clock. With these I hoped to pass the infantry during the night, abandoning our baggage, and leaving a detachment to capitulate for the town's people and the sick

[30]Cornwallis was commander of British forces at Yorktown. Clinton was an American-born general who had joined the British as early as Bunker Hill. There was great animosity between the two. Clinton's overall plan focused on New York and a northern defense. Cornwallis was convinced that the subduing of Virginia was key to victory. Clinton at first proposed that Cornwallis take a southern position and hold it with a Red Coat force. Cornwallis chose to hold Yorktown; Clinton's failure to send reinforcements gave Cornwallis a reason (along with the weather) for his defeat. The bad blood between the two did not end with the American victory. They engaged in a post-war battle of words in the London press for years.

[31]A "post" is a military term for a place assigned to a soldier for duty. The term is still used today.

and wounded; on which subject a letter was ready to be delivered to General Washington . . .

At this critical moment the weather, from being moderate and calm, changed to a most violent storm of wind and rain and drove all the boats, some of which had troops on board, down the river. It was soon evident that the intended passage was impracticable, and the absence of the boats rendered it equally impossible to bring back the troops that had passed . . . In this situation, with my little force divided, the enemy batteries opened at daybreak . . . The boats having now returned, they were ordered to bring back the troops that had passed during the night, and they joined us in the forenoon without much loss.

Our works in the mean time were going to ruin, and not having need able to strengthen them . . . my opinion entirely coincided with that of the engineer and principal officers of the army, that they were in many places assailable in the forenoon, and that by the continuance of the same fire for a few hours longer, they would be in such state as to render it desperate with our numbers to attempt to maintain them. We at that time could not fire a single gun . . . Our numbers had been diminished by the enemy's fire, but particularly by sickness, and the strength and spirits of those in the works were much exhausted by the fatigue of constant watching and unremitting duty.

Under all these circumstances, I thought it would have been wanton and inhuman to the last degree to sacrifice the lives of this small body of gallant soldiers, who had behaved with so much fidelity and courage, by exposing them to an assault, which from the numbers and precautions of the enemy could not fail to succeed. I therefore proposed to capitulate.

Source: *The London Magazine.* (London: R. Baldwin, January 1781), 599–600.

Exchange of Letters on Surrender: Cornwallis and Washington,[32] October 17, 1781

Cornwallis to Washington

I propose a cessation of hostilities for twenty four hours, and that two officers may be appointed by each side, to meet at Mr. Moore's house, to settle terms for the surrender of the posts of York and Gloucester.

[32]This correspondence reveals Washington's demands as both generous and fair: the British Army surrendered to the Americans; the navy surrendered to the French; officers kept their arms and property. Cornwallis was permitted to return to England. Cornwallis, pleading illness, did not participate in the exchange of swords that was a key feature of the surrender ceremony. His second in command, General O'Hara, gave up his sword to General Lincoln, Washington's second.

Washington to Cornwallis

I have had the Honor of receiving Your Lordship's Letter of this Date. An ardent Desire to spare the further effusion of human blood will readily incline me to listen to such Terms for the Surrender of your Posts and Garrisons at York and Gloucester, as are admissible.

I wish, previous to the Meeting of Commissioners, that your Lordship's proposals in writing may be sent to the American Lines: for which Purpose, a Suspension of Hostilities during two Hours from the Delivery of this Letter will be granted.

Cornwallis to Washington

I have this moment been honored with your Excellency's letter, dated this day. The time limited for sending my answer will not admit of entering into the detail of articles, but the basis of my proposals will be, that the garrisons of York and Gloucester shall be prisoners of war, with the customary honors. And, for the convenience of the individuals which I have the honour to command, that the British shall be sent to Britain, and the Germans to Germany, under engagement not to serve against France, America, or their allies, until released or regularly exchanged. That all arms and public stores shall be delivered up to you; but that the usual indulgence of side-arms to officers, and that the interest of several individuals, in civil capacities and connected with us, shall be attended to.

If your Excellency thinks that a continuance of the suspensions of hostilities will be necessary, to transmit your answer, I shall have no objection to the hour that you may propose.

Washington to Cornwallis

To avoid unnecessary Discussions and Delays, I shall at Once, in Answer to your Lordship's Letter of Yesterday, declare the general Basis upon which a Definitive Treaty and Capitulation must take place. The Garrisons of York and Gloucester, including the Seamen, as you propose, will be received Prisoners of War. The Condition annexed, of sending the British and German Troops to the parts of Europe to which they respectively belong, is inadmissible.

Instead of this, they will be marched to such parts of the Country as can most conveniently provide for their Subsistence; and the Benevolent Treatment of Prisoners, which is invariably observed by the Americans, will be extended to them . . . The Shipping and Boats in the two Harbors, with all their Guns, Stores, Tackling, Furniture and Apparel, shall be delivered in their present State to an Officer of the Navy, appointed to take possession of them. The Artillery, Arms, Accoutrements, Military Chest and Public Stores of every Denomination, shall be delivered unimpaired to the Heads of Departments, to which they respectively belong. The Officers shall be indulged in retaining their Side Arms, and the Officers and Soldiers may preserve their Baggage and Effects, with this Reserve, that Property taken in the Country, will be reclaimed . . . I have to add, that I expect the Sick and Wounded will be supplied with their own Hospital Stores, and be attended by British Surgeons, particularly charged with the Care of them. Your Lordship will be pleased to signify your Determination either to accept or reject the Proposals now offered, in the Course of Two Hours from the Delivery of this Letter, that Commissioners may be appointed to digest the Articles of Capitulation, or a Renewal of Hostilities may take place.

Cornwallis to Washington

I agree to open a treaty of capitulation upon the basis of the garrisons of York and Gloucester, including seamen, being prisoners of war, without annexing the condition of their being sent to Europe; but I expect to receive a compensation in the articles of capitulation for the surrender of Gloucester in its present state of defence. I shall, in particular, desire, that the sloop of war *Bonetta* may be left entirely at my disposal, from the hour that the capitulation's signed, to receive an aide-de-camp to carry my dispatches to Sir Henry Clinton. Such soldiers as I may think proper to send as passengers in her, to be manned with fifty men of her own crew, and to be permitted to sail without examination, when my dispatches are ready; engaging, on my part, that the ship shall be brought back and delivered to you . . . that the crew and soldiers shall be accounted for in future exchanges, that she shall carry off no officer without your consent, nor public property of any kind; and I shall likewise desire, that the traders and inhabitants may preserve their property, and that no person may be punished or molested for having joined the British troops. If you choose to proceed to negotiation on these grounds, I shall appoint two field officers of my army to meet two officers from you, at any time and place that you think proper, to digest the articles of capitulation.

Source: Henry P. Johnston, *The Yorktown Campaign and the Surrender of Cornwallis.* (New York: Harper and Bros, 1881), 185–187.

Journal of Dr. James Thatcher,[33] October 19

This is to us a most glorious day, but to the English, one of bitter chagrin and disappointment. Preparations are now making to receive as captives that vindictive, haughty commander and that victorious army, who, by their robberies and murders, have so long been a scourge to our brethren of the Southern states . . . The stipulated terms of capitulation are similar to those granted to General Lincoln at Charlestown last year. The captive troops are to march out with shouldered arms, colors cased[34] and drums beating a British or German march, and to ground their arms at a place assigned for the purpose. The officers are allowed their side-arms and private property, and the generals and such officers as desire it are to go on parole to England or New York. The marines and seamen of the king's ships are prisoners of war to the navy of France; and the land forces to the United States. All military and artillery stores to be delivered up unimpaired. The royal prisoners to be sent into the interior if Virginia, Maryland and Pennsylvania in regiments, to have rations allowed them equal to the American soldiers, and to have their officers near them, Lord Cornwallis to man and despatch the "Bonetta" sloop of war with dispatches to Sir Henry Clinton at New York without being searched, the vessel to be returned and the hands accounted for.

At about twelve o'clock, the combined army was arranged and drawn up into lines extending more than a mile in length. The Americans were drawn up in a line on the right side of the road, and the French occupied the left. At the head of the former, the great American commander, mounted on his nobel courser, took his station, attended by his aide. At the head of the later was posted the excellent Count Rochambeau and his suite. The French troops, in complete uniform, displayed a martial and noble appearance; their bands of music, of which the timbrel formed a part, is a delightful novelty and produced while marching to the ground[35] a most enchanting effect. The Americans, though not all in uniform, nor their dress so neat, yet

[33]Dr. Thatcher, intrepid observer of the revolution, concludes his "military journal" with a commentary on the surrender ceremony.

[34]Colors cased meant there were no flags flying.

[35]The "ground" was the field of surrender.

exhibited an erect, soldierly air, and every countenance beamed with satisfaction and joy. The concourse of spectators from the country was prodigious, in point of numbers was probably equal to the military, but universal silence and order prevailed.

It was about two o'clock when the captive army advanced through the line formed for their reception. Every eye was prepared to gaze upon Lord Cornwallis . . . but he disappointed our anxious expectations; pretending indisposition, he made General O'Hara his substitute as the leader of his army. This officer was followed by the conquered troops in a slow and solemn step, with shouldered arms, colors cased and drums beating a British march. Having arrived at the head of the line, General O'Hara, elegantly mounted, advanced to his excellency the commander-in-chief, taking off his hat, and apologized for the non-appearance of Earl Cornwallis. With his usual dignity and politeness, his excellency pointed to Major-General Lincoln for directions, by whom the British army was conducted into a spacious field, where it was intended they should ground their arms.

The royal troops, while marching through the line formed by the allied army, exhibited a decent and neat appearance, as respects arms and clothing, for their commander opened his store and directed every soldier to be furnished with a new suit complete, prior to the capitulation. But in their line of march we remarked a disorderly and unsoldierly conduct, their step was irregular, and their ranks frequently broken. But it was in the field, when they came to the last act of the drama, that the spirit and pride of the British soldier was put to the severest test: here their mortification could not be concealed. Some of the platoon officers appeared to be exceedingly chagrined when giving the word "ground arms," and I am a witness that they performed this duty in a very unofficer like manner; and that many of the soldiers manifested a sullen temper, throwing their arms onto pile with violence, as if determined to render them useless. This irregularity, however, was checked by the authority of General Lincoln. After having grounded their arms and divested themselves of their accoutrements, the captive troops were conducted back to Yorktown and guarded by our troops till they could be removed to the place of their destination . . .

We are not to be surprised that the pride of the British officers is humbled on this occasion, as they have always entertained an exalted opinion of their own military prowess and affected to view the Americans as a contemptible, undisciplined rabble. But there is no display of magnanimity when a great commander shrinks from the inevitable misfortunes of war; and when it is considered that Lord Cornwallis has frequently appeared in splendid triumph at the head of his army, by which he is almost "adored," we conceive it incumbent on him cheerfully to participate in their misfortunes and degradations, however humiliating; but it is said he gives himself up entirely to vexation and despair.

Source: James Thatcher, *A Military Journal during the American Revolutionary War*. (Boston: Richardson and Lord, 1823), 343–349.

SECTION III

A Nation of Amazons

Introduction

Women who actively supported the rebellion informally styled themselves "Daughters of Liberty." They borrowed the term from the "Sons of Liberty" organized by Samuel Adams in Boston. While the Sons were engaged in sometimes violent protests (the Boston Tea Party is the most famous), Daughters engaged in boycotts of British goods, the manufacturing of clothing for the army, and fund-raising. It is ironic that the term "Sons of Liberty" was not the invention of American patriots. It was taken from a speech by Colonel Isaac Barre, a member of Parliament who supported the American cause during the debates over the Stamp Act (1765). He described the patriots as victims of "persons sent to rule over them . . ." [these actions], he said "have caused the blood of those sons of liberty to recoil within them."

George Washington recognized the importance of women's activities and wrote that "the contribution of the association they represent exceeded what could have been expected, and the spirit that animated the members of it, entitles them an equal place with any who have preceded them in the walk of female patriotism. They have embellished the American character with a new trait; by proving that the love of country is blended with those softer domestic virtues, which have always been allowed to be more peculiarly their own."

Patriotic Sentiments of an American Woman in Advocacy of the Revolution

(June 1780)

INTRODUCTION

This letter, published in a Philadelphia paper, contains historical references to women who served as political leaders. Especially potent is the author's mention of Joan of Arc, whose inspiring leadership freed France from British tyranny.

On the commencement of actual war, the women of America manifested a firm resolution to contribute as much as could depend on them, to the deliverance of their country . . . They aspire to render themselves more really useful . . . I glory in all that which my sex has done, great and commendable. I call to mind with enthusiasm and with admiration, all those acts of courage, of constancy and patriotism, which history has transmitted to us . . . So many famous sieges, where the women have been seen forgetting the weakness of their sex, building new walls, digging trenches with their feeble hands, furnishing arms to their defenders, they themselves darting the missile weapons on the enemy, resigning the ornaments of their apparel and their fortune,[1] to fill the public treasury, and to hasten the deliverance of their country . . .

Born for liberty, disdaining to bear the irons of a tyrannic government, we associate ourselves to the grandeur of those sovereigns, cherished and revered, who have held with so much splendor the scepter of the greatest states . . . The Elizabeths, the Maries, the Catherines,[2] who have extended the empire of liberty, and, contented to reign by sweetness and justice, have broken the chains of slavery, forged by tyrants in the times of ignorance and barbarity. . . . We call to mind . . . that it was a French maid[3] who kindled up amongst her fellow citizens, the flame of patriotism buried under long misfortunes; It was the maid of Orleans who drove from the kingdom of France the ancestors of those same British, whose odious yoke we have just shaken off and whom it is necessary that we drive from this continent . . .

[1] Women contributed jewelry and raised money to defray the costs of war.

[2] The author references women who were outstanding political leaders: Queen Elizabeth I, Marie de Medici, and Catherine, empress of Russia.

[3] Joan of Arc.

We are at least certain, that he cannot be a good citizen who will not applaud our efforts for the relief of the armies which defend our lives, our possessions, our liberty . . . Brave Americans . . . your courage, and your constancy will always be dear to America, as long as she shall preserve her virtue. We know that, at a distance from the theatre of war, if we enjoy any tranquility, it is the fruit of your watchings, your labors, your dangers . . . if our barns, our orchards are safe at the present time from the bands of those incendiaries, it is to you that we owe it. And shall we hesitate to evidence to you our gratitude? Shall we hesitate to wear a clothing more simple; hair-dresses less elegant, while at the price of this small privation, we shall deserve your benedictions?[4] Who amongst us, will not renounce, with the highest pleasure, those vain ornaments, when she shall consider that the valiant defenders of America will be able to draw some advantage from the money which she may have laid out in these; that they will be better defended from the rigors of the seasons; that, after their painful toils, they will receive some extraordinary and unexpected relief; that these presents will perhaps be valued by them at a greater price, when they will have it in their power to say: This is the offering of the ladies.

The time is arrived to display the same sentiments which animated us at the beginning of the revolution, when we renounced the use of teas,[5] however agreeable to our taste, rather than receive them from our persecutors: when we made it appear to them that we placed former necessaries in the rank of superfluities, when our liberty was interested; when our republican and laborious hands spun the flax, prepared the linen intended for the use of our soldiers . . .

Let us not lose a moment; let us be engaged to offer the homage of our gratitude at the altar of military valor, and you, our brave deliverers, while mercenary slaves combat to cause you to share with them, the irons with which they are loaded,[6] receive with a free hand our offering, the purest which can be presented to your virtue.

Source: H. Niles, *Principles and Acts of the Revolution in America.* (Baltimore: Printed by W.O. Niles, 1822), 212–213.

[4]This references the boycott of British goods, designed to hurt British commercial wealth.

[5]The tea embargo by women was a complement to the Boston Tea Party.

[6]That is, while those loyal to Great Britain—their political "slaves"—fight against the revolution hoping to make our soldiers slaves to British tyranny.

The Voice of Aristocracy: Mary Morris

(June 10, 1780)

INTRODUCTION

Mary Morris was a member of a distinguished Philadelphia family whose members included signers of the Declaration of Independence and delegates to the Constitutional Convention. The recipient of this letter, Catherine Livingston of New Jersey, had an equally distinguished pedigree. The Livingstons were wealthy aristocrats whose support for the revolution was based on a desire to preserve their social and economic hegemony. The letter reflects this background; for Morris, money is the important thing: money to support the cause and money to reward the soldiers.

"Instead of waiting for the donations being sent, the ladies of each ward go from dore to dore[1] and collect them and I am one of those harrowed with this business. Yesterday we began our tour of duty and had the satisfaction of being successful . . . Of all absurdities— the ladies all going about for money exceeded everything; they were so extremely importunate that people were obliged to give them something to get rid of them."[2]

[1]"Dore" is an 18th-century spelling of door.

[2]The ladies were so persistent in their requests people gave them money in order to get rid of them.

"An idea prevails among the ladies that the soldiers will not be so much gratified by bestowing an article to which they are entitled from the public,[3] as in some other method which will convey more fully the idea of a reward for past services and an incitement to future duty. Those who are of this opinion propose the whole of the money to be changed into hard dollars and giving each soldier two; to be entirely at his own disposal."

[3]Uniforms.

Source: William Brooke Rawle, "Laurel Hill and Some Colonial Dames Who Once Lived There." *Pennsylvania Magazine of History and Biography* 35, no. 4 (1911): 398.

Eyewitness to Independence: The Adams's Correspondence
(July 1776)

INTRODUCTION

The correspondence of John and Abigail Adams reflects the events and developing social attitudes of the revolutionary period. After the revolution, John Adams would serve as vice president under George Washington and succeed him as president. Adams had a thorough understanding of the issues of forming a new government; his *Thoughts on Government* (1774) was widely read and was influential in building support for the revolution.

Abigail Smith Adams was a great correspondent and a great personality. Her letters show that she was a woman of spirit and great self-confidence. John Adams was not immune to the prejudice of his age that relegated women to a secondary role in public affairs.

John Adams to Mrs. Adams, Philadelphia, July 3, 1776

. . . Yesterday the greatest question was decided which ever was debated in America; and a greater, perhaps, never was or will be decided among men. A resolution was passed, without one dissenting colony: "That these United Colonies are, and of right ought to be, free and independent states; and, as free and independent states, they have, and of right ought to have, full power to make war, conclude peace, establish commerce, and to do all other acts and things which other states may rightfully do." You will see, in a few days, a declaration, setting forth the causes which have impelled us to this revolution, and the reasons which will justify it in the sight of God and man. A plan of confederation will be taken up in a few days. When I look back to the year 1761, and recollect the argument concerning Writs of Assistance,[1] in the superior court, which I have hitherto considered as the commencement of the controversy between Great Britain and America, and run through the whole period from that time, to this, and recollect the series of political events, the chain of causes and effects, I am surprised at the suddenness as well as greatness of this revolution.

[1] The Writs of Assistance were general court orders allowing the authorities to search a man's home for smuggled articles. It was part of a program by Parliament to control colonial trade.

Britain has been filled with folly, and America with wisdom; at least this is my judgement—time must determine. It is the will of Heaven that the two countries should be sundered forever. It may be the will of Heaven that America shall suffer calamities still more wasting, and distresses still more dreadful. If this is to be the case, it will have this good effect at least, it will inspire us with many virtues which we have not, and correct many errors, follies, and vices, which threaten to disturb, dishonor, and destroy us. The furnace of affliction produces refinement in states as well as individuals. And the new governments we are assuming in every part, will require a purification from our vices, and an augmentation of our virtues, or they will be no blessings. The people will have unbounded power; and the people are extremely addicted to corruption and venality, as well as the great. I am not without apprehensions from this quarter; but I must submit all my hopes and fears to an over ruling Providence, in which, unfashionable as it may be, I firmly believe.

John Adams

. . . The second day of July, 1776, will be a memorable epocha[2] in the history of America. I am apt to believe that it will be celebrated by succeeding generations, as the great Anniversary Festival. It ought to be commemorated, as the day of deliverance by solemn acts of devotion to God Almighty. It ought to be solemnized with pomp, shows, games, sports, guns, bells, bonfires and illuminations, from one end of the continent to the other, from this time forward forever. You will think me transported with enthusiasm; but I am not. I am well aware of the toil, and blood and treasure, that it will cost us to maintain this Declaration, and support and defend these States. Yet, through all the gloom, I can see the rays of ravishing light and glory. I can see that the end is more than worth all the means. And that posterity will triumph in that day's transaction, even though we should rue[3] it, which I trust in God we shall not.

John Adams

Mrs. Adams to John Adams,[4] July 7, 1776

. . . Remember the Ladies and be more generous and favorable to them than your ancestors. Do not put such unlimited power into the hands of the Husbands. Remember, all men would be tyrants if

[2]This is a word for the beginning of a new period.

[3]Feel sorrow.

[4]Here, Abigail attempts to shape her husband's thought in favor of a more balanced view of the role of women in the new republic John and his male associates were shaping.

they could. If particular care and attention is not paid to the Ladies, we are determined to foment a rebellion, and will not hold ourselves bound by any laws in which we have no voice or Representation.

That your sex are so naturally tyrannical is a truth so thoroughly established as to admit of no dispute; but such of you as wish to be happy willingly give up the harsh title of master for the more tender and endearing one of friend. Why, then, not put it out of the power of the vicious and lawless to use us with cruelty and indignity with impunity? Men of all sense in all ages abhor these customs which treat us only as the vassals of your sex; regard us then as beings placed by Providence under your protection, and in imitation of the Supreme Being make use of that power only for our happiness.

Source: Charles Francis Adams, ed., *Familiar Letters of John Adams and His Wife Abigail.* (Boston: Houghton Mifflin Company, 1875), 191–194, 149–150.

"Dirty Kate": The Hero of the Battle of Fort Washington

(1779)

INTRODUCTION

Fort Washington in northern Manhattan was an important repository of supplies and materiel. When the installation fell to the British, 3,500 troops were taken prisoner. Margaret Corbin was among them. She was eventually released and returned to her native Pennsylvania. The injuries she suffered never healed completely, and she lost the use of her arm. She was made a permanent member of the Invalid Regiment stationed at West Point, New York. When the regiment was disbanded, she remarried and took up residence in Highland Falls, New York, not far from the U.S. Military Academy. She soon gained a reputation for her unpleasant personality. Perhaps that can be attributed to the fact that she was allowed to receive rations from the quartermaster—including liquor. In 1782, she requested 257 gills (1 gill is about 1½ oz) of whiskey, which she received in dribs and drabs.

Her eccentricities soon earned her the nickname "Dirty Kate," and in her declining years, she was often seen fishing in the Hudson River wrapped in an old artilleryman's coat. She died in 1800. In 1926, it was said the Daughters of the American Revolution had her remains reburied with full military honors in the West Point Cemetery. However, recent excavations of the cemetery at West Point unearthed the remains in what was supposed to be Dirty Kate's grave. The bones were discovered to be those of a male Revolutionary War soldier. Therefore, her final resting place remains a mystery. These documents detail her exploits.

Resolution of the Board of War of the Continental Congress,[1] June 6, 1779

[1]This resolution formally recognizes Corbin's contribution.

Resolved: That Margaret Corbin, who was wounded and disabled in the attack on Fort Washington, whilst she heroically filled the part of her husband who was killed by her side serving a piece of artillery, do receive, during her natural life, or the continuance of said disability, the one-half of the monthly pay drawn by a soldier in the service of these states; and that she receive out of the public stores one complete suit of clothes, or the value thereof in money.

Source: *Journals of the Continental Congress*, Volume 14. (Washington, DC: Government Printing Office, 1909), 805.

[2] Both the state of Pennsylvania and the Continental Congress awarded Corbin pensions for her service.

The Action of the Supreme Council of Pennsylvania,[2] Tuesday, June 29, 1779

. . . orders were drawn on the Treasurer . . . in favor of Margaret Corbin, for Thirty Dollars, to relieve her present necessities, she having been wounded and utterly disabled by three grape-shot, while she filled with distinguished bravery the post of her Husband, who was killed by her side, serving a piece of artillery at Fort Washington.

Ordered, That the case of Margaret Corbin, who was wounded and utterly disabled at Fort Washington, while she heroically filled the post of her husband, who was killed by her side serving a piece of Artillery, be recommended to a further consideration by the Board of War. This Council being of opinion that notwithstanding the rations which have already been allowed her, she is not provided for as her helpless situation really requires.

Source: *Minutes of the Supreme Executive Council of Pennsylvania*, Volume 12. (Harrisburg: Theo. Fenn & Co., 1853), 34–35.

[3] Here, further details of her service are given, and the financial stipend augmented by provisions of clothing.

The Action of the Continental Congress,[3] July 6, 1779

The board having received information that Margaret Corbin . . . for her gallant conduct in serving a piece of artillery when her husband was killed by her side still remains in a deplorable situation in consequence of her wounds, by which she is deprived of the use of one arm, and in other respects much disabled and probably will continue a cripple during her life. Beg leave to report:

Resolved, that Margaret Corbin receive annually, during her natural life, one compleat suit of cloaths, out of the public stores, or the value thereof in money, in addition the provision made for her by the act of Congress of July 6, 1779.

Source: *Journals of the Continental Congress*, Volume 17. (Washington, DC: Government Printing Office, 1910), 664.

Dear Shaw: No Liquor for Women!! Even Heros?,[4] Col. Tilghman's Appeal

[4]Male prejudice against equal recognition of women's contribution extended even to the issue of a ration. Here, Colonel Tilghman appeals to the quartermaster at West Point to make an exception in Corbin's case.

It is not in my power to transmit to you the resolve of Congress of the 10th Sept 1782, West Point, respecting Mrs. Corbin, Her case is a peculiar one. Her husband killed and herself wounded in the service were misfortunes of so aggravated a nature as justly rendered her worthy of public attention. I saw Col. Nicola just now, who told me that the resolve of Congress referred to, gave her, in consequence of the distress she was involved in, a complete ration per day and half pay for life and that Congress afterward passed the subsequent resolution which I have already sent you. Both these resolves were founded on Col. Nicola's application in her behalf, but however benevolent the intention, the poor woman has derived very little advantage from it, having received only her ration, and a few articles of clothing, by no means adequate to one suit annually. Her present application is in consequence of the rum or whiskey which composed part of her ration being stopped by . . . common custom in the issue to women . . . Hers being so singular a case, she thinks this regulation should not extend to her, and prays she may have an order for what has been detained from her, and that the Commissary be directed to issue the full ration in the future. With this back allowance she will be able to procure sundry necessaries that will render her present wretchedness a little more tolerable . . . I am sorry to trouble you again on this subject but the woman is truly an object of compassion. Her present husband is a poor crippled invalid who is of no service to her rather adds to her trouble . . .

It appears clearly to me that the order forbidding the issue of rum to women does not extend to Mrs. Corbin. Granting provision at all, to women who are followers of the army, is altogether a matter of courtesy, and therefore the Commanding General may allow them such Ration as he thinks proper. But Mrs. Corbin is a pensioner of Congress, and therefore, upon producing the Resolve made in her favor, Genl. Knox, as Commandant, may direct the Contractor to commute her Retained Rations of Liquor. Perhaps it would not be prudent to give them to her all in liquor.

I am, Yours affecty,
T. Tilghman

Source: Tench Tilghman to Samuel Shaw, September 11, 1782. The Gilder Lehrman Institute of American History, GLC02437.01597. Used by permission.

Mercy Otis Warren: Poet and Propagandist

(1774)

INTRODUCTION

In colonial America, the role of woman was defined by both custom and the exigencies of the "times that tried men's [and women's] souls." The feminine ideal of, in the words of John Adams, "refinement, delicacy, modesty, and non-assertiveness" was met head on by many women of all classes who refused to be defined in thought or action by male stereotyping. No one epitomized this conflict more than Mercy Otis Warren.

A gifted poet, playwright, and patriotic propagandist, Warren's writings were influential in bringing many to support the cause of the revolution. She refused to bend to criticism when she became openly involved in politics, although many of her works were originally published anonymously in radical journals such as the *Massachusetts Spy*. Her activities in support of the revolution were not limited to her literary work. On November 2, 1772, the first Massachusetts Committee of Correspondence was formed at her home in Plymouth by Samuel Adams to spread revolutionary propaganda. Soon there were over 80 such committees in Massachusetts alone. They shaped public opinion throughout the colonies in the years immediately before the outbreak of hostilities.

[1]This poem was directed at upper-class ladies who refused to go along with the boycott of British finery.

[2]Lustrings were glossy silk fabric; mecklin was a delicate lace used for dresses.

[3]Cardinals were short red cloaks worn by women; dyes refer to colors.
[4]Embroidery.
[5]Shoulder capes.

[6]Heavy corded silk dress fabrics.

[7]Loose gown.

[8]Rough homespun fabric.

To the Ladies[1]

. . .

With lawns and lustrings, blond, and mecklin laces,[2]
Fringes and jewels, fans and tweezer-cases,
Gay cloaks and hats of every shape and size,
Scarfs, cardinals, and ribands, of all dyes.[3]

With ruffles stamped, and aprons of tambour,[4]
Tippets[5] and handkerchiefs at least threescore . . .
Add feathers, furs, rich satins and ducapes,[6]
And head-dresses in pyramidal shapes . . .

Yet Clara quits the more dressed negligee[7]
And substitutes the careless Polanee[8]

Until some fair one from Britannia's court
Some jaunty dress or newer taste import;
This sweet temptation could not be withstood,
Though for her purchases paid her father's blood . . ."

Source: Rufus Griswold, ed., *Female Poets of America*. (Philadelphia: Carey and Hart, 1849).

Phillis Wheatley: Young Black Phenomenon
(1773)

INTRODUCTION

Phillis Wheatley was a person of exceptional ability, at once outstanding and unsuspected. Born a slave in West Africa, she was sold at the age of seven to a wealthy Boston merchant, John Wheatley. It was her good fortune to have entered a family of a sincerely religious nature. She had been destined to be educated in those virtues that would suit her to be a useful maid to Mrs. Wheatley, but she soon displayed a temperament that revealed her to be a person of exceptional gifts. She spoke no English, but soon adapted to the atmosphere of the Wheatley household. She was treated as one of the children of the family. She had her own room and was educated by her older siblings.

In less than two years, she was reading classical works and the Bible. At age 18 she began writing poetry. Her major themes were religious but that, and her personal history of redemption from slavery, led easily to her embrace of the cause of revolution.

People would visit the Wheatleys just to enjoy her company and conversation. Accompanied by her older brothers, she made a triumphant tour of England where she was received by the most prestigious households, her published poems and reputation having preceded her.

Lord Dartmouth, the secretary of state for the colonies, was a sincerely religious man. He was a humanitarian and philanthropist. He was living evidence that not all British leaders were opponents of colonial freedom. This poem reflects Wheatley's hopes for the cause of freedom based on the personal liberation she had achieved by virtue of her faith and talent.

To Lord Dartmouth

No more, America, in mournful strain
Of wrongs, and grievance unredress'd[1] complain,
No longer shall thou dread the iron chain,
Which wanton[2] Tyranny with lawless hand
Had made, and with it meant t'enslave the land.

[1]Uncorrected.

[2]Unjustified.

Should you, my Lord, while you peruse my song,[3]
Wonder from whence my love of freedom sprung,
Whence flow these wishes for the common good,
By feeling hearts alone best understood,
I, young in life, by seeming cruel fate
Was snatch'd from Afric's fancy'd happy seat![4]
What pangs excruciating must molest[5]
What sorrows labour in my parent's breast?

Steel'd[6] was that soul and by no misery moved
That from a father seiz'd his babe belov'd:
Such, such my case. And can I then but pray
Others may never feel tyrannic sway?

[3]Should the Earl of Dartmouth, secretary for North America read her poem.

[4]People suppose that Africa is a happy place.

[5]Injure and disturb.

[6]Strongly resistant.

Book: Phillis Wheatley, *Poems on Various Subjects, Religious and Moral.* (London: A. Bell, 1773), 74.

Anna Winslow: A Boston Schoolgirl Writes Home

(1771)

INTRODUCTION

Anna Winslow was 12 when her mother sent her to school in Boston. In this letter home, she reports on the activities of an older family acquaintance who engaged in sexual actions with British soldiers encamped on Boston Common. A combination of innocent girlish gossip and patriotic fervor, this excerpt preserved in her diary presents a unique view of the Boston occupation. The Winslows were prominent silversmiths and associates of the most famous of the Boston artisans, Paul Revere.

January 17

. . . our treat was nuts, raisins, Cakes, wine, punch, hot and cold, all in great plenty. We had a very agreeable evening from 5 to 10 o'clock.

February 21

[1]"Daughters of Liberty" were women and girls who met to spin homespun cloth and refused to wear fabric or textiles from England. They also refused to drink imported tea.
[2]A chip was a bonnet; lineing was underwear.

As I am (as we say) a Daughter of Liberty[1] I chuse to wear as much of our own manufactory as possible . . . I will go on to save my money for a chip and a lineing, etc.[2]

February 25

[3]A British regiment.

[4]"Gaol" is an archaic term for jail.
[5]In the colonies, criminal activity was discouraged by public humiliation and punishment.

Dear mamma, I suppose that you would be glad to hear that Betty Smith who has given you so much trouble, is well and behaves herself well and I should be glad if I could write you so. But the truth is, no sooner was the 29th regiment[3] encamp'd upon the common but miss Betty took herself among them (as the Irish say) and there she stay'd with Bill Punchion awhile. The next news of her was, that she was got into gaol[4] for stealing: from whence she was taken to the publick whipping post.[5]

March 6

. . . from . . . my unkle, aunt and cousin Sally, I had an account of yesterday's publick performances and exhibitions,[6] but aunt says I need not write about 'em because no doubt there will be printed accounts. I should have been glad if I could have seen and heard for myselfe.

[6]The first anniversary of the Boston Massacre (March 5, 1770) was the occasion for city-wide observances with mass meetings and church observances.

Diary: Alice Morse Earle, *Diary of Anna Green Winslow: A Boston School Girl of 1771.* (Boston: Houghton Mifflin and Company, 1894), 17, 32, 36, 40.

A Soldier's Daughter's Pride

(1876)

INTRODUCTION

The women of Boston in the 1770s, witness to British abuses and the heroic actions of the Continental militia, carried the spirit of patriotic fervor all their lives. In this account, published in *Woodworth's Literary Casket*, an anonymous daughter preserves for posterity a family legend of the revolution.

At the commencement of the revolutionary war, my father had attained the age when the mind yields most easily to the passion for military glory, and he was among the first who were enrolled under the banner of American liberty.

What follows is an example of female heroism and tenderness, which if recorded on the page of history, might form a counterpart to the story of the Roman mother, who died from the effect of joyful surprise, when her son, whom she thought dead, was restored to her arms.

"My mother received the news that her darling had fallen in battle, but she shed no tears. Her son had done his duty, and what more in these times of peril could a virtuous mother desire? Agreeably to the primitive custom of our fathers the whole family appeared at church the next Sabbath, clothed in habiliments of sorrow and in the note, in which the minister read for the deceased, was an expression of triumph that he had fallen for liberty. The next morning as my mother sat by her window, intently watching some little shrubbery which the hand of her departed child had planted, she discovered, through the vista of the trees that embowered our peaceful dwelling, a litter, slowly winding along the road.

The hope of being able to afford relief or refreshment to a wounded soldier, drew my mother to the little gate that separated her own cultivated lawn from the highway. 'Will you stop and rest?' said she to the man who conducted the litter. 'We go no farther,' was the reply. She heard no more; the truth flashed across her mind and she fainted.

'Long and tenderly was I nursed by that heroic woman, and though she sympathized in every pain I felt, she never breathed a regret for the part I had acted, and when I was again able to join my regiment, she mingled with her parting blessing a fervent prayer that all her children might prefer death to slavery.'[1] Such was my father's tale—could I hear it and ever forget that I am a soldier's daughter? Never, never. Recollections of patriotism are impressed on every page of my existence, and sentiments of freedom twined with every fibre of my heart. . . . The spirit of my father glows with undiminished ardor, and it is my pride and my boast that I am a Soldier's Daughter."

Source: H. Niles, *Principles and Acts of the Revolution in America*. (Baltimore: Printed by W.O. Niles, 1822), 490–492.

[1] This quote is from the mother's son.

Nancy Hart: Terror of the Georgia Tories

INTRODUCTION

That Nancy Hart existed there can be no doubt. If the epitaph on her tombstone is to be believed, she was "big-boned, cross-eyed, illiterate and rude in speech." Joel Chandler Harris, creator of the "Uncle Remus" stories, devoted an entire chapter in his *Stories of Georgia* to her exploits as a heroine of the revolution.

Georgia was probably the scene of the most vicious colonial events of 1775–1783. While the rest of the newly born nation embraced "Revolution," Georgia proclaimed a "War of Extermination." No mercy was to be shown to Tory Loyalists; Aunt Nancy's exploits epitomized this attitude. As recently as 1927, a marker to her memory was set in Transylvania Park in Atlanta with this wording:

"Nancy Hart sleep, we come to praise thee,
And leave tardy honors in thy lonely grave,
A patriot, a woman, a lover of freedom,
While above thee forever Old Glory shall wave."

Annie Dennis Hart

. . . it was for her military exploits that Nancy was especially renowned, and has acquired a name in history. When the tempest of revolution swept over the land, she was among the first and the most ardent in support of liberty. She encouraged the "liberty boys," as she called them; and on more than one occasion showed that she was ready "to do or to die" for her country. . . .

Many anecdotes are told of her. One evening as she was at home in her log-cabin, with her children around her, and a pot of soap boiling over the fire, her keen eye discovered some one peeping through the crevices. With the quickness of lightning she dashed a ladleful of the boiling soap in the face and eyes of the lurking Tory. Blinded and scalded, he roared with pain and terror. Nancy coolly walked out, and, all the while amusing herself with jibes and taunts upon him, bound him fast as her prisoner.

. . . On one occasion a company of five Tories, that were scouring the country, suddenly entered the cabin of Nancy Hart. Her only greeting was a scowl of defiance; but in this instance it seemed rather impotent. The suddenness of their descent had completely surprised her. They charged her with complicity in the escape of a noted rebel who had been pursued by the king's troops, and would have been hung if taken. With a defiant and exulting air, she confessed that she was the means of his escape. She said that when she saw him coming, she let down the bars a few steps from her cabin, and motioned him to enter and pass directly through her house; and then to take himself to the swamp and secure himself there as well as he could. It was all the work of a moment. The bars were instantly put up, and she entered the house and closed the doors. She had hardly accomplished this when the pursuing Tories rode up and called out to her in a most boisterous manner. Muffling up her head and face, she opened the door and inquired why they disturbed a sick, lone woman. They inquired if a man had passed on horseback. She replied no; but she had seen a man on a sorrel[1] horse turn out of the path into the woods, some two or three hundred yards back. "That must be the fellow," said the Tories, and they were instantly off in the pursuit. "Well fooled," she continued, "they went in an opposite direction to that of my Whig[2] boy; when if they had not be so lofty-minded, but had looked on the ground inside the bars, they would have seen his horse-tracks . . . as plain as you can now see the horse's tracks on this very floor, and out of the other door down the path to the swamp."

[1] Reddish brown.

[2] Also known as patriots, Continentals, or revolutionaries were colonials who rebelled against British control during the revolution. Not to be confused with members of the Whig Party (1836–1856) who advocated limitation of presidential power and support for industry.

Source: D. W. Clark, "Nancy Hart." *The Ladies' Repository* 17, no. 2 (February 1857): 82–83.

Deborah Sampson Gannett: A Wolf in Wolf's Clothing

INTRODUCTION

The career of Deborah Sampson Gannett is perhaps the oddest history of an American female patriot. Her adventures as a soldier of distinguished accomplishment, and later as a lecturer and entertainer who used her wartime experiences as a springboard for public amusement, are unique—and in its way, typically American. Composed of equal parts of gallantry, inventiveness, pluck, and enrichment, it is at once original and typical. No career before or since can boast anything like it.

Gannett spent her youth, like so many of her generation, in laborious farm drudgery. At age 20, fed up with her routine life, she set out in search of adventure. A single woman traveling alone stood in danger of rape by marauding private soldiers of the Crown, so she decided to disguise herself by binding her breasts tightly to her chest with strips of cotton. Her hair was worn tied back with a short "pony tail"—typical of 18th-century male fashion.

In 1782, the Continental Army was badly in need of recruits, and Gannett enlisted under the name of "Timothy Thayer." But her smooth face and soft features soon betrayed her, and she was discharged. Still, that was not enough to discourage her. She enlisted again as a private soldier in the Fourth Massachusetts Regiment commanded by Colonel Henry Jackson. At the time, many teenagers were accepted into service as drummers, so Gannett's smooth features did not give her away. She used her brother's name (Robert Shurtleff), and it is under that name that her service was recognized.

These documents testify to the enlistment money she received at the beginning of her service. "Robert" was stationed at West Point and in June 1782 was sent on a mission to spy on the British encampment north of New York City. She was wounded in battle at Eastchester.

Mrs. Gannett's Service in the Continental Army,[1] Boston, August 11, 1786

These may certify that Robert Shurtleff was a soldier in my regiment in the Continental Army, for the town of Uxbridge in the Commonwealth of Massachusetts, and was inlisted for the term of three years—that he had the confidence of his officers, did his duty as a faithful and good soldier, and was honorably discharged from the Army of the United States.

Henry Jackson, Late Col. in the American Army

The Battle of Eastchester[2]

I considered this as a death wound, or as being equivalent to it; and must, I thought, lead to the discovery of my sex. Covered in blood from head to foot I told my companions I fear I have received a mortal wound and I begged them to leave me to die on the spot, preferring to take the small chance I should in this case have of surviving, rather than to be carried to the hospital. To this my comrades would not consent; but one of them took me before him on his horse and in this painful manner I was borne 6 miles to the hospital of the French Army . . . On coming in sight of the hospital my heart again failed me. In a paroxysm of despair, I actually drew a pistol from the holster, and was about to put an end to my own life. That I did not proceed to the fatal act, I can ascribe only to the interposition of Divine Mercy.

The French surgeon . . . was alert, cheerful, humane. "How you lose so much blood at this early hour? Be any bone broken?" was his first salutation; presenting me and the other wounded men of our party with two bottles of choice wine. My head having been bound up and a change of clothing becoming a wounded soldier being ready, I was asked . . . whether I had any other wound. He had observed my extreme paleness and that I limped in attempting to walk. I readily replied in the negative—it was a plump falsehood! . . .

Meanwhile I had procured in the hospital a silver probe, a needle, some lint, a bandage, and some of the same kind of salve. . . . I found that the ball had penetrated my thigh about two inches and the wound was still moderately bleeding. The wine had revived me, and God, by His kind care watched over me. At the third attempt I extracted the ball . . . Before the wound in my thigh was half healed I rejoined the army on the lines.

We came upon the Indians unexpectedly . . . and our first fire dealt terrible destruction among them.[3] Raising their horrid war-whoop they returned our fire. [Many] made their escape into the woods. Observing one man, light of foot, entering the forest I happened to be foremost in pursuit of him . . . he cried for quarter.[4] My first impulse was to bayonet him, but an instant sympathy turned away the pointed steel.

[2]This account in her own words was first published in the *Dedham (Massachusetts) Register*, December 1820. It was an attempt to preserve the personal recollections of Revolutionary War participants for posterity.

[3]Deborah had joined a large detachment of Washington's army from New Windsor and was sent north to stop Indian incursions against settlements.

[4]Mercy.

[5]In 1783, Deborah Sampson was afflicted with malignant fever and hospitalized at Philadelphia. At the hospital, the doctor questioned her.

[5]In 1783, Deborah Sampson was afflicted with malignant fever and hospitalized at Philadelphia. At the hospital, the doctor questioned her.

[6]At the end of the war, Sampson rejoined her regiment at West Point. She brought a letter from the doctor who had cared for her addressed to the West Point Commandant. It revealed her sex. "Robert Shurtleff" was honorably discharged in October 23, 1783, but continued to dress in men's civilian clothing until she met Benjamin Gannett. In the spring of 1784, they were married and became parents of Carl, Mary, and Patience. But this is not the end of the story of this remarkable woman. Her young family was soon in financial distress. Deborah applied to the Massachusetts General Court for a pension that had never been paid. Her petition was approved by Governor John Hancock, and her service was duly recognized. The court paid her 34 pounds per year, a generous sum for the time.

[7]The House of Representatives' Committee on Revolutionary Pensions recognizes her contribution.

[8]Money remained a problem for Gannett. To raise funds to support her family, she agreed to lecture to audiences about her adventures. Her presentation ended with her performance of the military "manual of arms," an impressive physical exercise that set her audiences cheering. The income from her theatricals and her pension provided the family with a fine home on 100 acres of farmland where she once again took up the responsibilities of the agricultural life she had escaped so many years before. She died peacefully on April 29, 1827, and is buried in Sharon, Massachusetts.

[9]Paul Revere, speaking here, supported Gannett's pension application. Up to this point, a military pension had never been asked by or for a woman. Thus, Gannett received a supplemental payment of $4 a month from the federal government, later raised to $8 a month for the rest of her life.

Her True Sex Discovered[5]

Thrusting his hand into my bosom to ascertain if there were motion at the heart, he was surprised at finding an inner vest lightly compressing my breasts . . .

A Grateful State Rewards Her Service[6]

"[She] did actually perform the duty of a soldier in the late army of the United States to the 23rd day of October 1783 for which she received no compensation. And whereas it further appears that the said Deborah exhibited an extraordinary instance of female heroism by discharging the duties of a faithful gallant soldier, and at the same time preserving the virtue and chastity of her sex unsuspected and unblemished."

From the Congressional Record[7]

. . . the whole history of the American revolution records no case like this, and furnishes no other similar example of female heroism, fidelity and courage.[8]

Source: Herman Mann, *The Female Review. Life of Deborah Sampson, the Female Soldier in the War of the Revolution.* (Boston: J.K. Wiggin & Wm. Parsons Lunt, 1916), 19, 121–122, 128, 136, 18, and 17.

And a Grateful Nation Follows Suit, Led by Paul Revere[9]

We commonly form an idea of the person whom we hear spoken of as a soldier and I formed the idea of a tall masculine female, who had a small share of understanding, without education, and one of the meanest of her sex. When I saw and discoursed with her I was agreeably surprised to find a small, effeminate, and conversible woman, whose education entitled her to a better station in life.

Source: Letter from Paul Revere to William Eustis, February 20, 1804. Miscellaneous bound manuscripts collection. http://www .masshist.org/database/326. Massachusetts Historical Society. Used by permission.

Prudence Wright and the Women's Guard

INTRODUCTION

In the years leading to the beginning of the conflict, the population of colonial America divided into roughly two camps: those who wished to remain loyal to the king and those who supported armed insurrection. It should come as no surprise that these divisions existed not only on the level of groups within society but also within families. These later divisions—parents against children, brother against brother (or sister)—were perhaps the most painful of all. And when, as in the case of Prudence Wright, that sister was a natural leader of rebellion and adept at combat, the division could become not only painful but bloody.

Prudence Wright's family was one of split loyalties. Her brothers were loyalists. She was a daughter of the revolution. The following document is an account of an action by the women's guard.

The Guard assembled at dark one night a few days after the nineteenth of April, when they heard the rumor that British messengers were expected to cross the town[1] . . . When two horsemen approached from the north they heard the women's voices . . . One of the horsemen recognized it as that of his sister whose fearless, determined spirit he knew full well . . . and galloped away. The other, being a military man was not so much impressed by the voices of the women and rode on into the midst of the "Guard" before he realized the nature of the force he had to face.[2] The women surrounded him, seized his horse and . . . compelled him to dismount and submit to search. In his boots were found treasonable papers. The women marched their prisoner to the middle of the town . . . and guarded their prisoner until morning, when they . . . delivered him into custody. The papers were sent to the Committee of Safety at Charlestown.

[1]Shortly after the skirmishes at Lexington and Concord, word came that British spies were about to pass through with information about the location where the minutemen had hidden their armaments.

[2]Prudence gathered a group of 30–40 women dressed in men's clothing to ambush any Tories at the Pepperell Covered Bridge.

Source: Mary L. P. Shattuck, *Prudence Wright and the Women Who Guarded the Bridge*. (Nashua: Wheeler Print, 1899).

Patience Lovell Wright: Sculptress and Spy

INTRODUCTION

In the annals of wartime American covert operations, there is no stranger figure than Patience Lovell Wright. A gifted sculptress, she used her artistic talent to make wax figures of important New Yorkers. Long before the establishment of Madame Tussaud's waxworks, Wright set up a small museum where patrons paid admission to view her images.

In 1771, a fire destroyed much of New York City, and armed with letters of reference from many of the prominent figures she had immortalized in wax, she emigrated to London to set up shop in fashionable Pall Mall. Her amusing eccentricities proved to be an excellent cover for her revolutionary activities. She was an ardent supporter of the American cause, but the British never suspected that she might be an active courier of military secrets. They looked at her as an American oddball. But they were very wrong. She obtained information in casual conversation with the upper-class ladies who visited her atelier and sent secret communication to members of Congress. An anonymous letter in the papers of Benjamin Franklin quotes John Hancock's recognition of her work. She concealed her notes in wax images that she sent to her sister in Philadelphia.

[1]It is only natural that little documentary evidence exists concerning the activities of spies during the revolution since the keeping of written records would have endangered their success. There were several female spies actively supporting the American cause. The Quakers of Philadelphia provided many of them. Patience Wright was a Quaker and another Quaker, Lydia Darrah, is credited with once saving Washington's army.

She soon found out the avenues to get information of almost every design which was agitated or intended to be executed in America,[1] and was the object of the most active confidence of Doctor Franklin and others, with whom she corresponded, and gave information during the whole war. As soon as a General was appointed to go out to mount the tragic-comic stage in America, from the commander in chief to the brigadier, she instantly found some access to a part of the family, and discovered the number of troops to be employed, and the ends of their destination.

Source: *The Scots Magazine*, Volume 48. (March 1786), 154–155.

The wild flights of her powerful mind stamped originality on all her acts and language. She was a tall and athletic figure; walked with a firm, bold step, and erect as an Indian . . . Her sharp glance was appalling; it had almost the wildness of the maniac. The vigor and originality of her conversation corresponded with her manners and appearance. She would utter language . . . that would put her hearers to the blush . . . The peculiarity of her character, and the excellence of her wax figures, made her rooms in Pall Mall a fashionable lounging-place for the nobility and distinguished men of England.[2] Here her deep penetration and sagacity, cloaked by her apparent simplicity of purpose, enabled her to gather many facts and secrets important to "dear America"—her uniform expression in referring to her native land, which she dearly loved.

Source: Winslow C. Watson, *Men and Times of the Revolution*. (New York: Dana and Company, 1856), 117–118.

[2] Among her most distinguished patrons were King George III and his queen. The upper crust were shocked and amused when Patience dared to address them as "George and Caroline." William Pitt, the creator of England's colonial empire and a faithful friend of America, was a frequent visitor. He was created a peer as the Earl of Chatham, and one of Patience's best images—that of Pitt—may be seen today in Westminster Abby.

SECTION IV

The Songs of Liberty

Introduction

"Nothing is certain but death and taxes." Truer words were never spoken, and it's certain that in 1765 the British Americans who lived in the colonies knew it. In order to maintain their local government, the colonists had taxed themselves for years. Those taxes had been imposed by local elected assemblies. That pattern of self-imposed taxation had implications far beyond its economic aspect; it was a reflection of colonial pride in self-rule that was perhaps more of an issue to the colonists than the even more famous "taxation without representation."

Wars are expensive, and the Seven Years' War was no exception. Known in America as the "French and Indian War," it was the most tremendous conflict of the 18th century. In Europe, it aligned the forces of France, Austria, Spain, and Russia against Frederick the Great of Prussia. England was Frederick's ally, and the war brought it into conflict with France for colonial supremacy in America. Britain won, but it became a debtor nation and since much of the war expense had been incurred for the defense of its American colonies, the leaders of Parliament felt that it was only fair for the Americans to shoulder the economic costs of their defense.

During the war, Britain had asked each colony to provide economic support. The response was not promising. Some colonies did respond in a positive way, some half-heartedly, and others not at all. There was no way Parliament would tolerate that sort of dilatory response. The colonists were, after all, British subjects and had the responsibilities that went with that status. Consequently, Parliament decided to tax the colonies. In 1764, a sugar tax was passed. When the result was less than adequate, Sir George Grenville, chancellor of the exchequer (secretary of the Treasury), suggested the Stamp Act, under which all colonial legal documents, newspapers, and almanacs would have to be printed on paper embossed with an official water mark, or carry a stamp, much as cigarettes and liquor carry stamps today. These papers would be sold by agents of Parliament, and sales would raise the needed funds.

In fairness to the colonists, this tax was not imposed immediately. The British government gave the Americans a year to come up with another proposal if they objected to the government plan. The colonists' only suggestion was to keep the old system: self-taxation by the colonial assemblies. But that had been tried—unsuccessfully.

Benjamin Franklin (1706–1790) was Philadelphia's leading citizen, a universal genius, and guiding spirit of the revolution. During his lifetime, he conducted experiments with electricity, invented the Franklin stove, served as postmaster general, shaped the Declaration of Independence, served as minister to France, worked on the Albany Plan of

Union, helped write the Articles of Confederation and the Constitution, and published *Poor Richard's Almanac* (a collection of aphorisms like "a penny saved is a penny earned") and an autobiography that still stands as a classic of the type. At the time of the Stamp Act crisis, Franklin was sent to London to plead for the old method of raising revenue in the colonies. When Franklin admitted that he could not guarantee colonial payments, Parliament passed the Stamp Act.

The Americans protested, but the members of Parliament felt they had been more than fair to their subjects. The colonies exploded; Parliament had never before levied a direct internal tax on their economic activities. The colonists felt the act threatened their right—as Englishmen—to self-government.

Of course, Parliament had previously put taxes on external colonial trade, but only with the consent of the colonies. Parliament insisted that, as English subjects, the colonists were "virtually" represented—as were all Englishmen—wherever they lived. The colonists rejected that idea. For them, representation meant a government *directly* elected by those who were taxed. Anything else they famously saw as "tyranny."

Songs have been an integral part of the American experience since colonial days. The first book published in the colonies was the *Massachusetts Bay Psalm Book*, used along with an invented form of musical notation known as "shape notes" to enrich worship services. The music was largely an adaptation of English-Scottish-Irish folk melodies, not all of them devotional. The "Star-Spangled Banner" was sung to the tune of a ribald drinking song, "To Anacreon in Heaven." The ballads excerpted here first appeared in the popular press or in single-sheet publications known as "broadsides." Many of these songs were used by soldiers to relieve the weariness of the long marches typical of the war effort. The ballads are presented in archaic spelling and language.

Peter St. John's "American Taxation"

(1765)

INTRODUCTION

Peter St. John was a native of Norwalk, Connecticut. During the early days of the revolution, he taught school and wrote many pieces. This ballad references the Stamp Act Crisis (1765) and its aftermath: war and victory.

While I relate my story
Americans give ear
Of Britain's faded glory
You presently shall hear;
I'll give a true relation,
Attend to what I say
Concerning the taxation
Of North America[1]

The cruel lords of Britain,
Who glory in their shame,
The project they have hit on
They joyfully proclaim;
'Tis what they're striving after
Our right to take away,
And rob us of our charter
In North America.

There are two mighty speakers,
Who rule in Parliament,
Who ever have been seeking
Some mischief to invent:
T'was North, and Bute his father,[2]
The horrid plan did lay
A mighty tax to gather
In North America . . .

His comrades were pursuing
A diabolic way,

[1] In the 18th-century ballad style, "America" was pronounced "Americay," so this rhymes with "say." This will hold true for all the ballads in this section.

[2] Lord Frederick North (1732–1792) was first Lord of the Treasury and prime minister. He served first as assistant to the Earl of Bute, who, among other things, was the tutor of King George III.

231

For to complete the ruin
Of North America . . .

[3]A biblical reference to the "promised land" of Canaan.

Their land with milk and honey,[3]
Continually doth flow,
The want of food or money
They seldom ever know:
They heap up golden treasure,
They have no debts to pay,
They spend their time in pleasure
In North America.

On turkeys, fowls and fishes,
Most frequently they dine,
With gold and silver dishes,
Their tables always shine.
They crown their feasts with butter,
They eat, and rise to play:
In silks their ladies flutter,
In North America.

With gold and silver laces
They do themselves adorn,
The rubies deck their faces,
Refulgent as the morn!
Wine sparkles in their glasses,
They spend each happy day
In merriment and dances
In North America.

[4]"Our suit" was the appeal by the colonists to the goodwill of King George III. The king ignored the communications.

Let not our suit affront you,
When we address your throne,[4]
Oh King, this wealthy country
And subjects are your own,
And you, their rightful sovereign,
They truly must obey,
You have a right to govern
This North America.

Oh King, you've heard the sequel
Of what we now subscribe,
Is it not just and equal
To tax this wealthy tribe?

The question being asked,
His majesty did say,
"My subjects shall be taxed
In North America."

Invested with a warrant,
My publicans shall go,[5]
The tenth of all their current
They surely shall bestow;[6]
If they indulge rebellion,
Or from my precepts stray,
I'll send my war battalion
To North America.

I'll rally all my forces
By water and by land,
My light dragoons and horses
shall go at my command:
I'll burn both town and city,
With smoke becloud the day,
I'll show no human pity
For North America . . .

O George! You are distracted,[7]
You'll by experience find
The laws you have enacted
Are of the blackest kind,
I'll make a short digression,
And tell you by the way,
We fear not your oppression.
In North America.

Our fathers were distressed,
While in their native land;
By tyrants were oppressed
As we do understand;
For freedom and religion
They were resolved to stray,[8]
And trace the desert regions
Of North America.

Heaven was their sole protector
While on the roaring tide,

[5]The king issued a legal order allowing an officer ("publican") to seize property.
[6]The king demanded that the colonies provide 10 percent of their income to defray the costs of their defense in the French and Indian War.

[7]The Americans respond, knowing it was an insult to His Majesty to address him by his name.

[8]The original settlers of the New England colonies had come to escape religious persecution by the Church of England. The church demanded uniformity of belief and worship as a symbol of its authority. Any nonconformity was seen as leading to political rebellion as well.

Kind fortune their director,
And Providence their guide.
If I am not mistaken,
About the first of May,
This voyage was undertaken
For North America.[9]

If rightly I remember,
This country to explore,
They landed in November
On Plymouth's desert shore.[10]
The savages were nettled,
With fear they fled away.
So peaceably they settled
In North America.

We are their bold descendants,
For liberty we'll fight,
The claim to independence
We challenge as our right;
Tis what kind Heaven gave us,
Who can take it away.
O, Heaven, sure will save us,
In North America.

We never will knock under,
O, George! We do not fear
The rattling of your thunder,
Nor lightning of your spear:
Though rebels you declare us,
We're strangers to dismay
Therefore you cannot scare us
In North America.

To what you have commanded[11]
We will never consent,
Although your troops are landed
Upon our continent;
We'll take our swords and muskets,
And march in dread array,
And drive the British red-coats
From North America.

[9]The pilgrims initially left England for Holland. They found religious tolerance there, but soon felt that their children were becoming "Dutchified." They left on July 31, 1621, on the *Speedwell*; when that ship proved unseaworthy, they finally sailed on the *Mayflower* on September 16, 1620.

[10]In fact, after sighting land on November 19, they arrived at Provincetown (not Plymouth) on November 21. They reached Plymouth on December 21.

[11]This refers to the 10 percent tax.

We have a bold commander,
Who fears not sword or gun,
The second Alexander,
His name is Washington.[12]
His men are all collected,
And ready for the fray,
To fight they are directed
For North America . . .[13]

Proud George, you are engaged
All in a dirty cause,
A cruel war have waged
Repugnant to all laws.[14]
Go tell the savage nations
You're crueler than they,
To fight your own relations
In North America . . .

Confusion to the tories,[15]
That black infernal name,
In which Great Britain glories,
For ever in her shame;
We'll send each foul revolter
To smutty Africa,
Or noose him in a halter,
In North America.

A health to our brave footmen,
Who handled sword and gun,
To Greene and Gates and Putnam[16]
And conquering Washington
Their names be wrote in letters
Which never will decay,
While sun and moon do glitter
On North America.

Success unto our allies
In Holland, France, and Spain,[17]
Who man their ships and galleys,
Our freedom to maintain;
May they subdue the rangers
Of proud Britannia,
And drive them from their anchors

[12]George Washington is compared to Alexander the Great, Greek conqueror of the classical world.

[13]During the French and Indian War, the governor of Virginia sent George Washington to what is today Pittsburgh to remove the French from what was considered English territory (1754). He fought the French and Indians at the Battles of Great Meadows. He and his men were defeated. A year later, a British force under General Braddock was again defeated, but Washington's reputation as a commander grew. His gallant conduct in rallying his men, in spite of the fact that his horse was twice shot out from under him and his uniform riddled with bullet holes, prevented a rout and lay the basis for his reputation as a military leader.

[14]Here, "cruel war" refers to the king's conflict with the colonies: not yet a shooting war, but a conflict between Englishmen. Such a war between brothers is seen as more "savage" than the battle against Native Americans.

[15]Americans who were loyal to the king.

[16]Nathanael Greene (frequently misspelled Nathaniel) was a great military leader, second only to Washington. Horatio Gates was major general at the Battle of Camden. Colonel Rufus Putnam was commander at the Battle of Saratoga.

[17]Holland, France, and Spain were England's opponents, if not militarily then commercially. Thus, they were allies to the colonists.

In North America.
Success unto the Congress

Of these United States,
Who glory in the conquests
Of Washington and Gates;
To all, both land and seamen
Who glory in the day
When we shall all be freemen
In North America.

Success to legislation,
That rules with gentle hand,
To trade and navigation,
By water and by land,
May all with one opinion
Our wholesome laws obey,
Throughout this vast dominion
Of North America.

Source: George Cary Eggleston, *American War Ballads and Lyrics*, Volume 1. (New York: G.P. Putnam's Sons, 1889), 60–71.

"The World Turned Upside Down"

(1767)

INTRODUCTION

This song was an expression of the desire by many in America to find a way to make peace between Great Britain ("The Old Woman," "Goody Bull," later "John Bull") and the colonies ("The Daughter").

Why, as late as 1767, would there be a sizable portion of the citizens of colonial America who wanted to make peace with the mother country? By this time, Parliament had passed several acts which the colonists saw as injurious to their rights as Englishmen: rights to prosperity and self-government. But, in fact, since the establishment of British settlements in the early 17th century, the new world empire had been an "empire of consent"; because of the physical distance between America and the mother country, the bonds that had been provided for a union within the empire had of necessity been bonds of fraternal affection. The colonists were proud to be British Americans. Their governments, the physical settlements, and local traditions reflected their admiration for the British model. In the six decades leading up to the outbreak of armed conflict (1775), depredation after depredation had been followed by a repeated desire to fix things up. The issues (representation, taxation, and centralization of political authority in Parliament) were seen by a substantial percentage of the population as growing pains that could be alleviated through protest and pushback.

The effectiveness of the Stamp Act Congress (1765) seemed to support this position. And although eloquent and effective voices had been raised in support of independence, by 1767, it was by no means a sure thing that the only route to a redress of colonial grievances would be a resort to arms. Many still felt that the world of British America could be turned "upside down" without violence.

This ballad, a depiction of the conflict between a mother and her rebellious teenaged daughter, argues for a settlement of differences and uses humor to diffuse a tense and potentially explosive family fight. But note well that it is framed in terms of family, and nowhere is divorce or separation contemplated as a solution.

Goody Bull and her daughter together fell out.[1]
Both squabbled, and wrangled, and made a [damn] rout,

[1] In 18th-century slang, a "goody" was a woman of the lowest class. Thus, "goody bull" is an insult to Great Britain, personified by "John Bull" the line then means lowlife Britain and her daughter (the colonies) had a quarrel.

But the cause of the quarrel remains to be told,
Then lend both your ears, and a tale I'll unfold.

The old lady, it seems, took a freak in her head,
That her daughter, grown woman, might earn her own bread,
Self applauding her scheme, she was ready to dance;
But we're often too sanguine in what we advance.

For mark the event; thus by fortune we're crossed.
Nor should people reckon without their good host;
The daughter was sulky, and wouldn't come to,
And pray, what in this case could the old woman do?

In vain did the matron hold forth in the cause,
That the young one was able; her duty, the laws:
Ingratitude vile, disobedience far worse;
But she might e'en as well sung psalms to a horse.

Young, froward[2] and sullen, and vain of her beauty,
She tartly replied that she well knew her duty,
That other folks' children were kept by their friends,
And that some folks loved people but for their own ends . . .

"She be [damned]," says the farmer,[3] and to her he goes,
First roars in her ears, then tweaks her old nose,
"Hallo, Goody, what ails you? Wake! Woman, I say;
I am close to make peace, in this desperate fray . . ."

"Alas!" Cries the old woman, "and must I comply?
But I'd rather submit than the huzzy should die;"[4]
"Pooh, prithee be quiet, be friends and agree,
You must surely be right, if you're guided by me."

Unwillingly awkward, the mother knelt down,
While the absolute father[5] went on with a frown,
"Come, kiss the poor child, there come, kiss and be friends!
There kiss your poor daughter, and make her amends."

"No thanks to you, mother;" the daughter replied;
"But thanks to my friend here, I've humbled your pride."

Source: Burton E. Stevenson, *Poems of American History*. (Boston: Houghton Mifflin Company, 1908), 130.

[2]Habitually disposed to disobedience and opposition.

[3]After independence had been declared, a committee with John Dickinson of Pennsylvania as chairman was formed to prepare a plan of confederation. The result was the Articles of Confederation, an early attempt to provide a government for the colonies. Dickinson had been an advocate of reconciliation during the meetings of the Continental Congress, an advocate of peace and harmony. He was a delegate to the constitutional convention and signed the document for Pennsylvania. He was the author of the series of "Letters from a Farmer in Pennsylvania."

[4]Huzzy is an old spelling of Hussy.

[5]George III.

"The Liberty Song" and Its Parodies

(1768)

INTRODUCTION

A patriotic expression of support for the American cause, this song gained wide popularity. It was sung to the popular tune "Hearts of Oak" in the streets of Boston and the taverns throughout New England. Loyalist Tories, not to be outdone, were quick to provide a parody.

John Dickinson, the author of this ballad, was an unlikely candidate to pen such a radical song, which became so popular among the leaders of the revolution that it inspired parody after parody among the supporters of loyal allegiance to the Crown. Dickinson was a reluctant revolutionary. He was an advocate of moderation in all things political. As governor of both Delaware and Pennsylvania and author of a series of "Letters from a Farmer in Pennsylvania" (1767), he had become the voice of the middle colonies. He looked upon Samuel Adams and his Boston mob with serious reservations. He advocated support of the cause of freedom as a step-by-step process by which the American colonies could incrementally achieve their political goals. He promoted the formation of the Continental Congress as an alternative to a more radical "Solemn League and Covenant" advocated by the Boston Committee of Correspondence.

But by 1768, as events reached crisis proportions, Dickinson was moved to compose what he called "A Song for the American Freedom." It was published under the title "The Liberty Song" in the *Boston Gazette* (July 18, 1768); soon after, a loyalist parody appeared. Not to be outdone, that parody was soon itself parodied by anonymous leaders of the revolution. And so, before Lexington and Concord, the battle was joined in the pages of the popular press.

The Liberty Song

. . . Then join hand in hand brave Americans all,
By uniting we stand, by dividing we fall;
In so righteous a cause let us hope to succeed,
For Heaven approves of each generous deed.

All ages shall speak with amaze and applause,
Of the courage we'll show in support of our laws;
To die we can bear, but to serve we disdain,
For shame is to freemen more dreadful than pain . . .

[chorus]
In Freedom we're born and in Freedom we'll live,
Our purses are ready. Steady, friends, steady;
Not as slaves, but as Freemen our money we'll give.[1]

The Parody[2]

Come shake your dull noddles[3], ye pumpkins, and bawl,
And own that you're mad at fair Liberty's call;
No scandalous conduct can add to your shame,
Condemn'd to dishonor, inherit the same.

In folly you're born, and in folly you'll live,
To madness still ready,
And stupidly steady,
Not as men, but as monkeys, the tokens you give . . .

Then plunder, my lads, for when red coats appear,
You'll melt like the locusts when winter is near;
Gold vainly will glow, silver vainly will shine,
But, faith, you must skulk, you no more shall purloin . . .

Gulp down your last dram, for the gallows now groans,
And, over depress'd, her lost empire bemoans;
While we quite transported and happy shall be,
From mobs, knaves and villains, protected and free.

The Massachusetts Liberty Song (1768)[4]

Come swallow your bumpers, ye tories, and roar.
That the sons of fair Freedom are hamper'd once more;
But know that no cut-throats our spirits can tame,
Nor a host of oppressors shall smother the flame.

In freedom we're born, and, like sons of the brave,
We'll never surrender,
But swear to defend her,
And scorn to survive, if unable to save . . .

Source: Percy Boynton, *American Poetry.* (New York: Charles Scribner's Sons, 1921), 61–62.

[1]Dickinson wrote this note: "The Ministry have already begun to give away in pensions the money they lately took out of our pockets, without our consent. Our purses are ready to replace these funds in service of the course of liberty."

[2]This parody was published in the *Boston Gazette* (September 26, 1768) with this comment: "Last Tuesday, the following song made its appearance from a garret at Castle William. The author is unknown."

[3]"Noddles" is a mid-18th-century form of the verb "to nod or wag" and referred to the head.

[4]This parody is typical of the spirit of the times in which it was written. It was published in London in the *St. James Chronicle* (November 8, 1768) and soon found its way to America. It was so popular in Britain that it was still sung there during the War of 1812.

"To Our Ladies"
(1769)

INTRODUCTION

The passage of the Townsend Acts in 1767 resulted in a boycott of British products that badly hurt the British economy. These verses were written to encourage patriotic women to support the revolutionary cause. The song suggested the benefits of women refusing to purchase or wear fashionable clothing from England and wearing their own "homespun." This boycott of British textiles—at this time, the textile industry was the great engine of the British Industrial Revolution—was quite successful, and resulted in a decline of income from $11,800,000 in 1768 to $8,170,000 in 1769.

Yet, it would be a mistake to limit an understanding of women's contribution to the revolution to such relatively passive activities. There is considerable evidence that women served in the army as soldiers in uniform, as nurses in military hospitals, and as support personnel traveling with the Continental Army. The "feminine ideal" of refinement, delicacy, and modesty reflected in the correspondence of John and Abigail Adams was frequently abandoned as a result of a nation struggling for freedom.

On March 31, 1776, while Adams was at Philadelphia developing the Constitution, his wife wrote to him that "if particular care and attention is not paid to the ladies, we are determined to foment [stir up] a rebellion, and will not hold ourselves bound by any laws in which we have no voice or representation."

Young ladies in town, and those that live round,
Let a friend at this season advise you;
Since money's so scarce, and times growing worse,
Strange things may soon hap and surprise you;

First then throw aside your high topknots of pride;[1]
Wear none but your own country linen;
Of economy boast, let your pride be the most,
To show clothes of your own make and spinning.

What if homespun they say is not quite so gay
As brocades, yet be not in a passion,

[1] Ornamental hair ribbons.

241

For when once it is known this is much worn in town,
One and all will cry out—'Tis the fashion! . . .

No more ribbons wear, not in rich silks appear;
Love your country much better than fine things;
Begin without passion, 'twill soon be the fashion,
To grace your smooth locks with a twine string . . .

These do without fear, and to all you'll appear,
Fair, charming, true, lovely and clever;

²May come courting.

Though the times remain darkish, young men may be sparkish,²
And love you much stronger than ever

Them make yourselves easy, for no one will teaze ye,
Nor *tax* you, if chancing to sneer
At the sense-ridden tools, who think us all fools;
But they'll find the reverse far and near.

Source: Frank Moore, *Songs and Ballads of the American Revolution*. (New York: D. Appleton &
Company, 1856), 48–50.

"A New Song"

(1774)

The Boston Tea Party, which occurred on December 16, 1773, brings up images of Boston patriots, their faces blackened with soot from blacksmith foundries and wrapped in blankets, boarding three British tea ships in Boston harbor and consigning their cargo of 344 chests of India Tea to the depths.

But the Tea Party wasn't about tea itself. Tea was the item; it was not the cause. By 1770, Parliament had eliminated most of the import and export taxes it had imposed on the American colonies. Tea was the exception. By 1775, the British East India Company was in bad shape. Its activities in India had almost led to its bankruptcy and its warehouses were loaded with excess tea. To help, Parliament authorized the sale of 10 million pounds of tea in America at low prices. The Americans, in order to avoid paying the tea tax, had been patronizing tea smugglers; they saw this authorization as more than just a way to help the company. They saw it as a revival of Parliament's attempt to impose nonrepresentational taxes on the colonies. So, once again, it was the taxation issue, the issue of who had the authority to impose a tax, that surfaced.

The sale of tea in the colonies was in fact a British monopoly, and the cheap import tea was seen as an attempt to undersell American merchants. What is more, Americans seemed addicted to tea. It was said that women "would rather go without their dinner than without a dish of tea." Tea drinking now became an issue of patriotism. To drink the "accursed, detested stuff" became anti-American.

Even physicians joined the battle and claimed that tea drinking led to most American girls of age 20 losing their teeth; that tea "weakened the tone of the stomach, and therefore of the whole system, inducing tremors and spasmodic affections."

When the tea ships arrived in Boston harbor, Governor Hutchinson refused to allow them to leave port. When a last minute meeting failed to persuade Hutchinson to change his mind, the Sons of Liberty went into action. Groups of 50 men each boarded the ships, masquerading as Indians. Hundreds of citizens lined the waterfront as the "Indians," armed with axes, broke open the tea chests and, aided by the sailors, threw them overboard.

The battle had been joined. Governor Hutchinson saw no middle ground: either Parliament or the colonists were supreme—or as King George III put it, "We must either master them or totally leave them to themselves and treat them as Aliens!"

As near beauteous Boston lying,
On the gently swelling flood,
Without jack or pendant flying,
Three ill-fated tea-ships rode.[1]

Just as glorious Sol was setting,
On the wharf a numerous crew,
Sons of freedom, fear forgetting,
Suddenly appeared in view . . .

Quick as thought the ships were boarded,
Hatches burst and chests display'd;
Axes, hammers, help afforded;
What a glorious crash they made!

Squash into the deep descended,
Cursed weed of China's coast;[2]
Thus at once our fears were ended;
British rights shall ne'er be lost.

Captains! once more hoist your streamers,
Spread your sails, and plough the wave!
Tell your masters they were dreamers,
When they thought to cheat the brave.

[1] The tea ships were the *Dartmouth*, the *Beaver*, and the *Eleanor*.

[2] "Cursed weed" refers to the tea from the East India Company's Chinese warehouses.

Source: *The Muse's Mirror, Being a Collection of Poems*, Volume 1. (London: Robert Baldwin, 1778), 202–203.

Meshech Weare's "India Tea"

(1774)

INTRODUCTION

The distaste of the colonists for "pestilential" tea was encouraged by ballads such as "India Tea," attributed to Meshech Weare, president of the state of New Hampshire in 1776.

Noxious effluvia sending out,[1]
From its pernicious store,
Not only from the foaming mouth,
But every lifeless pore.

To view the same enrolled in tea,
Besmeared with such perfumes,
And then the herb sent o'er the sea,
To us it tainted comes

Some of it tinctured with a filth,
Of carcasses embalmed;
Taste of this herb, then, if thou wilt,
Sure me it cannot charm.

Adieu! away, oh yes! begone!
Salute our taste no more;
Though thou art coveted by some
Who're destined to be poor.

[1] The goal was to make tea sound as unpalatable as possible.

Source: Everett Tomlinson, *Stories of the American Revolution*, Part 2. (Boston: Thos. R. Shewell & Company, 1898), 46.

"Pennsylvania Song"

(1775)

INTRODUCTION

Pennsylvania, Delaware, New Jersey, and Rhode Island all had sizable Quaker populations, who were well known to hold pacifist sentiments. In the decade before the outbreak of the shooting war, many residents of these colonies fell under suspicion of disloyalty to the patriot cause. In the popular mind, Samuel Adams, his Sons of Liberty, and the Massachusetts Committee of Correspondence were the leaders of radical forces championing armed conflict with Great Britain.

Then how is it that this marching war song that reflects the strongest of patriotic sentiments was born in the heart of pacifist country? The common people had for decades suffered under Quaker domination. The rulers of Pennsylvania were Quaker, and many citizens objected to that rule as much as to the rule of the British. The Pennsylvania Constitution (1776) represents a democratic triumph: the triumph of the farmers of western Pennsylvania over the eastern Philadelphia ruling class. It was written by Thomas Paine (who wrote *Common Sense*) and Benjamin Franklin and called for universal manhood suffrage and religious freedom.

The gentry saw it as an expression of "mobocracy," the creation of a social order where lower-class types would meet in "taverns and dram shops" and organize a lower-class government. Yet, it was these same lower-class types who fought the war and achieved the triumph over privilege—both foreign and domestic. It was that democratic spirit that achieved popular expression in the "Pennsylvania Song."

'The Earl of Sandwich was a virulent opponent of the American cause. He belittled the Continental Army accusing them of cowardice. He rejoiced at the prospect of a large American Army being formed because "if they did not run away, they would starve themselves into compliance with our measured force." As first Lord of the Admiralty, he was to blame for Britain's naval weakness during the revolution. He was also the center of many scandals. His wife was insane, his son a spendthrift, and his mistress was murdered.

We are the troop that ne'er will stoop
To wretched slavery,
Nor will our seed, by our base deed
Despised vassals be;
Freedom we will bequeathe to them,
Or we will bravely die:
Our greatest foe, ere long shall know,
How much did Sandwich lie.[1]

[chorus]
And all the world shall know,
Americans are free;
Nor slaves nor cowards we will prove,[2]
Great Britain soon shall see.

We'll not give up our birthright,
Our foes shall find us men;
As good as they, in any shape,
The British troops shall ken.[3]

Huzza! brave boys, we'll beat them
On any hostile plain;
For freedom, wives, and children dear,
The battle we'll maintain.

What! can those British tyrants think,
Our fathers crossed the main,
And savage foes, and dangers met,
To be enslaved by them?

If so, they are mistaken,
For we will rather die;
And since they have become our foes,
Their forces we defy.

> **Source:** Frank Cowan, *Southwestern Pennsylvania in Song and Story*. (Greensburg, PA: Printed by the Author, 1878), 336–337.

[2]This line expresses opposition to tyranny in all its forms and proclaims the democratic cause.

[3]Know or acknowledge.

"Alphabet for Little Masters and Misses"

(1775)

INTRODUCTION

Normal school copybooks have a long history of combining educational goals with societal agendas. Here, a verse designed to teach the alphabet to children also has the objective of instilling support for the patriot cause. This production appeared in a ballad sheet in the early part of 1775 and was afterward reprinted in the *Constitutional Gazette*.

A, stands for Americans, who scorn to be slaves;
B, for Boston, where fortitude their freedom saves;
C, stands for Congress, which, though loyal, will be free;
D, stands for defence, 'gainst force and tyranny.
Stand firmly, A and Z,
We swear for ever to be free!

E, stands for evils, which a civil war must bring;
F, stands for fate, dreadful to both people and king;
G, stands for George, may God give him wisdom and grace;[1]
H, stands for hypocrite, who wears a double face.

J, stands for justice, which traitors in power defy,[2]
K, stands for king, who should to such the axe apply;
L, stands for London, to its country ever true,
M, stands for Mansfield, who hath another view.[3]

N, stands for North, who to the House the mandate brings,[4]
O, stands for oaths, binding on subjects not on kings:
P, stands for people, who their freedom should defend,
Q, stands for *quere*, when will England's troubles end?

R, stands for rebels, not at Boston but at home,[5]
S, stands for Stuarts, sent by Whigs abroad to roam,[6]
T, stands for Tories, who may try to bring them back,
V, stands for villains, who have well deserved the rack.[7]

[1] George Washington had recently been appointed "Generalissimo" (commander in chief) of the Continental Army.

[2] In the 18th century, the letters "I" and "J" were interchangeable in spelling and considered a single letter.

[3] Lord Mansfield was an advocate of the bill closing the port of Boston as punishment for the tea party. He said, "The sword is drawn; you must throw away the scabbard."

[4] Lord North was prime minister of Great Britain.

[5] Massachusetts was proclaimed in rebellion against the Crown. This line asserts that the true rebellion was not at Boston, but that the royal action was a rebellion against the traditional rights of Englishmen.

[6] Charles Stuart, son of Charles I, was exiled by Oliver Cromwell, leader of the Whig Party. Tories, those loyal to the royal house of Stuart, did indeed return him to power as Charles II.

[7] There is no "U"; "Y" and "U," both descendants of the Greek letter Upsilon, were interchangeable.

W, stands for Wilkes, who us from warrants saved,[8]
Y, for York, the New, half corrupted, half enslaved,[9]
Z, stands for Zero, but means the Tory minions,
Who threaten us with fire and sword, to bias our opinions.
Stand firmly A and Z,
We swear for ever to be free!

[8]John Wilkes was a sort of parliamentary Thomas Paine. A champion of the colonial cause, he attempted to "save" the colonies from the official orders, the Intolerable Acts, that led to armed rebellion.

[9]During the run up to the revolution, New York City was divided in its loyalties. Some citizens opposed a "rebellion." This position was seen as corrupt by others who were willing to fight, and thus were not willing to remain enslaved to British tyranny.

Source: Lydia Newcomb, "Songs and Ballads of the Revolution." *The New England Magazine* 13/19 (September 1895–February 1896): 508–509.

"Adam's Fall, or the Trip to Cambridge"

(1775)

INTRODUCTION

In 1775, the Continental Congress appointed George Washington commander in chief of the ragtag Continental Army. Washington immediately set off to join the troops stationed at Cambridge, Massachusetts. His "triumphal" journey was witnessed by the disdainful royal troops who ridiculed him in this, one of the very few ballads making fun of the newly minted general. It was sung to the tune of "Yankee Doodle."

When Congress sent great Washington
All clothed in power and breeches,
To meet old Britain's warlike sons
And make some rebel speeches;

'Twas then he took his gloomy way
Astride his dapple donkeys,[1]
And travelled well, both night and day,
Until he reached the Yankees

Away from camp, 'bout three miles off,
From Lily he dismounted,
His serjeant brushed his sunburnt wig
While he the specie counted.[2]

All prinked up in full bag-wig;[3]
The shaking notwithstanding,[4]
In leathers tight, oh! glorious sight!
He reached the Yankee landing.

The women ran, the darkeys too;
And all the bells, they tolled;
For Britain's sons, by Doodle doo,
We're sure to be consoled.

Old mother Hancock with a pan[5]
All crowded full of butter,

[1] Washington was known for riding a white stallion. This parody has him astride a "lily white" donkey.

[2] "Specie" refers to his pay.

[3] Groomed with excessive care.
[4] Despite his trembling.

[5] A reference to Mrs. John Hancock.

Unto the lovely Georgius ran,
And added to the splutter.[6]

Says she, "Our brindle has just calved,[7]
And John is wondrous happy.
He sent this present to you, dear,
As you're the 'country's papa' . . ."

Full many a child went into camp,
All dressed in homespun Kersey,[8]
To see the greatest rebel scamp
That ever crossed o'er Jersey.

The rebel clowns, oh! what a sight !
For awkward was their figure.
T'was yonder stood a pious wight,
And here and there a nigger.

Upon a stump, he placed himself,
Great Washington did he,
And through the nose of lawyer Close[9]
Proclaimed great Liberty.

The patriot brave, the patriot fair,
From fervor had grown thinner,
So off they marched, with patriot zeal,
And took a patriot dinner.[10]

[6]"Splutter" refers to spitting out bits of food when talking excitedly.

[7]A "brindle" is a spotted animal.

[8]Proper dress.

[9]Major Lee Close, Washington's confidential assistant.

[10]Corn pudding and rum.

Source: Benson Lossing, *The American Historical Record*, Volume 1. (Philadelphia: Chase & Town, 1872), 502.

Verses from "Yankee Doodle"

(1775)

INTRODUCTION

This is the most famous song of the revolutionary period. It is probably the only one that is still familiar to 21st-century Americans. During the period of its creation, it was so popular that over 200 stanzas were composed to be sung to the popular melody. No one knows for sure who the original author is. What is certain is that both the British and the colonials adopted it; the Americans as a patriotic war song, the British as a satirical portrait of the colonials and their pretensions. The most famous stanza comes from the British, making fun of the Americans.

[1]The word "doodle" is a corruption of "noodle," which in 18th-century English is similar in meaning to our "bobble"—as in "bobble-head doll"—meaning to wag your head foolishly up and down.

[2]In 18th-century British slang, macaroni meant dressing up in absurdly grotesque finery. So the stanza means: "A Colonial jerk went to the city dressed up in what he thought was the finest fashion—but in fact, he looked like a fool."

Yankee Doodle[1] came to town
Riding on a pony
Stuck feather in his hat
And called it "macaroni."[2]

Source: Oscar Sonneck, Report on "the Star-Spangled Banner," "Hail Columbia," "America," "Yankee Doodle." (Washington, DC: Government Printing Office, 1909), 127.

Another Version of "Yankee Doodle"

[3]An obscure reference likely made up to provide a rhyme for "pudding."

Father and I went down to camp,
Along with Captain Gooding,[3]
There we see the men and boys
As thick as hasty pudding.

Yankee Doodle keep it up,
Yankee Doodle dandy;
Mind the music and the step,
And with the girls be handy.

252

And there was Captain Washington
And gentle folks about him,
They say he's grown so tarnal proud
He will not ride without 'em![4]

Source: "Yankee Doodle," published by Charles Magnus, Rare Book and Special Collections Division, Library of Congress.

And there was Gen'ral Washington
Upon a snow-white charger[5]
He look'd as big as all outdoors
Some thought he was much larger.

Source: George T. Tobin, *Our National Songs.* (New York: Frederick A. Stokes Company, 1898), 97–98.

[4]George Washington insisted on having an honor guard wherever he went, to protect both him and the important papers and money that traveled with him. This stanza ridicules Washington for his arrogance.

[5]Horse.

John Mason's "Liberty's Call"

(1776)

INTRODUCTION

A patriot ardently devoted to the cause of liberty, John Mason published many of his ballads privately. Mason was a native of Maryland who moved to Philadelphia to work in the office of the *Pennsylvania Packet*, a paper devoted to the revolution. He ridiculed loyalists who accused him of being an eccentric. He set up shop as an upholsterer and circulated his writings from there. When the British marched into Philadelphia, Mason marched out, returning after the war to his dual role as gadfly and citizen where "slavery could not thrive, because liberty there springs spontaneous."

[1] The interest here is his image of liberty as a woman welcoming the downtrodden of the world to America's shores; 110 years before Emma Lazarus' poem "The New Colossus" was inscribed on the Statue of Liberty (Give me your poor, your huddled masses yearning to breathe free), Mason used the same metaphor. One wonders if Lazarus knew this poem.

[2] Londonderry in Northern Ireland was a center of anti-British agitation that eventually broke out in militant rebellion in 1797.

[3] Benefit.

High on the banks of Delaware,
Fair Liberty she stood[1];
And waving with her lovely hand,
Cried, "Still thou roaring flood.

Be still ye winds, be still ye seas,
Let only zephyrs play!"
Just as she spoke, they all obeyed;
And thus the maid did say:

Welcome my friends, from every land
Where freedom doth not reign;
Oh! hither fly from every clime,
Sweet liberty to gain.

Mark Londonderry's brave defence.[2]
'Gainst tyranny that swayed;
Americans, the example's great!
Like them, be not dismayed.

Expect not that on downy beds,
This boon[3] you can secure;

At peril's smile, rouse up your souls!
War's dangers to endure . . .

Book: Frank Moore, *Songs and Ballads of the American Revolution.* (New York: D. Appleton & Company, 1856), 83–86.

Benjamin Dearborn's "A War Song"

(1776)

INTRODUCTION

Benjamin Dearborn was the printer of the *Freeman's Journal*, or *New Hampshire Gazette*, in which many songs were published.

[1]Pay attention.

HARK, hark, the sound of war is heard,
And we must all attend;[1]
Take up our arms and go with speed,
Our country to defend.

Our parent state has turn'd our foe,
Which fills our land with pain;
Her gallant ships, manned out for war,
Come thundering o'er the main . . .

Our pleasant land they do invade,
Our property devour;
And all because we won't submit
To their despotic power.

Then let us go against our foe,
We'd better die than yield;
We and our sons are all undone,
If Britain wins the field.

[2]Colonists who support Britain.

Tories[2] may dream of future joys,
But I am bold to say,
They'll find themselves bound fast in chains,
If Britain wins the day.

Husbands must leave their loving wives,
And sprightly youths attend,
Leave their sweethearts and risk their lives,
Their country to defend.

May they be heroes in the field,
Have heroes' fame in store;
We pray the Lord to be their shield,
Where thundering canons roar.

Source: William McCarty, *Songs, Odes, and Other Poems on National Subjects*, Part 3. (Philadelphia: Wm. McCarty, 1842), 444–445.

"Off from Boston," or Military Song

(1776)

INTRODUCTION

On June 15, 1775, the Continental Congress appointed George Washington commander in chief of the army. He took charge of the militia at Cambridge and soon had transformed a ragtag force into an efficient fighting machine. Too late to reverse the British victory at the Battle of Bunker (Breeds') Hill (June 17, 1775), it became clear to Washington that his first job was to drive the British from Boston. To do that, the Americans needed artillery. In November 1775, he arranged to have heavy guns moved from northern New York, where the Americans had captured artillery after defeating the British at Ticonderoga, across the snowy Berkshire Mountains to the heights of Dorchester just south of Boston. This amazing transport was completed by early March 1776. General Howe, the British commander, realized that the Americans had taken the high ground and loaded his troops into ships on March 17, 1776. The evacuation seemed a triumph of strategy for Washington and gave a much-needed boost to the spirits of his troops.

As the British departed, Washington marched into the city and was received with this song as the "deliverer of his country."

---

[1] The triumph was short-lived; by July 1776, Howe's army had taken control of New York City.

Sons of valor, taste the glories
Of celestial liberty,
Sing a triumph o'er the tories,[1]
Let the pulse of joy beat high.

Heaven hath this day foil'd the many
Fallacies of George the King;
Let the echo reach Britan'y.
Bid her mountain summits ring.

See yon navy swell the bosom.
Of the late enraged sea;
Where're they go, we shall oppose them,
Sons of Valor must be free . . .

War, fierce war, shall break their forces,
Nerves of tory men shall fail,

Seeing Howe with alter'd courses,
Bending to the western gale.

Thus from every bay of ocean,
Flying back with sails unfurl'd,
Tossed with ever-troubled motion,
They shall quit this smiling world . . .

> **Source:** Frank Moore, *Songs and Ballads of the American Revolution.* (New York: D. Appleton & Company, 1856), 122–125.

Jonathan Sewall's "On Independence"

(1776)

INTRODUCTION

The authorship of this song, celebrating the publication of the Declaration of Independence, is curious. J. M. Sewall was an orphan raised by his uncle, a member of a prominent colonial family. He had a distinguished career in law in New Hampshire and supported the revolutionary cause. Jonathan Sewall of Massachusetts was also orphaned and raised by his uncle and had a distinguished career in the law. He was a close friend of John Adams and John Hancock. He was also a staunch loyalist who urged Adams not to join the First Continental Congress. He claimed to be neutral but supported the British constitutional government. The patriotic fervor expressed in these verses would indicate that J. M. S. is the author, but J. S. was a close friend of both supporters of independence.

Come all you brave soldiers, both valiant and free,
It's for Independence we all now agree;
Let us gird on our swords and prepare to defend,
Our liberty, property, ourselves and our friends.

In a cause that's so righteous, come let us agree,
And from hostile invaders set America free,
The cause is so glorious we need not to fear,
But from merciless tyrants we'll set ourselves clear.

Heaven's blessing attending us, no tyrant shall say
That Americans e'er to such monsters gave way,
But fighting we'll die in America's cause
Before we'll submit to tyrannical laws.

George the Third, of Great Britain, no more shall he reign,
With unlimited sway o'er these free states again;
Lord North, nor old Bute, nor none of their clan,[1]
Shall ever be honor'd by an American.

May heaven's blessing descend on our United States,
And grant that the union may never abate;

[1] North was prime minister of Britain. Bute was the political mentor of George III.

260

May love, peace, and harmony ever be found,
For to go hand in hand America round.

Upon our grand Congress may heaven bestow,
Both wisdom and skill our good to pursue;
On heaven alone dependent we'll be,
But from all earthly tyrants we mean to be free.

Unto our brave Generals may heaven give skill,
Our armies to guide, and the sword for to wield,
May their hands taught to war, and their fingers to fight,
Be able to put British armies to flight.

And now, brave Americans, since it is so,
That we are independent, we'll have them to know,
That united we are, and united we'll be,
And from all British tyrants we'll try to keep free.

May Heaven smile on us in all our endeavours,
Safe guard our seaports, our towns, and our rivers,
Keep us from invaders by land and by sea,
And from all who'd deprive us of our liberty.

Source: Evert Duyckinck and George Duyckinck, *Cyclopaedia of American Literature*, Volume 1. (Philadelphia: Baxter Publishing, 1881), 464.

"To the Commons"

(1776)

INTRODUCTION

This ballad is addressed to the House of Commons on their reconvening to consider the colonial problem after a recess. It is a warning to Parliament that the colonists' determination to secure their rights should not be underestimated. They would prevail. First published in the *Middlesex Journal* in 1776, it was reissued as a broadside, dated 1777. The author, who only identified himself by the signature "M," wrote, "I have the temerity to republish, in a more portable form, and try the royal brutes again."

[1]The colonists.

[2]Cups.

The folks on t'other side the wave[1]
Have beef as well as you, sirs;
Some chines,[2] and turkeys too, they have
And as they bake they brew, sirs.

What, tho' your cannon raze their towns,
And tumble down their houses,
They'll fight like devils, blood and 'oons,
For children and for spouses.

Another truth, nay, 'tis no boast,
Nor yet the lie o' th' day, sirs;
[3]"Saints" refers to the descendants of the pilgrims who emigrated for religious freedom.
The saints on Massachusetts coast[3]
Gain if they run away, sirs.

For further than your bullets fly,
A common man may run, sirs.
And wheat will grow beneath a sky
Where cannot reach a gun, sirs.

Source: Frank Moore, *Songs and Ballads of the American Revolution*. (New York: D. Appleton & Company, 1866), 141–143.

The British Lamentation or "The Dying Redcoat"

(1776)

INTRODUCTION

This is an example of what was known as "gallows literature." The execution of a felon was an important public event. Crowds gathered to witness the last words of the condemned. Standing on the brink of extinction during his last moments, the dying man prepared a message summarizing his fate. Here, the author imagines the last memoir of a dying redcoat.

'Twas on that dark and dismal time,
When we set sail for the northern clime;
Our drums did beat and trumpets sound,
And unto Boston we were bound.

And when to Boston we were come,
We thought by sounding British drums,
To drive those rebels from the place,
Which filled our souls with sore disgrace.

But to our sad and sore surprise,
We saw them like grasshoppers rise:
They fight like heros much enrag'd,
Which surely frighten'd General Gage.[1]

We saw those brave American sons,
Spread death and slaughter from their guns;
"Freedom or death!" those heros cry,
I'm sure theyre not afraid to die.
Like lions watching for their prey,
They fear no danger or dismay;
True British blood runs through their veins,
And them with courage yet sustains.

We sailed to York,[2] as you've been told,
By the loss of many a Briton bold,

[1] General Thomas Gage was governor of Massachusetts and commander of the British forces in America.

[2] New York.

263

To make those rebels own their king,
And daily tribute to him bring . . .

They said it was a garden place,
And that our armies might be safe;
Burn down your towns, lay waste your land,
In spite of all your boasting bands.

A garden place it was indeed,
And in it grows a bitter weed,
Which will put down our brightest hopes,
And sorely wound our British troops.

It is a year the nineteenth day,
Since first we came to America;
Full fifteen hundred have been slain,
Bold British heros every one.

Now I've receivd my mortal wound,
I bid adieu to Old England's ground;
My wife and children mourn for me,
When I lay cold in America.

Fight on, fight on, American boys,
Old England's thundering noise,
Maintain your rights from year to year,
God your side—you need not fear.

Source: "British Lamentation and Green on the Cape." American Song Sheets, Rare Books and Special Collections, Library of Congress.

The Battle of Trenton: A Drinking Song

(1777)

INTRODUCTION

After a string of defeats on Long Island and Manhattan, Washington withdrew his army to the west bank of the Delaware River. Both his reputation and his army were in tatters. It was a bitter winter of 1776 and, worst of all, most of his troops' enlistments expired on December 31. Trenton was in the hands of a small British garrison, supported by Hessian mercenaries. Washington and a small detachment of Continentals crossed the ice-jammed Delaware River at 3:00 A.M. on Christmas night and surprised the garrison, inflicting a huge defeat on the soldiers who had been celebrating Christmas. Washington's reputation was rehabilitated and his troops, scenting the possibility of victory, reenlisted.

On Christmas-day in seventy-six,
Our ragged troops with bayonets fixed,
For Trenton marched away.
The Delaware see! the boats below![1]
The light obscured by hail and snow!
But no signs of dismay.

Our object was the Hessian[2] band,
That dared invade fair freedom's land,
And quarter in that place.
Great Washington he led us on,
Whose streaming flag, in storm or sun,
Had never known disgrace.

In silent march we pass'd the night,
Each soldier panting for the fight,
Though quite benumb'd with frost,
Greene, on the left, at six began,[3]
The right was led by Sullivan,[4]
Who ne'er a moment lost.

The pickets storm'd, the alarm was spread,
That rebels risen from the dead

[1] The crossing took 10 hours.

[2] Professional German soldiers from the state of Hesse who had been hired to join the British forces.

[3] Washington had divided his army into three parts. Washington led the main force above Trenton. Greene's men were to attack at Trenton to prevent the Hessians from escaping.

[4] General John Sullivan had moved the troops under his command from Philadelphia to join Washington's army. According to Washington, they were the weakest element of his force. Sullivan's men crossed at Bordertown to distract the Hessian troops. Greene's and Sullivan's troops failed to gain their objectives, but Washington's men attacked in the early hours of December 26, overpowering the 1,000 Hessian troops.

265

Were marching into town.
Some scamper'd here, some scamper'd there,
And some for action did prepare;
But soon their arms laid down.

Twelve hundred servile miscreants,
With all their colors, guns, and tents,
were trophies of the day.
The frolic o'er, the bright canteen[5]
In center, front, and rear was seen
Driving fatigue away.

Now, brothers of the patriot bands,
Let's sing deliv'rance from the hands
Of arbitrary sway.
And as our life is but a span,
Let's touch the tankard while we can,
In mem'ry of that day.

[5] A shop set up on a military post to provide enlisted men with provisions.

Source: "Revolutionary Heroes, No. XI." *The National Magazine* 13 (December 1858).

"A Fable"

(1778)

For decades, the British and French had struggled for control of the riches of the New World. The central economic theory of the times embraced by both nations was mercantilism. This doctrine championed the idea that a great nation must base its prosperity in creating a favorable balance of trade, based on the establishment of a colonial empire where wealth would be channeled into the coffers of the mother country.

The war that ended in 1763 (known in England as the Seven Years' War and in the New World as the French and Indian War) concluded with a victory for England. After the Treaty of Paris, France was stripped of her possessions in Canada but allowed to retain islands in the Caribbean. On the surface, this seemed like a victory for England. In fact, it proved just the opposite, for the sugar islands were a source of great wealth for France, while Canada was largely a wasteland and proved of little economic value to England.

But there was an even more fateful result of the geographic realignment. While France and her Native American allies ruled the north country, the American colonies welcomed England's military presence as a defense against the French. With that threat removed, the colonists felt more secure and when, in order to pay for colonial expenses Parliament began to tax the colonists for sugar and tea, the spirit of revolution was nourished by the colonists' increased sense of security.

As Britain and its colonies moved closer and closer to conflict, no one was happier to watch the development than France, seeing an opportunity for revenge for its losses of 1763. When the Americans revolted, France was ready to intervene—but not openly. France followed a policy of secretly assisting the Americans. At the outbreak of the revolt, there was no assurance it would be a success. In fact, the first year of the war was characterized by a series of defeats for the Continental Army. The French sent munitions and supplies to the Americans, while still proclaiming their so-called neutrality.

Subterfuge and trickery were typical of French diplomacy, and it is that element that is emphasized in this ballad of 1778. The French had at first refused to enter into an alliance with the Americans; that would have resulted in war with Britain. The tipping point came with the American victory at Saratoga in October 1777. It was a near thing; after the British defeat, England sent a peace delegation to America to try and set up an arrangement where the Americans would enjoy independence and remain part of the British Empire.

France rushed to recognize American independence (February 6, 1778) and sign a Treaty of Friendship to promote commerce with France as a guarantor of American independence.

These verses "A Fable addressed to Americans, upon their treaty with France" reflect the British reaction to the event, warning the Americans about the dangers of an alliance with perfidious France. It has been suggested that the author was David Matthews, mayor of New York City during the revolution. It was published in *Rivington's Royal Gazette* in 1778. James Rivington faced harsh criticism for his paper's perceived loyalist leanings, including the destruction of his property and press. After the revolution, there was increased speculation that he was, in fact, a spy and supporter of Washington's Culper ring, using his position as editor of the weekly newspaper to act as a double agent for Washington.

REJOICE, Americans, rejoice!
Praise ye the Lord with heart and voice!
The treaty's signed with faithful France,
And now, like Frenchmen, sing and dance!

But when your joy gives way to reason,
And friendly hints are not deemed treason,
Let me, as well as I am able,
Present your Congress with a fable.

Tired out with happiness, the frogs[1]
Sedition croaked through all their bogs;
And thus to Jove the restless race,[2]
Made out their melancholy case . . .

"Great Jove," they croaked, "no longer fool us,
None but ourselves are fit to rule us:
We are too large, too free a nation,
To be encumbered with taxation!

We pray for peace, but wish confusion,
Then right or wrong, a revolution!
Our hearts can never bend to obey;
Therefore no king—and more we'll pray."

Jove smiled, and to their fate resigned
The restless, thankless, rebel kind;
Left to themselves, they went to work,
First signed a treaty with king Stork.[3]

[1] "Frogs" was an insulting nickname for the French among the British.

[2] Jove, or Jupiter, was king of the gods in Greek mythology.

[3] Louis XVI, king of France, was tall and thin, resembling (to the poet) a "stork."

He swore that they, with his alliance,
To all the world might bid defiance;
Of lawful rule there was an end on't,
And frogs were henceforth independent.[4]

At which the croakers one and all,
Proclaimed a feast, and festival!
But joy today brings grief tomorrow;
Their feasting o'er, now enter sorrow!

The Stork grew hungry, longed for fish;
The monarch could not have his wish;
In rage he to the marshes flies,
And makes a meal of his allies.

Then grew so fond of well-fed frogs,
He made a larder of the bogs!
Say, Yankees, don't you feel compunction,
At your unnatural, rash conjunction?

Can love for you in him take root,
Who's Catholic, and absolute?
I'll tell these croakers how he'll treat 'em;
Frenchmen, like storks, love frogs—to eat 'em.

[4]This refers to the alliance concluded between the French and the Americans.

Source: E.C. Stedman and E.M. Hutchinson, *A Library of American Literature*, Volume 3. (New York: Charles L. Webster & Company, 1888), 353–354.

"Our Women"

(1780)

INTRODUCTION

By the time this was published, American women had shown themselves to be a vital force in support of the cause of independence.

"Daughters of Liberty" met to spin cloth for uniforms and refused to drink "cursed tea." Loyalist women suffered. Many lost their homes and property. Many were subject to physical abuse by the marauding redcoats. But it would be a mistake to limit our appreciation of women's activities to such events. In the skirmishes, which made up the vast majority of military activism of the war, women used hatchets, guns, farm implements, and pots of boiling oil to defend their homes and families. They also served as couriers of war messages and as spies. Their contribution was recognized and widely praised.

[1]Although feminist leaders like to trace their activities to the mid-19th century, it should be clear that the role of women in revolutionary society was recognized and praised. The significance of a line like "all hail, superior sex" is not open to misinterpretation.

All hail! superior sex, exalted fair,[1]
Mirrors of virtue, Heaven's peculiar care;
Formed to enspirit and ennoble man
The immortal finish of Creation's plan!

Accept the tribute of our warmest praise
The soldier's blessing and the patriot's bays!
For fame's first plaudit, we no more contest
Constrained to own it decks the female breast . . .

And now ye sister angels of each state,
Their honest bosoms glow with joy elate,
Their gallant hearts with gratitude expand
And trebly feel the bounties of your hand . . .

Then freedom's ensign thus inscribed shall wave,
"The female patriots who their country save!"
Till time's abyss, absorbed in heavenly lays,
Shall flow in your eternity of praise.

Source: William C. Armstrong, *Patriotic Poems of New Jersey*. (New Jersey: Society Sons of the American Revolution, 1906), 6–7.

"Address to the Vile Traitor"
(1780)

INTRODUCTION

Benedict Arnold was perhaps the most perplexing figure of the revolutionary period. He was by turns a great hero and a great traitor to the American cause. A distinguished soldier who had defeated Burgoyne at the Battle of Saratoga, he felt himself insulted by Washington who passed him over for promotion.

Furious at the commander in chief's action, Arnold contacted the British, became a turncoat, and planned to betray the fortification of West Point to the British. The plot was discovered and foiled, but Arnold escaped to join the conflict in Virginia, conducting raids against the Continental Army. He finally got his long sought promotion as the British commissioned him brigadier general. Under his command, the redcoats followed a scorched earth policy, setting fire to crops and war materiel. Washington sent a force under Lafayette to oppose Arnold to no avail; nothing could defeat the newly minted general.

To the Traitor Arnold:

ARNOLD! the name, as heretofore,
Shall now be Benedict no more;[1]
Since, instigated by the devil,
Thy ways are turned from good to evil.

'Tis fit we brand thee with a name,
To suit thy infamy and shame;
And since of treason thou'rt convicted,
Thy name should now be maledicted.[2]

Unless by way of contradiction,
We style thee Britain's Benediction;
Such blessings she, with lavish hand,
Confers on this devoted land . . .

Then, in this class of Britain's heroes,
The Tories, savage Indians, Negroes,
Recorded Arnold's name shall stand,

[1] Benedict comes from the Latin "bene" meaning "good." Benedict means a blessing as indeed Arnold was in the early days of the war.

[2] A malediction is a curse.

While Freedom's blessings crown our land.
And odious for the blackest crimes,
Arnold shall stink to latest times.[3]

[3]His name shall give off an offensive smell forever.

Source: Burton E. Stevenson, *Poems of American History*. (Boston: Houghton Mifflin Company, 1908), 328.

"Cornwallis Burgoyned"

(1781)

INTRODUCTION

General Burgoyne had been defeated by Benedict Arnold at the Battle of Saratoga in 1777. Burgoyne had attacked relentlessly, but Arnold's daring leadership forced him to retreat, and he soon was encircled by the American forces. A similar situation arose at the Battle of Yorktown, where French and American troops defeated General Cornwallis. The French fleet blocked the entrance of Chesapeake Bay to prevent Cornwallis's escape by sea. At the same time, Washington rushed his forces to trap the British in a pincer movement on land. Cornwallis knew the game was up as the Americans closed in on him and forced his surrender on October 19, 1781. The title "Cornwallis Burgoyned" refers to the defeat of British, but also to the triumph of American military strategy.

Although the surrender of Yorktown is often characterized as the final battle of the revolution, it was not. The hostilities continued in certain areas for two more years.

WHEN British troops first landed here,
With Howe commander o'er them,[1]
They thought they'd make us quake for fear,
And carry all before them;
With thirty thousand men or more,
And she without assistance,
America must needs give o'er,
And make no more resistance.

But Washington, her glorious son,
Of British hosts the terror,
Soon, by repeated overthrows,[2]
Convinced them of their error . . .

Be peace, the glorious end of war,
By this event effected;
And be the name of Washington,
To latest times respected;
Then let us toast America,

[1] Howe, commander of British troops, had been forced by Washington to evacuate Boston. Washington tried to defend New York, but Howe drove his army from Brooklyn, Long Island, across New Jersey to the western bank of the Delaware River.

[2] Washington crossed the Delaware on Christmas night 1776, defeated the British at Trenton, defeated Cornwallis at Princeton, and began a series of victories that led to eventual triumph at Yorktown.

And France in union with her;
And may Great Britain rue the day
Her hostile bands came hither.

Source: Burton E. Stevenson, *Poems of American History.* (Boston: Houghton Mifflin Company, 1908), 256–257.

"Thanksgiving Hymn"

(1783)

INTRODUCTION

The Treaty of Paris negotiated with the British by Benjamin Franklin, John Adams, and John Jay was signed on September 3, 1783. It recognized the independence of the United States and specified its borders, granted fishing rights off the coast of Nova Scotia, and restored property that had been confiscated from loyalists during the conflict. The last British soldier left New York City in November 1783.

This patriotic hymn celebrated the end to a war in which 7,200 Continentals had lost their lives, 8,200 had been wounded, 10,000 had died of disease, and 8,500 had died in British captivity.

In light of the costs in lives and treasure, these super patriotic verses lose some of their luster. Praise for Washington, praise for the Congress, and invocation of the lord's blessing on them and the nation are typical of the literature of the period.

The Lord above, in tender love,
Hath sav'd us from our foes;
Through Washington the thing is done,
The war is at a close.

America has won the day,
Through Washington, our chief;
Come let's rejoice with heart and voice,
And bid adieu to grief.

Now we have peace, and may increase
In number, wealth, and arts;[1]
If every one, like Washington,
Will strive to do their parts.

Then let's agree, since we are free,
All needless things to shun;
And lay aside all pomp and pride,
Like our great Washington . . .

[1] Most soldiers who survived were penniless. Some were given certificates for land in the West but were forced to sell them to raise cash. Thirty years later, Congress finally agreed to pay pensions to the few veterans who survived.

The Thirteen States, united sets,
In Congress simply grand;
The Lord himself preserve their health,
That they may rule the land . . .

But all should try, both low and high,
Our freedom to maintain;
Pray God to bless our grand Congress,
And cease from every sin.

Then sure am I, true liberty
Of every sort will thrive;
With one accord we'll praise the Lord,
All glory to Him give . . .

Source: Frank Moore, *Songs and Ballads of the American Revolution.* (New York: D. Appleton & Company, 1856), 376–379.

Timeline of Events

1764, April 5

The Sugar Act, an attempt to extend the legislative power of Parliament (especially the power to tax) over the colonies, takes effect, and is seen as an invasion of colonial liberties. Violations are to be tried by a court in Nova Scotia. The burden of proof is on the accused. The decision is that of a judge; no jury trial is permitted.

1765, March 22

The Stamp Act takes effect. All legal documents are to be printed on special paper bearing an official stamp. The purpose is to raise revenue (essentially a tax by another name).

1765, May 15

The first Quartering Act requires colonies to provide housing and support for British troops. This provision is later restated as one of the intolerable acts of 1776.

1765, October 7–25

The Stamp Act Congress meets in New York City, with delegates from nine colonies, and publishes a statement of "rights and grievances." It is an early step toward union.

1766, March 4

The Declaratory Act repeals the Stamp Act and reserves Parliament's right to legislate laws for the colonies.

1767

The Townshend Acts aim to raise money by taxing glass, paper, lead, and tea, thus becoming an issue of "taxation without representation."

1770, March 5

The Boston Massacre occurs. Tension between colonists and British soldiers escalates into armed conflict and several citizens are killed. It becomes a rallying point for colonial anger.

1773, May 10

The Tea Act gives a monopoly to the East India Company to aid its economic ills. The change in the tea tax causes great agitation in the colonies. The tea ships become symbols of "taxation tyranny."

1773, December 16

The Boston Tea Party is a formal protest against the tea act. Colonists disguised as Indians board tea ships and destroy 90,000 pounds of tea.

1774

The Intolerable Acts are enacted, punishing Boston for the tea party. The acts close the port of Boston, attack colonial courts and town meetings, require that trials be held at British courts, and impose the quartering of British troops.

1774, September 5

The First Continental Congress, an advisory body of the colonies, meets in Philadelphia. The purpose is to protect colonial rights violated by Parliament. It also advocates the boycott of British goods.

1775, April 19

In the Battles of Lexington and Concord, the first encounters of the war, 49 Americans and 73 British soldiers are killed. The skirmish shows the Americans that they could defeat the British with guerilla tactics.

1775, May 10
At the Second Continental Congress, colonial representatives meet in Philadelphia. Washington is appointed "generalissimo" of the Continental troops. "The Declaration of Causes and Necessity of Taking up Arms" is published.

1775, June 12
In the Battle of Bunker Hill, the Continentals try to force the British from Boston; 2,000 Americans defend the heights above Charlestown. The British, under Sir William Howe, attack twice and are repulsed. The third attack is a frontal movement supported by close bayonet contact. The Continentals, low on ammunition, retreat. The casualties were 441 Americans and 1,054 British. The battle is a costly "victory" for the Crown.

1776, January
Thomas Paine's *Common Sense* is published with an initial print run of 120,000 copies. Paine denounces those who would remain loyal to the Crown, calling them "dreamers." He supports colonial independence in terms that convince many who were undecided that the only wise course is separation from Britain.

1776, March 12
The British evacuate Boston. During the winter following the British victory at Bunker Hill, Washington reorganizes the several militias into a unified force. Cannon captured at Ticonderoga are moved on sledges and boats through the Berkshire mountains to Dorchester Heights, taking command of Boston where the British are encamped. Realizing the futility of an offensive move, the British embark for Nova Scotia, and Washington immediately occupies the city.

1776, July 4
The Declaration of Independence is adopted. On June 19, Congress appointed a committee (consisting of Thomas Jefferson, John Adams, Benjamin Franklin, Roger Sherman, and Robert Livingston) to prepare a declaration in support of independence. Although Jefferson's text was somewhat altered, the declaration is essentially his work. The most important change is the elimination of a paragraph on the slave trade.

1776, August 27
The Battle of Long Island is a British victory. Howe moves his army from Staten Island to Gravesend, Brooklyn. Washington's army is encamped at Brooklyn Heights; he moves his force to Long Island and is attacked by Howe. Although the attack is successful, Howe neglects to push his advantage, and Washington is able to withdraw to Manhattan. The successful escape ends by August 30, 1776.

1776, September 15
The British occupy New York City. In 1776, the city limits end half way up the island of Manhattan. Washington occupies New York in April 1776, but his defeat in the Battle of Long Island leads to his evacuation of the city. New York remains in the hands of the British until the end of the war.

1776, December 26
In the Battle of Trenton, Washington's surprise attack defeats the Hessian garrison. The Hessians held the Continental Army in contempt and had not fortified the city. Washington, after a series of defeats, had a badly demoralized force. On Christmas night, with 2,500 men, he crosses the Delaware River to attack the garrison at Trenton. A storm of sleet and snow and a river choked with ice delay his movement; he reaches the village in broad daylight. However, the Hessians are completely surprised and lose. There are 22 men killed, 84 wounded, and 1,000 captured. The victory heartens Washington's

army, and together with victory at Princeton, nearly frees New Jersey from British control.

1777, January 3
The Battle of Princeton takes place. Washington's victory at the battle of Princeton is a tribute to his generalship but is also attributed to the arrogant attitudes of his opponent, Cornwallis, who is determined to settle the score for the American victory at Trenton. Washington's army occupies a precarious position, with its escape route blocked by the Assunpink River. Cornwallis unwisely decides to delay his attack until morning light. At midnight, leaving his campfires burning to give the British the impression that he had hunkered down for the night, Washington moves his army via a back road to the rear of the British camp. As his army approaches Princeton, it encounters a force of redcoats moving to reinforce Cornwallis. Vicious fighting follows, which results in British losses of 400–600 killed, wounded, and captured. Cornwallis withdraws his army to New Brunswick; Washington's army, flush with victories at Trenton and Princeton, settles in at Morristown, full of new hope and enthusiasm.

1777, September 11
The British win at Brandywine Creek, Chester, Pennsylvania. The British force of 18,000 badly outnumbers the American force of 11,000. The Americans fight bravely, but the odds are too great and they are forced to retreat to Chester.

1777, September 19
At the first battle of Freeman's Farm (Saratoga), Gates defeats Burgoyne.

1777, September 26
The British occupy Philadelphia.

1777, October 4
Washington is defeated at Germantown, Pennsylvania.

1777, October 7
In the second battle of Freeman's Farm (Saratoga), the British are defeated.

1777, October 17
Burgoyne surrenders after the Battle of Saratoga.

1777, December 19
Washington establishes winter quarters at Valley Forge.

1778, February 6
The United States and France sign an alliance.

1778, June 28
The Battle of Monmouth Courthouse occurs. General Howe had occupied Philadelphia the previous September, but in May 1778 he was replaced by Clinton. Clinton abandons the city and intends to attack New York. Washington is determined to defeat his plan and attacks Clinton's flank at Monmouth Court House, but Clinton's army escapes. In the fall, Clinton marches south and occupies Georgia. Washington sets up a new base of operations at White Plains, New York.

1779, February 25
The British surrender Vincennes. Vincennes and Detroit had been established as important centers of resistance to colonial settlements of the Ohio Valley and the northwest. General Clark attacks the British stronghold at Vincennes, and after a 36-hour battle, the British yield to Clark's forces. Clark retains control of the southern section of the northwest territory until the end of the revolution; this is an important factor in granting the U.S. control of the northwest territory under the Treaty of Paris (1783).

1779, September 23
John Paul Jones' ship *Bonhomme Richard* captures the British ship *Serapis* in one of the important naval engagements of the war. Jones is sailing up

the east coast of England in search of English cargoes when he encounters the *Serapis* carrying valuable stores; Jones attacks it. There is a terrible battle with tremendous losses on both sides. When challenged to surrender, Jones famously replies, "I have not yet begun to fight." Jones essentially forces the British to surrender.

1780, May 12
The British capture Charleston, attacking the city both by land and by sea. The fall of Charleston paralyzes the Continental cause in the Carolinas.

1780, August 16
The patriots lose the Battle of Camden, one of the most devastating losses of the southern campaign. General Gates is replaced by General Greene.

1781, January 17
The patriot victory at Cowpens is one of the most brilliant of Continental victories. General Greene organizes his troops into three lines: Line one, the light infantry, is ordered to fire on the British when they were 50 yards distant, then fall back. Line 2, the militia, is ordered to fire twice and retreat. The British think they have won an easy victory and advance, only to encounter Greene's third line of fresh troops. Their deadly fire and bayonet charge result in huge British losses.

1781, March 1
The Articles of Confederation are ratified in an attempt to create a unified authority for the colonies. Internal disputes and weaknesses would occur until, in desperation, a constitutional convention is called to review the articles.

1781, March 15
The Battle of Guilford Courthouse, one of the longest and bloodiest battles of the war, is an engagement between Greene and Cornwallis. Greene retreats after five hours and Cornwallis, victorious, retreats and abandons the Carolinas. It is a military victory for the British but a strategic victory for the Americans.

1781, September 5
The French fleet damages the British at Chesapeake Bay. This key event leads to the Continental victory at Yorktown, preventing the escape and reinforcement of British troops.

1781, October 19
In the final victory of the war, Cornwallis surrenders at Yorktown.

1782, November 30
The United States and Britain sign a preliminary peace treaty at Paris, France.

1783, April 15
Congress ratifies the Treaty of Paris

1783, September 3
The United States and Britain sign the final peace treaty at Paris, France.

Further Reading

Adams, C.F., ed. *Letters of Mrs. Adams*. Boston: Little, Brown, 1848.

Adams, C.F., ed. *The Works of John Adams*. Boston: Little, Brown, 1856.

Bailyn, B., ed. *The Ideological Origins of the American Revolution*. Cambridge, MA: Harvard University Press, 1967. (The influence of British political ideas on American revolutionary thought.)

Bailyn, B., ed. *Pamphlets of the American Revolution 1750–1776*. Cambridge, MA: Belknap Press of Harvard University Press, 1965. (Presents a collection of contemporary press coverage of the major events leading to war.)

Becker, C. *The Declaration of Independence*. New York: Alfred A. Knopf, 1942. (The best discussion of the philosophy underlying the founding document.)

Bill, A.H. *Valley Forge*. New York: Harper and Bros., 1955. (Account of the process by which a dispirited force was transformed into a fighting unit by Washington and von Steuben.)

Burnett, E.C. *The Continental Congress*. New York: Macmillan, 1941. (This is the classic discussion of the organization, conflicts, and personalities that shaped the first attempt to achieve colonial unified action.)

Carter, C.E., ed. *The Correspondence of General Thomas Gage*. New Haven, CT: Yale University Press, 1931.

Conway, M.D., ed. *The Writings of Thomas Paine*. New York: G.P. Putnam's Sons, 1894.

Davis, Burke. *George Washington and the American Revolution*. New York: Random House, 1975. (Focuses on Washington's genius as a military leader and his inspiring personality.)

Dexter, F.B., ed. *The Literary Diary of Ezra Stiles*. New York: Charles Scribner's Sons, 1901.

Dorson, Richard M., ed. *American Rebels: Narratives of the Patriots*. New York: Pantheon Books, 1953. (Personal reminiscences of leading patriots.)

Ernest, R., and Dupuy, T.N. *The Compact History of the American Revolutionary War*. Portland, OR: Hawthorne Books, 1963. (Military history, thorough and easy to follow with excellent maps and illustrations of battle tactics and strategies.)

Fitzpatrick, J.C., ed. *The Diaries of George Washington*. Boston: Houghton Mifflin, 1971.

Freneau, P.M. *Poems Written and Published during the American Revolutionary War*. Philadelphia: The Press of Lydia R. Bailey, 1809.

Gipson, L.H. *The Coming of the Revolution*. New York: Harper and Bros., 1954. (The most detailed discussion of the precipitating events 1763–1776.)

Goss, E.H. *The Life of Col. Paul Revere*. Boston: J.C. Cupples, 1891.

Greene, G.W. *The Life of Nathanial Greene, Major General in the Army of the Revolution*. New York: G.P. Putnam's Sons, 1867.

Handlin, O.A. *A Restless People: Americans in Rebellion 1770–1787*. New York: Doubleday, 1982. (Underlying causes of the rebellion festering for decades.)

Hutchinson, Thomas, ed. *Diary and Letters of Thomas Hutchinson*. Boston: Houghton Mifflin, 1984.

Johnston, H.P. *The Yorktown Campaign and the Surrender of Cornwallis, 1781*. New York: Harper and Bros.

Ketchum, R.M. *The Battle for Bunker Hill*. New York: Doubleday, 1974. (Detailed Study of the battle and the personalities involved.)

Ketchum, R.M. *The Winter Soldiers*. New York: Doubleday, 1973. (A tribute to the resilience and fortitude of the first American army.)

Knollenberg, B. *Origin of the American Revolution*. New York: Macmillan Co., 1965. (Presents the thesis that it was the British attempt to usurp colonial rights long established that was the sole cause of the conflict.)

Labaree, B.W. *The Boston Tea Party*. New York: Oxford University Press, 1964. (An exhaustive discussion that brings to light personal involvement and colonial reaction to the event and to the British response to it.)

Lafayette, Marquis de. *Memoirs*. New York: Saunders and Otley, 1837.

Mackesy, P. *The War for America*. Cambridge, MA: Harvard University Press, 1964. (Presents the revolution as part of an international struggle for European imperial superiority.)

Martin, J.P. *Private Yankee Doodle*. G.F. Scheer, ed. New York: Popular Library, 1942. (Anecdotal accounts of "dangers and suffering" of Continental soldiers.)

Moore, Frank, ed. *Songs and Ballads of the American Revolution*. New York: D. Appleton and Co., 1856.

Morgan, E.S. *The Birth of the Republic.* Chicago: University of Chicago Press, 1957. (Discusses the most important events leading to the revolution.)

Morgan, E.S., and H. Morgan. *The Stamp Act Crisis.* Chapel Hill: University of North Carolina Press, 1953. (A useful examination of political and social aspects of colonial outrage.)

Morris, R.B. *The American Revolution Reconsidered.* New York: Harper and Bros., 1968.

Niles, H., ed. *Principles and Acts of the Revolution in America.* New York: A.S. Barnes and Co., 1876.

Royster, C. *A Revolutionary People at War.* Chapel Hill: University of North Carolina Press, 1979. (How the military experience shaped the American character.)

Sabine, L. *The Loyalists of the American Revolution.* Springfield, MA: The Walden Press, 1957. (An in-depth consideration of the motives and actions of colonial Tories.)

Sanderlin, G.W. 1776: *Journals of American Independence.* New York: Harper and Row, 1968. (Eyewitness reports of events of the revolution.)

Schlesinger, A.M. *Prelude to Independence.* New York: Alfred A. Knopf, 1958. (Presents a review of the role of the press during the revolution.)

Stone, W.L., ed. *Ballads and Poems Relating to the Burgoyne Campaign.* Albany, NY: Joel Munsell, 1893.

Tourtellot, A. *Lexington and Concord.* New York: W.W. Norton, 1959. (A popular account of the initial conflicts.)

Van Doren, C. *Secret History of the American Revolution.* New York: The Viking Press, 1941.

Willcox, William B., ed. *The American Rebellion by Sir Henry Clinton.* New Haven, CT: Yale University Press, 1954.

Index

abattis, 133
Abercrombie, James, 110
Adams, Abigail, 117, 130, 206–208
Adams, John, 32, 60, 70, 275
  Abigail's letter to, 117, 130, 207–208
  on government structure, 77–78
  letter to Mrs. Adams, Philadelphia, July 3, 1776, 206–207
  Palmer's letter to, 117
  Prescott's letter to, 107–108, 120–121
  on representative assembly, 77, 78
  republic defined by, 77
  Thoughts on Government, 76–79, 206
Adams, Samuel, 60, 86, 94, 97, 201, 246
  Boston Committee of Correspondence report, 10–12
  Boston Tea Party and, 21
  Committee of Correspondence, 27
  Sons of Liberty Tea Resolutions, 19–20
"Adam's Fall (Trip to Cambridge)," 250–251
"Address to the Vile Traitor," 271–272
affray, 5
African corsairs, 42
aide-de-camp, 110
Ainslie, Thomas, 126–127
Alexander the Great, 235
Allen, Ethan, 123
allowed no quarters, 188
"Alphabet for Little Masters and Misses," 248–249
American Army, parts of, 138
American Crisis Papers #1, 85
American Navy, 71
American Revolution, road to
  American Crisis Papers #1, 85
  Boston Committee of Correspondence, 10–12
  Boston Massacre reports, 5–9
  Boston Tea Party, accounts of, 21–24
  Committee of Correspondence and, 27–29

Common Sense (Paine), 61–75
  Declaration of Causes and Necessity of Taking Up Arms, 52–58
  Henry speech to House of Burgesses, 46–47
  Intolerable Acts and, 25–26
  introduction to, 1–3
  Jefferson's letter hoping for reconciliation, 59–60
  Jefferson's letter to Dr. Small, 48–49
  Navigation Acts and, 1–2
  Sons of Liberty Tea Resolutions, 1773, 19–20
  stamp tax and, 2
  Suffolk Resolves and, 30–35
  Sugar/Molasses Act and, 2
  Tea Act, 1773, 2–3, 13–18
  "Thoughts on Government," 76–79
  timeline of events, 277–280
  Townsend and, 2
  Unanimous Declaration of the Thirteen United States of America, 83–84
  Virginia Declaration of Rights, 80–82
  Washington and Continental Army, 50–51
"American Taxation" (St. John), 231–236
Anburey, Thomas, 178
Andrews, John, 22–23, 129–130
Arcadia, 79
Archbald, Edward, 8
Archbald, Francis, 8
Armstrong, John, 153–154
Arnold, Benedict, 123
  "Address to the Vile Traitor," 271–272
  at Battle at Saratoga, 175
  Camp Stillwater correspondence with Gates, 170–172
  letter to Schuyler, 123–124

  letter to Hannah, 125–126
  at second battle of Freeman's Farm, 176
Articles of Confederation, 238, 280
Atwood, Samuel, 8

baggage, 138
banditti, 114
Barker, John, 92–93
Barre, Isaac, 201
Barrell, William, 129–130
Barrett, William, 22
Barton, William, 154
batteaux, 123–124
batteries, 106, 108, 115, 189
Battle of Trenton: A Drinking Song, 265–266
battlefield concept, 89
battles of liberty
  Boston, siege of, 129–136
  Brandywine, Valley Forge, and Paoli Massacre, 150–156
  Bunker Hill, 106–122
  introduction to, 89–90
  Lexington and Concord, letters on, 91–105
  Long Island, Northern Manhattan, White Plains, 137–140
  Monmouth, 157–161
  Montreal and Quebec, invasion of, 123–128
  Sag Harbor, skirmish of, 147–149
  Saratoga, 162–179
  Trenton, 141–146
  Yorktown, 180–199
  See also *individual battles*
Bay Psalm Book, 230
bayonets, 107
bayonets fixed, 97
Beaver (tea ship), 244
Black troops, emancipation of, 160–161
Blair, John, 154

blockhouse, 125

blunderbuss, 94

bohea tea, 13, 16

Bonhomme Richard (ship), 279–280

Bostnick, Elisha, 143–144

Boston, evacuation of, 134–135, 278

Boston, siege of, 129–136

    Abigail's letter to John Adams, 130

    Andrews' letter to Barrell, 129–130

    evacuation of Boston, 134–135

    introduction to, 129

    Larrabee's pension application, 132

    Newell journal, 134

    officer at Boston letter sent to
        England, 131–132

    officer of distinction letter to person
        in London, 131

    Stuart's letter to Bute, 133–134

    Washington's proclamation on,
        135–136

Boston Centinel, 134

Boston Committee of Correspondence,
    10–12

Boston Gazette, 239, 240

Boston Gazetteer, 23–24

Boston Massacre, 5–9, 277

    American report of, 5–7

    British report of, 8–9

    introduction to, 5

Boston Port Act, 25, 54, 55

    Jefferson on, 40

    Maryland's reaction to, 25–26

Boston Tea Party, 21–24, 277

    Andrews' account of, 22–23

    Boston Gazetteer account of, 23–24

    Hewes's account of, 21–22

    introduction to, 21

    New Daily Advertiser account of,
        23–24

    song about, 243–244

Boughes, 8

Brandywine, Battle of, 150–156, 279

    Armstrong's letter to Gates,
        153–154

    Barton's letter to father from Valley
        Forge, 154

    Burke's letter to Sullivan, 152–153

    Hutchinson's description of Paoli
        Massacre, 155–156

    introduction to, 150–151

    Pickering's journal of, 151

Seldon's letter to Mather, 154–155

    Washington's report on defeat at,
        151–152

brass fender, 97

brass fieldpieces, 177

breastwork, 120

Breed's Hill, 107–108

Brigham, Johnathan, 115

brindle, 251

British America rights, Jefferson
    summary view of, 36–45

broadsides, 121, 230

Brown, Peter, 118–119

Brown, Samuel, 141–142

Bruce (tea ship), 22

Bunker Hill, Battle of, 57, 106–122,
    278

    Abigail's letter to John Adams, 117

    Brigham's application for pension,
        115

    British officer's critique of, 113–114

    broadside, 121

    Brown's letter to mother, 118–119

    Burgoyne's propaganda letter to
        nephew, 116

    Burgoyne's report to nephew, 111

    casualty lists, 106

    Farnsworth's diary of, 106–107

    Gage's account of, 112, 122

    Howe's account of, 110–111

    Hutton's account of, 114

    Ober's diary entry, 117–118

    Palmer's letter to Adams, John, 117

    Prescott's letter to Adams, John,
        107–108, 120–121

    as Pyrrhic victory, 106

    Rawdon's account of, 109

    Thacher's eyewitness narrative of,
        108–109

    Waller's account of, 119–120

Burgoyne, John, 162

    Bunker Hill report to nephew, 111

    letter to Germain, 167–168

    plays written by, 163

    proclamation by, 162–164

    propaganda letter to nephew, 116

    reply to proclamation by, 164–167

Burke, Edmund, 55

Burke, Thomas, 152–153

Bute, Lord, 133–134

Butler, Richard, 186, 187

Camden, Battle of, 280

Carleton, Guy, 57, 123

Castle William, 22, 132

cataracts, 165

Cemetery (light ship), 113

ceremony of soldiery, 186

Charleston, fall of, 280

chevaux de freze, 134

Clinton, Henry, 193–194

Close, Lee, 251

Coercive Acts, 30

Coffin (tea ship), 22

colony committees, 27

colors cased, 197

columns, moving in, 113

Commissions, 138

Committee of Correspondence,
    Massachusetts, 27–29, 180, 246

Common Sense (Paine), 46, 60, 61–75, 278

    biblical references and, 66

    British trade monopoly and, 62

    colonial prosperity and, 62

    Continental Congresses and, 68

    Declaration of Independence
        compared to, 74–75

    free trade and, 63

    introduction to, 61

    Massanello and, 69

    mercantilist doctrine and, 67

    natural law and, 66

    purpose of, 61

    race wars and, 69

    reconciliation and, 64–65

    religions and, 63

Concord, Battle of. *See* Lexington and
    Concord, Battles of

Concord bridge, stand at, 95–96

"Concord Hymn" (Emerson), 95

Constitutional Gazette, 248

Continental Congress, 3, 54, 60, 68, 162

Continentals, 138, 162

Copernicus, 66

Corbin, Margaret (Dirty Kate), 209–211

    Action of the Continental Congress,
        July 6, 1779, 210

    Action of the Supreme Council of
        Pennsylvania, June 29, 1779, 210

    Resolution of the Board of War of
        the Continental Congress, June 6,
        1779, 209–210

    Tilghman's appeal for exception, 211

Cornwallis, Lord
   letter to Henry Clinton, 193–194
   Washington's letters to, on Yorktown
      surrender, 194–197
"Cornwallis Burgoyned," 273–274
county committees, 27
Cowpens, patriot victory at, 280
Cromwell, Oliver, 43, 95
crow feet, 134
Crozier, John, 94–95
cursed weed, 244
cutlass, 97

Darrah, Lydia, 226
Dartmouth (tea ship), 244
Daughters of Liberty, 201, 216
Daughters of the American Revolution,
   209
Dawes, William, 97
de Grasse, Comte, Washington letter
      to, 184–185
Dearborn, Benjamin, 256–257
declarant, 115
Declaration of Causes and Necessity of
      Taking Up Arms, 52–58
Declaration of Independence, 83, 278
   Common Sense comparisons to, 74–75
Declaratory Act, 277
Dedham (Massachusetts) Register, 223
Delpht manufactory, 9
deponent, 127
Devil's Disciple, The (Shaw), 162
Dickinson, John, 238
   "Liberty Song, The," 239–240
Digby, William
   October 7, 1777, journal entry,
      175–176
   October 17, 1777, journal entry,
      178–179
   September 19, 1777, journal entry,
      169
Dirty Kate. *See* Corbin, Margaret
      (Dirty Kate)
disposition, 152
doodle, 252
dore, 205
drum beat to arms, 126, 132
Duke of Wellington, 89
Duncan, James, 186–187
duties of customs, drawback of, 13
"Dying Redcoat, The," 263–264

East India Company, 2, 13–14, 16–17, 21,
      40, 243
Eleanor (tea ship), 244
Elysium, 79
embrasures, 133, 187
Emerson, Ralph Waldo, 95
Emerson, William, 95–96
eminence, 95
emoluments, 81
Empress of Russia (frigate), 94
entrenching tool, 133
epocha, 79, 207
excise tax, 15
exhalters, 143
extempore arbitrary decrees, 11

"Fable addressed to Americans, upon
      their treaty with France, A"
      (Matthews), 267–269
Farnsworth, Amos, 106–107
fascine knife, 133
fascines, 133
Federalist Papers, 160
Fifth Amendment, 81
First Amendment, 82
First Continental Congress, 277
ford, 151
Fort Washington, Battle of, 209–211
Francis, Lord Rawdon, 109
Franklin, Benjamin, 48, 52, 229–230, 246,
      275
freedom of religion, 73
Freeman's Farm
   first battle of, 279
   second battle of, 176–178, 279
French and Indian War, 167, 229
frigate ship, 71
frogs, 268
froward, 163

Gage, Thomas, 55, 56–57, 91
   on Battles of Lexington and
      Concord, 93–94
   on Bunker Hill, 112, 122
   British officer's critique of, 114
   Farnsworth on, 107
Galileo, 66
Gannett, Deborah Sampson, 222–224
   at Battle of Eastchester, 223
   career of, 222
   in Continental Army, 222

pension application, 224
Revere on, 224
service recognition of, 224
sex of, discovered, 224
Gates, Horatio, 153–154, 162, 235
   Camp Stillwater correspondence
      with Arnold, 170–172
George II, king, 14–15
George III, king, 31, 43–44, 55, 232
   Howe's letter to, 110–111
Germain, George, letters to Knox,
      William, 168–169
Germantown, Pennsylvania,
      Washington defeat at, 279
Glorious Revolution, 43
goody, 237
goody bull, 237
government elections, 81
government powers
   derived from people, 80
   limited, 81
   separation of, 81
grape shot, 176
Greene, Nathanael, 235
grenadiers, 138, 176
Grenville, George, 229
Guilford Courthouse, Battle of, 280

Hall (tea ship), 22
Hamilton, Alexander, 157, 160–161, 187
Hancock, John, 2, 60, 86, 94, 97
Harris, Joel Chandler, 220
Harrison, Richard, 158–159
Hart, Nancy, 220–221
"Hearts of Oak," 239
"Heiress, The" (Burgoyne play), 163
Henry, Patrick, 59, 60
   Fairfax Resolutions, 46
   House of Burgesses speech, 46–47
Hessians, 89, 112, 137–138, 144–145, 175,
      265
Hewes, George, 21–22
Hicks, John, 8
Hobbes, Thomas, 76–77
horrid massacre, 6–7
hors de combat, 177
House of Hanover, 41
House of Stuart, 41
House of Tudor, 41
House of Windsor, 41
Howe, William, 110–111, 167, 168–169

howitzers, 189
husband, 18
Hutchinson, Thomas, 7
Hutchinson, William, 155–156
Hutton, Ann, 114

imparlance, 15
inch of candle, 17
"India Tea" (Weare), 245
infantry, 89
Inquiry into the Source of the Wealth of Nations, An (Smith), 38
Intolerable Acts, 277
    Maryland's reaction to, 25–26
intrepidity, 6

jagers, 185
Jay, John, 52, 160–161, 275
Jefferson, Thomas, 36, 52, 60
    on Boston Massacre, 41
    on Boston Port Act, 40
    letter hoping for reconciliation with Britain, 59–60
    letter to Dr. Small, 48–49
    on Navigation Acts, 37–38
    rights of British America, summary view of, 36–45
    on slavery, 42
    on Sugar and Stamp Acts, 39
Jennings, Nathan, 147–149
Joan of Arc, 203
Jones, John Paul, 279–280
journeymen, 5
Jove, 268

Kepler, 66
Knox, Henry, 144–145
Knox, William, letters from Germain, George, 168–169

Lafayette, Marquis de, 151–152, 157
    letter to Vergennes, 180–181
    memoirs of, 158
    Yorktown campaign letter from Washington, 181–182
Larrabee, Samuel, 132
laws of planetary motion, 66
Lazarus, Emma, 254
Lee, Richard Henry, 83
Leech, John, 8
Legislative, rights of, 11

Leigh, Benjamin, 9
"Letters from a Farmer in Pennsylvania" (Dickinson), 238, 239
Leviathan (Hobbes), 76–77
Lexington and Concord, Battles of, 56, 62, 277–278
    anonymous letter from Boston, 98–99
    Barker's account of, 92–93
    British officer's diary entry of, 91–92
    Crozier's account of, to Dr. Rogers, 94–95
    Emerson's description of stand at Concord bridge, 95–96
    female reaction to, 104
    Gage's account of, for propaganda purposes, 93–94
    letter from British source, 102–103
    letter from gentleman of Boston, 100–101
    letter from gentleman of rank in New England, 99–100
    letter from private soldier in Boston, 101–102
    Massachusetts Committee of Safety appeals for help, 104–105
    minuteman's account of, 96–98
    overview of, 91
Liberty (ship), 2
liberty cap, 92, 102
Liberty Pole, 92, 102
"Liberty Song, The" (Dickinson), 239–240
    parodies of, 240
"Liberty's Call" (Mason), 254–255
line formation, 89, 90
Livingston, Catherine, 205
Livingston, Henry Brockholst, letter to Schuyler, 172–173
Livingston, William, 52
Lobster, 5
local committees, 27
Locke, John, 10, 80
Long Island, Battle of, 137–140, 278
    introduction to, 137
    Miles's description of, 137–139
    officer in General Frazier's battalion letter, 139
    Washington's proclamation, 139–140

Louis XVI, king of France, 182, 268
Loyalist, described, 154

macaroni, 252
Machiavelli, Niccolo, 76
magazine, 92
"Maid of the Oaks" (Burgoyne play), 163
makeweight, 64
mandamus, 33
Martin, James Sullivan, 159–160
    Battle of Yorktown narrative, 187–191
Mason, George, 80
Mason, John, 254–255
Massachusetts Committee of Correspondence, 27–29, 180, 246
Massachusetts Committee of Safety appeals for help, 104–105
Massachusetts Spy (journal), 212
Massanello, 69
Mather, Samuel, 154–155
Matthews, David, 268
Mattoon, Ebenezer, letter to Schuyler, 175
Mayflower (ship), 234
Merchant, Wm., 8
Middlesex Journal, 262
Miles, Samuel, 137–139
"Military Song," 258–259
military-industrial complex, 71
minutemen, 91, 138
mobocracy, 246
moiety, 15
Monmouth, Battle of, 157–161, 279
    Hamilton's letter to Jay on emancipation of Black troops, 160–161
    Harrison's testimony at Lee court martial, 158–159
    introduction to, 157
    Marquis de Lafayette's memoirs, 158
    Martin, narrative attributed to, 159–160
Montgomery, Richard, 123, 124–125
Montreal and Quebec, invasion of, 123–128
    Ainslie's journal, 126–127
    Arnold's letter to Schuyler, 123–124

Arnold's letter to wife, 125–126
    introduction to, 123
    Stocking's journal on Montgomery
        death, 124–125
    Vining's pension application,
        127–128
Morgan, Daniel, 169–170
Morgan's Raiders, 173–174
Morris, Mary, 205
mortars, 189
musketry, 116

natural law, 66
natural rights, summary of, 84
"Natural Rights of the Colonists as
    Men, The" (Adams), 10–12
Navigation Acts, 1–2, 37–38
"New Colossus, The" (Lazarus), 254
New Daily Advertiser, 23–24
New York City, British occupation of,
    278
Newell, Isaac, 177
Newell, Timothy, 134
North, Frederick, 231
nullity, 38

Ober, Nathanial, 117–118
oeconomise, 184
"Off from Boston," 258–259
"Olive Branch" petition, 52
"On Independence" (Sewall), 260–261
"Our Women," 270

Paine, Thomas, 246
    Common Sense, 46, 60, 61–75
    "Crisis Papers," 85
Palmer, Joseph, 30
Paoli Massacre, 155–156
papists, 6
parricide, 31
passes, 130
Patriotic Sentiments of an American
    Woman in Advocacy of the
    Revolution (letter in Philadelphia
    paper), 203–204
Paxton, Charles, 5
Pennsylvania Constitution, 246
Pennsylvania Packet, 254
"Pennsylvania Song," 246–247
Percy, Earl, 97
philanthropy, 174

Pickering, Timothy, 151
pickets, 125, 176
Pitt, William, 49, 53, 55
Poor Richard's Almanac, 230
Pope Day battles, 6
post, 193
pounders, 113
Prescott, William, 107–108, 120–121
Preston, Thomas, 7
Prince, The (Machiavelli), 76
Princeton, Battle of, 279
privation, inured to, 181
propaganda, war and, 100
publicans, 233
puissant, 165
Putnam, Israel, 134
Putnam, Rufus, 235
Pyrrhic victory, 106

Quartering Act, 2, 277

race war, 69
Rall, Johann, 145
Randolph, John, 59
Randolph, Peyton, 60
ration, 124
recanter, 6
redoubts, 108, 176
redress, 37
Reed, Joseph, 142–143
regular elections, 81
republic, Adams's definition of, 77
Revere, Paul, 30, 48, 97
    account of his ride, 86–87
    in support of Gannett, 224
rising, 167
Rivington, James, 268
Rivington's Royal Gazette, 268
Rochambeau, Count de, 181
rod unit of length, 121, 175
Rolfe, John, 38
rope-walks, 5
Rowe, John, 23
rue, 207
Rutledge, John, 52

Sag Harbor, skirmish of, 147–149
saltpeter, 101, 117
sappers, 188
Saratoga, Battle of, 162–179, 279
    Anburey's letter, 178

Arnold/Gates's Camp Stillwater
    correspondence, 170–172
Burgoyne's letter to Germain,
    167–168
Burgoyne's proclamation, 162–164
Digby's journal, 169, 175–176, 178–179
Freeman's Farm, second battle of,
    176–178
Germain's letters to Knox, 168–169
introduction to, 162
Livingston's letter to Schuyler,
    172–173
Mattoon's letter to Schuyler, 175
reply to Burgoyne's proclamation,
    164–167
Wakefield's recollections of
    American army, 169–170
Wilkenson's memoirs, 173–175
Schuyler, Phillip, 123–124
    Livingston's letter to, 172–173
    Mattoon's letter to, 175
scorched earth policy, 134
Second Amendment, 82
Second Continental Congress, 278
Second Treatise of Government (Locke),
    10, 80
Seldon, Ezra, 154–155
separation of powers, 81
Serapis (ship), 279–280
Seven Years' War, 167, 229
Sewall, J. M., 260–261
shape notes, 230
Shaw, G. B., 162
shoats, 187
Shropshire Regiment, 169, 178–179
Shurtleff, Robert, 222
Sixth Amendment, 81
skirmishes, 89
slavery, 31, 52
    Jefferson and, 36, 42
slow-match, 125
Small, William, 48
Smith, Adam, 38
Soldier's Daughter's Pride, A
    (anonymous), 218–219
"Song for the American Freedom, A"
    (Dickinson), 239. *See also* "Liberty
    Song, The" (Dickinson)
songs of liberty
    "Adam's Fall (Trip to Cambridge),"
        250–251

"Address to the Vile Traitor,"
271–272
"Alphabet for Little Masters and
Misses," 248–249
"American Taxation," 231–236
Battle of Trenton: A Drinking Song,
265–266
Boston Tea Party, 243–244
"Cornwallis Burgoyned," 273–274
"Dying Redcoat, The," 263–264
"Fable addressed to Americans,
upon their treaty with France, A,"
267–269
"India Tea," 245
introduction to, 229–230
"Liberty Song, The," 239–240
"Liberty's Call," 254–255
"Military Song," 258–259
"Off from Boston," 258–259
"On Independence," 260–261
"Our Women," 270
"Pennsylvania Song," 246–247
"Thanksgiving Hymn," 275–276
"To Our Ladies," 241–242
"To the Commons," 262
"War Song, A," 256–257
"World Turned Upside Down, The,"
237–238
"Yankee Doodle," 252–253
Sons of Liberty, 246
Boston Tea Party and, 21, 243
New York, membership of, 20
Tea Resolutions, 1773, 19–20
specie, 250
Speedwell (ship), 234
spiking a gun, 102
splutter, 251
square formation, 89–90
St. James Chronicle, 240
St. John, Peter, 231–236
Stamp Act Congress, 2, 229, 230, 237,
277
"American Taxation" ballad,
231–236
stamp tax, 2, 39, 277
"Star-Spangled Banner," 189, 230
state militia Commissions, 138
state of nature, 39
Stockbridge Massachusetts Indians, 69
Stocking, Abner, 124–125

Stories of Georgia (Harris), 220
Stuart, Charles, 133–134
Suffolk Resolves, 30–35
Sugar/Molasses Act, 2, 39, 277
Sullivan, John, 137, 152–153, 265
surtout, 188
sycophant, 65

take benefit, 142
taxation without representation, 81,
229
Tea Act, 1773, 2–3, 13–18, 277
Thacher, Peter, 108–109
"Thanksgiving Hymn," 275–276
Thatcher, James
October 19 journal entry, 197–199
October 1781 journal entry, 191–192
Thompson, William, 30
Thoughts on Government (Adams),
76–79, 206
Tilghman, Tench, 211
tippling-house, 136
"To Anacreon in Heaven," 230
To Lord Dartmouth (Wheatley),
214–215
"To Our Ladies," 241–242
"To the Commons," 262
To the Ladies (Warren), 212–213
tobacco, 38, 62
Tory, described, 154, 235, 256
total war concept, 89
Townsend, Charles, 2, 15, 49
Townsend Revenue Acts, 1767, 15, 277
Treaty of Paris, 275, 280
Trenton, Battle of, 141–146, 278–279
Bostnick's Memoirs, 143–144
Brown's intelligence report, 141–142
introduction to, 141
Knox's letter to wife, 144–145
Officer's eyewitness account of, 145
Reed's letter to Washington,
142–143
Washington's letter to Continental
Congress, 145–146
Washington's response to Reed's
letter, 143
trial by jury, right to, 81
trimmers, 167
Trumbull, Johnathan, 185–186
Tucker, George, 182–183

Unanimous Declaration of the Thirteen
United States of America,
83–84. See also Declaration of
Independence
unrated goods, 17
unreasonable searches/seizures,
protection from, 81
usurpation, 31, 163

Valley Forge encampment, 154, 279
vault, 5
vaunts, 99
Vergennes, Count de, 180–181
Vincennes, British surrender of, 279
Vining, Richard, 127–128
Virginia Declaration of Rights, 80–82
von Steuben, Frederick, 154–155, 157,
187
Vose, Daniel, 30

Wakefield, E., recollections of
American army, 169–170
Waller, John, 119–120
"War Song, A" (Dearborn), 256–257
Warren, Joseph, 30, 86
Warren, Mercy Otis, 212–213
Washington, George, 100, 129, 235, 248
"Adam's Fall (Trip to Cambridge),"
250–251
on Common Sense, 61
Continental Army and, 50–51
Cornwallis's letters on Yorktown
surrender, 194–197
on importance of women's activities,
201
letter to Continental Congress,
145–146
letter to De Grasse, 184–185
letter to Lafayette, 181–182
proclamation on defeat for Long
Island and Manhattan, 139–140
proclamation on taking of Boston,
135–136
Reed's letter to, 142–143
report on defeat at Brandywine,
151–152
response to Reed's letter, 143
Wayne, Anthony, 156
Wheatley, Phillis, 214–215
Whigs, described, 154

Wilkenson, James, memoirs of, 173–175
William I, king, 69
William III, king, 16–17
Winslow, Anna, 216–217
women
    Adams, Abigail, 206–208
    Corbin, Margaret (Dirty Kate), 209–211
    Gannett, Deborah Sampson, 222–224
    Hart, Nancy, 220–221
    introduction to, 201
    Morris, Mary, 205
    Patriotic Sentiments of an American Woman in Advocacy of the Revolution (letter in Philadelphia paper), 203–204
    tea embargo by, 204
    Warren, Mercy Otis, 212–213

Washington recognition of, 201
Wheatley, Phillis, 214–215
Winslow, Anna, 216–217
Wright, Patience Lovell, 226–227
Wright, Prudence, 225
Women's Guard, 225
Woodruff, Samuel, 176
Woods, Sylvanus, 96–98
Woodward, Richard, 30
Woodworth's Literary Casket, 218
works (trenches), 175
"World Turned Upside Down, The," 237–238
Wright, Patience Lovell, 226–227
Wright, Prudence, 225
Writs of Assistance, 206

Yankee, defined, 98
"Yankee Doodle," 252–253
yeomanry, 115

Yorktown, Battle of, 180–199, 280
    Butler journal entries, 186, 187
    Cornwallis's letter to Clinton, 193–194
    Cornwallis/Washington's letters on surrender, 194–197
    Duncan's diary entries, 186–187
    introduction to, 180
    Lafayette's letter to Vergennes, 180–181
    Martin's narrative, 187–191
    Thatcher's journal entry, 191–192, 197–199
    Trumbull's journal entries, 185–186
    Tucker's letter to wife, 182–183
    Washington's letter to de Grasse, 184–185
    Washington's letter to Lafayette, 181–182

About the Author

Neil Gould teaches in the Department of History, Government, and Economics at Duchess Community College in Poughkeepsie, New York. For more than 25 years, he has taught his classes based on fundamental documents, covering the subjects of American history, government, the ancient world, Greece and Rome, and modern European history. His publications include *Victor Herbert: A Theatrical Life* and all forthcoming—*Princess: The Life of Sara Delano*, *Basic Documents of American History In Plain English*, and *Hitler and Goebbels Walk into a Bar: The Secret Humor of the 3rd Reich*. He is the winner of the Tona Sheppard Foundation Award through the Institute of International Education.